MW00586112

THE WORKINGMAN'S GAME

THE
WORKINGMAN'S
GAME

*Waverly, New York, the Twin Tiers and
the Making of Modern Baseball, 1887-1898*

WILLIAM H. BREWSTER

LUMINARE PRESS
WWW.LUMINAREPRESS.COM

The Workingman's Game
Copyright © 2019 William H. Brewster

All rights reserved. This book or any portion thereof may not be reproduced
or used in any manner whatsoever without the express written permission of
the publisher, except for the use of brief quotations in a book review.

Printed in the United States of America

Cover Design: Melissa K. Thomas

Luminare Press
442 Charnelton St.
Eugene, OR 97401
www.luminarepress.com

LCCN: 2019951048
ISBN: 978-1-64388-232-1

Dedicated with love and appreciation to
Nellie Lou Hemingway Brewster

TABLE OF CONTENTS

Notes on Sources
and Approach

> Unless otherwise indicated, all game accounts are based
  on historical box scores and news stories.

> Team mascots and nicknames are not used unless there is
  sufficient evidence that they were used by the applicable
  players/management/town at the time.

> Unless otherwise indicated, team rosters, player statistics,
  and player career movements are based on Society for
  American Baseball Research (SABR) records as documented on Baseball-Reference.com.

Preface

When I was growing up in the 1960s and '70s, my little hometown of Waverly, New York, was in the last vestiges of its economic heyday. I didn't know it at the time, but the busy downtown—with its three-story brick buildings, windowed storefronts, awnings, multiple locally-owned businesses, soda fountain, movie theater, Acme, Woolworth's, and six-story town clock, all congregated near an active passenger-train station–was about to be bypassed by a four-lane highway and eclipsed by suburban shopping malls.

Before that happened, though, commercial life in Waverly as a kid was idyllic. We regularly rode our bikes to the corner newsstand for baseball cards, magazines, and candy, and had at least a half-dozen other stores to check out along the way–toy stores, game stores, sporting goods stores, used book stores, the ice cream parlor, collectables stores, and so much more. We annoyed the shop owners who, fearing damage or theft, kept an extra close eye on us. As we grew older, we mowed lawns, tended gardens, shoveled sidewalks, and delivered newspapers to earn money. It was a childhood straight out of the old *The Little Rascals* short comedies.

In the pantheon of our idyllic small-town summer activities, baseball was at the top. When we were not playing ball for school or league teams, we played in the local schoolyards, free from adult supervision. We bought, sorted, and traded baseball cards; read *Sporting News* and *Baseball Digest*; and borrowed books about baseball from the Waverly Free Library. We listened to the Yankees' games on the radio and watched the Yankees and Mets on television. We regularly went to minor-league games in Elmira, visited the Hall of Fame in Cooperstown, and periodically made the 220-mile trek to New York City to visit Yankee Stadium or Shea Stadium.

On one such trip in 1978, when I was seventeen, three of my friends and I drove to the Yankee Old Timer's Day. All the great living Yankee stars were there, including Yogi Berra, Whitey Ford, Mickey Mantle, and Joe DiMaggio. Their friend and former teammate, Billy Martin, had recently been forced to resign as the Yankees' manager after describing his star outfielder, Reggie Jackson, and team owner, George Steinbrenner, to reporters: "one's a born liar and the other's convicted." Martin was fresh off of leading the Yankees to their first championship in over a decade and himself a star Yankee player from the team's heyday in the 1950s. As a manager, he was a protégé of Hall-of-Famer Casey Stengel, who in turn had learned from Hall-of-Famer John McGraw. In our opinion, Martin was on track to becoming a legitimate Hall-of-Famer himself. The Yankees seemed to be the right match for him, and we wanted him to return.

Following the introduction of the Old Timers, we joined the entire crowd in a cheer of surprise and glee when Bob Sheppard announced that Martin would return as the Yankees' manager in 1980. The announcement flashed across the scoreboard, and Martin ran out onto the field in his Yankee pinstripes with the familiar number "1." The cheering went on for so long that Joe DiMaggio said he would no longer return to Old Timer's Day if anyone was ever introduced after him without his permission. Martin later called it his "best day in baseball."[1]

Billy Martin might not have been the most naturally gifted player and manager, but what he was, was a hard worker–focused, studious, and smart–a true workingman's player. "When I was a little shaver, people kept telling me that if I wanted to succeed, I would have to play hard, aggressive baseball," Martin told a reporter early in his career.[2]

Martin's toughness came directly from his working class background, where succeeding at sports was a way to differentiate himself.

"None of us had much money," Martin said of his childhood in Berkeley, California. "We couldn't afford football equipment or baseball gloves, but we played football, we'd play tackle even though we didn't have helmets or pads. We'd get bloody noses and get all banged up, and then we'd go home for dinner and a little rest, and in the evening we'd meet back in the [James Kenney] park for capture the flag or boxing."[3]

The fans recognized his passion, admired his knowledge of inside baseball, and appreciated his winning attitude.

Following Martin's introduction and the crowd's response that day, the rest of the afternoon was downright anticlimactic. The Yankees defeated the Twins 7-3, and we drove back to Waverly very pleased with the whole day.

IN 2013, AFTER OVER TWENTY-FIVE YEARS OF LIVING IN BIG-city suburbs far away from Waverly, I read online that my little village once had its own professional baseball team–around the turn of the last century, from the 1890s through 1901. I had never heard of or even imagined such a thing before. Was this actually true, or just another piece of false Internet information?

Back in the 1890s, the downtown buildings, railroad station, and clock tower were still young and vibrant, and the town itself was still ambitious and aimed to compete with bigger towns like Elmira and Binghamton for commercial success. Could it be that the local townspeople actually supported a professional team? If so, whom did they play? Were they any good? What happened to the team and its players?

Curious, I started researching the players on those teams. I read local news stories from the time in libraries, historical societies, and archives. I searched online and went to the National Baseball Hall of Fame Library in Cooperstown. I also eventually contacted a number of the players' descendants.

What I discovered took me by surprise. Not only did my sleepy hometown enjoy several seasons of professional baseball from 1887 to 1901, but it earned national notoriety for its success and featured lineups that included prominent former and future major leaguers with close connections to some of the most significant historical and baseball events of the era. One newspaper even declared Waverly's 1900 team to be "the Champions of Western New York." Among these major league players were "Honest John" Clapp, one of the nineteenth century's most proficient catchers and the first manager of the New York Giants franchise; Harry Taylor, a solid first baseman who captained the 1893 Baltimore Orioles and later served as counsel for the Players Protective Association that was integral to the success of the new American League; "Wild Bill" Donovan, a star pitcher with 186 major league victories who mentored a young Ty Cobb in Detroit and later managed the Yankees; and Charles "Heinie" Wagner, a star infielder and long-time Boston Red Sox captain who mentored a young Babe Ruth.

The old newspapers and other sources connected Waverly

to a long legacy of working class ball players, stretching right up to Billy Martin and other modern characters. The sources revealed that most of the nineteenth century ballplayers in the Twin Tiers of Southern New York and Northern Pennsylvania were common laborers who lacked the skill, luck, persistence and/or skin color to make it to the major leagues. Their experiences as working men, particularly in the minor leagues, reflected the era, a time when economic dislocation, racial and labor strife, and record-high immigration levels led many to question whether instability was a permanent part of the American experience. It was also a period in which success was often predicated on ignoring these very questions and instead propelling oneself forward by being resourceful, hard-working, and opportunistic.

In many ways, it was a transitional era very similar to our own.

Workers then as today aspired to achieve success by climbing into what they perceived as ever higher and more secure social statuses. With formal education, workers could aspire to get into the professional ranks of white-collar work, but such opportunities were still relatively rare at the end of the nineteenth century. For the majority of workers who lacked formal education, there was a pecking order of working class status. For the 1865-1920 period, historian Melvyn Dubofsky categorized these statuses into three levels. At the top were the craftsmen who were in the most secure positions and were typically English speaking, Protestant and native-born or from Northern Europe. At the next level were the semi-skilled workers who were in less secure and less well paid positions and were typically non-English speaking, Catholic from Southern and Eastern Europe. At the lowest level were non-white and female workers who were in the least secure, most competitive and lowest paid positions, essentially the working poor.[4]

Despite the fact that working people from all three levels aspired to the same basic goals (steady work, higher wages, occupational advancement and acquisition of real property) the increasing anxiety brought about by immense social change, especially during economic recessions in the late 1890s, led to increasing rivalry among them. This was particularly true along the lines where working people most noticeably differed: by ethnicity, race and gender.

Within this working class context, the minor league baseball players in Waverly and other New York and Pennsylvania towns strived to achieve greater security and status while rubbing elbows with their factory and mine worker counterparts. Several would go on to become instrumental in transforming the sport from a leisure semi-skilled pastime to a craftsman profession. In 1901, this culminated in the creation of the American League and the National Association of Professional Baseball Leagues, developments that led to huge growth and crowds in big cities, while leaving little towns like Waverly behind.

This book represents the first part of the story, from 1887 to the wartime season of 1898. The second part of the story, with a focus on the 1899-1901 seasons, will be published in 2020.

PART ONE

Laying the Foundation

Waverly's First Professional Team

"One may work and struggle and drive,
and fall short all the same."

—SIRACH 11:11

CHAPTER 1

Why Waverly?

Waverly is a small town in central New York. It is located in the Penn-York Valley just north of the Pennsylvania border, and about five miles north of Tioga Point, where the Susquehanna and Chemung Rivers meet. The town originated in the early 1800s as a factory and mill town along a Susquehanna tributary named Cayuta Creek.[5] John Shepard's mill on the Creek constituted the northern border of a settlement called Factoryville, which was later eclipsed when the Erie Railroad came through in the early 1850s, resulting in the creation of an entirely new, larger settlement to the west of Factoryville, eventually named Waverly after Sir Walter Scott's 1814 novel.

Tioga Point, later renamed Athens, Pennsylvania, provided the area with a unique historical cache, since it was an important crossroad for aboriginal tribes for centuries; its name Anglicized from the Iroquoian "Te-a-o-ga" in the eighteenth century. Twentieth century anthropologist Elsie Murray translated this place name as meaning both "the meeting of the trails" and "the meeting of the waters."[6]

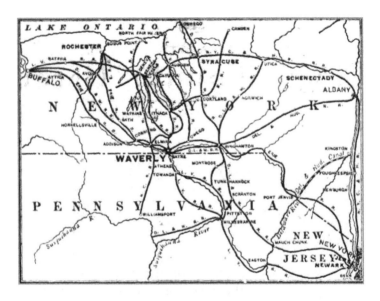

1907 map showing Waverly's central location.
From a Waverly Chamber of Commerce brochure.

Nineteenth century anthropologist and railroad attorney Lewis Henry Morgan, an adopted member of the Seneca Tribe, translated "Ta-yo-ga" as "at the forks"[7] and considered it one of the Iroquois confederacy's most significant locations. "The convergence of so many trails upon this point, preparatory to a descent upon the south, through Pennsylvania and into Virginia on the west side of the Blue Ridge," wrote Morgan, "rendered it an important and well known locality among the Iroquois."[8] Murray confirmed its centuries-long importance, terming Tioga Point "the junction of all trails – Algonkin, Andaste, Iroquois in turn." [9]

Waverly is located in New York's Tioga County, which derived its name from this location. Following the Revolution, this county was carved out of the southern portion of Montgomery County, which in 1790 comprised a significant portion of central New York. By the mid-1800s, pieces of Tioga County had been carved out into separate counties, so that it was much smaller than it had been originally, and its largest villages were Waverly and the county seat, Owego, its name a Europeanized version of its Iroquoian name, also interpreted by Morgan as "Ah-wa-ga," or "where the valley widens."[10] Today, Tioga County is in the center of New York's Southern Tier, which runs along the Pennsylvania border from just west of the Catskill Mountains to the state's western border. By the mid-1800s, as U.S. industrialization was picking up, the entire Southern Tier region's economy found itself lagging behind the Erie Canal towns of northern New York, the trade and transportation powerhouse of New York City, and the anthracite coal region of northeastern Pennsylvania. In exchange for agreeing to help fund the Erie Canal, the Southern Tier had been promised a railroad,[11] and, despite significant financial challenges, the Erie Railroad, stretching from the Hudson River to Lake Erie, came to the Southern Tier's rescue. Construction on the railroad began in 1836, and the first portion, running from Piermont to Goshen, opened in 1841. The line reached Binghamton in 1849 and opened fully to Dunkirk in May of 1851.[12] Both Waverly and Owego were along its stops.

New industry and economic activity followed the railroad throughout the Southern Tier. The region's largest town at the time, Elmira, had a population of less than 8,000 in 1850, but by 1870, it had almost doubled in population, with 15,863 people. The region's second-largest town at the time, Binghamton, also saw a phenomenal population increase during this period, more than doubling in size from 6,000 to 12,692 people.[13]

While the Erie Railroad was successful in siphoning some business away from the Erie Canal region and bringing industry to the Southern Tier, Pennsylvania's Northern Tier, fueled by railroad building and the anthracite coal industry, grew at an even greater pace. Scranton's population, for example, climbed from just 2,730 in 1850 to 35,092 in 1870.

The anthracite region was a hotbed of economic activity and, for many, human misery. For centuries, men and women had spent their peak physical years doing manual labor on farms and in homes, but by the late nineteenth century, fewer and fewer were working outdoors. Instead, more were working indoors in shops and factories or underground in mines.

"The factory system created a low-skilled low-wage proletariat labor force who worked long hours and had few holidays," explained historian Steven Riess. "In general, men engaged in physically exhausting work were often too tired for any after-hours activity more exerting than raising a beer to their mouths."[14]

Anthracite coal was in heavy demand after the Civil War, and the mining and railroading industries that provided and delivered it were indispensable. Reliable labor was in high demand, and owners pursued an increasing number of foreign-born workers to expand the labor pool. Working conditions were tough and wages were low, especially for relatively unskilled mine laborers.

"There was nothing strange about a twelve-year-old kid in the mines for 72 hours a week at a nickel an hour," ex-major leaguer Stanley Coveleski told Lawrence Ritter in the classic baseball book, *The Glory of Their Times*. Coveleski's father, Anthony, came to the U.S. from Poland, and was himself a miner in Shamokin, Pennsylvania.

An anonymous thirty-five-year-old anthracite miner in Pennsylvania explained in 1902:

> We were sent to school (such a school as there was in those days) until we were about twelve years of age, and then we were put into the screen room of a breaker to pick slate. From there we went inside the mines as driver boys. As we grew stronger we were taken on as laborers, where we served until able to call ourselves miners.
>
> I am only one of the hundreds you see on the street every day. Our daily life is not a pleasant one. When we put on our oil soaked suit in the morning we can't guess all the dangers which threaten our lives. We walk sometimes miles to the place–to the man way or traveling way, or to the mouth of the shaft on top of the slop. And then we enter the darkened chambers of the mines. On our

right and on our left we see the logs that keep up the top and support the sides which may crush us into shapeless masses, as they have done to many of our comrades.[15]

Waverly's location on the Pennsylvania-New York border in the middle of the Twin Tiers made it an ideal central transportation hub. Connecting Pennsylvania's anthracite coal with New York's factories and farms was a logistical challenge, given the hilly terrain between them. The North Pennsylvania Railroad aimed to make the connection as early as the 1850s, but the route was never completed for financial reasons. Surveyors in the 1850s recognized Waverly's unique geographic position in the center between coal country and the Great Lakes–noting to prospective investors that a railroad line from Philadelphia to Waverly would be shorter than any other route "both ways" from "Wyoming lines northwest to the Lakes" and "from the Lehigh mines southeast to the tidewater."[16]

*Waverly's Erie Railroad Station, on Fulton Street
just a block south of Broad Street.*

A few years later, in 1869, the Lehigh Valley Railroad finally accomplished the feat, uniting Wilkes-Barre with Waverly. Already a busy station on the Erie Railroad, Waverly now found itself in an extraordinary geographic and economic position: on two significant railroad lines, sixteen miles east of Elmira, thirty-nine miles west of Binghamton, and at the northern end of a large river valley that straddled the New York-Pennsylvania line. Waverly soon found itself to be a major transportation center, with a massive labyrinth of trestles, tracks and switches responsible for the transfer of millions of tons of coal and kerosene between Erie and Lehigh Valley destinations. Although this trestlework was dismantled in 1878 in favor of smaller, safer and more efficient works, the town's location remained at the nexus of railroad traffic.[17] Given the superb location, Waverly banker Howard Elmer convinced Lehigh Valley Railroad President Asa Packer and Superintendent Robert H. Sayre to develop a new town and major railroad repair facility in the vicinity.[18] Once the facility was built just south of Waverly, in Sayre, Pennsylvania, named for the Lehigh Valley Superintendent, local businessmen predicted it would guarantee significant industry for the area for the foreseeable future—perhaps Waverly would even end up rivaling the economic powerhouses of Elmira and Binghamton, or even Scranton and Wilkes-Barre.

Smaller, local railroads gradually emerged and connected their lines to the Erie and Lehigh Valley systems. By the 1880s, the Delaware, Lackawanna, and Western (DL&W) railroad had also made inroads into the region, acquiring a number of these smaller lines and competing with the other large systems for business and customers. The proliferation of railroads meant that major cities and industries became accessible within hours to all but only a very few small towns.

Waverly's location was tremendous for business, and among the businesses it could attract were entertainment businesses, like baseball and other sports.

Historian Harold Seymour explains:

America's march toward industrialization and urbanization, which had started in earnest a decade or so before the Civil War, proceeded with an irresistible rush in the latter half of the century. By 1900 the amount of capital invested in manufactures was nineteen times greater than in 1850. Only twenty-five years after Appomattox, the United States was the number one industrial country of the world, and by 1890, her railroad mileage exceeded that of all Europe.[19]

Just like business enterprises, towns and cities of all sizes competed for economic advantages during the late nineteenth century. Owego, for example, took advantage of its favorite son, Republican "Boss" Thomas Collier Platt, one of the nation's most influential Republican leaders in the last quarter of the century, to pull political and financial favors for the town. Elmira and Binghamton, meanwhile, leveraged their advantages in size to attract manufacturing. By 1880, Elmira continued to have the largest population in the region at 20,541, with Binghamton still trailing at 17,317.

Waverly (2,239) and Owego (5,525) still had much smaller populations at that point, but Waverly's growth trajectory toward the latter half of the decade, particularly in tandem with its Pennsylvania neighbor, Sayre, was tremendous. By 1887, Waverly had a thriving business community and had almost doubled its population, while Owego was seeing its population decline.[20]

It is against this backdrop of economic and political developments that we review Waverly's position at the crossroads of sporting developments, especially in regards to baseball.

The idea of baseball as a business, and as something more than a periodic pastime to be played at local fairs, festivals and carnivals, similar to how sports had been played for centuries in both urban and rural areas,[21] was still novel in the mid-19th century. Its viability as a commercial enterprise involving mass participation gained more credence following the Civil War. By the 1870s and 1880s, many civic-minded businessmen promoted sports as a way to positively motivate working class men. This equation was aligned with the idea of "Muscular Christianity" popularized by the growth of Young Men's Christian Associations (YMCAs) in Great Britain and the U.S., and intended to be a fresh-air healthy counter to "vile slum amusements,"[22] like gambling, drinking and promiscuity.

"It is very questionable whether there is any public sport so eminently fitted for the people it was made for as the American national game of baseball," proclaimed Albert Spalding in his *Official Baseball Guide of 1888*. "In every respect it is an outdoor sport admirably adapted for our mercurial population. It is full of excitement, is quickly played, and not only requires vigor of constitution and a healthy physique, but manly courage, steady nerve [and] plenty of pluck."[23]

Local young men from farms, mines, stores, and factories congregated in railroad towns like Waverly throughout the region. For an increasing number of these men, ball playing was an enjoyable competitive pastime when they were not working, and skill levels improved over time. Men who did not play, those who aspired to play and eventually women and children, watched the contests, and gradually the idea of charging admission prices gained favor. Hence baseball emerged as an entertainment business, like the circus. Teams began to pay some of the best players, and amateur and semi-pro teams and leagues popped up quickly, especially along established railroad lines. Many teams folded just as quickly as they formed if they could not maintain adequate attendance. The more prominent the team, the more likely it was that the player's pay would be guaranteed by contract. The less prominent the team, the more likely it was that his pay would be directly determined by the gate–or perhaps by wagers among local gamblers.

"Local boosters" found baseball teams a great source of public pride, and, according to historian Steven Riess, "regarded hometown support at the box office as an index of the community's progressive character."[24] It did not even matter if the town was part of an official league. Town teams sprouted up across the country and challenged their neighbors. When a league team folded, town teams pounced on the best players like vultures, making per-game guarantees of pay. Local newspapers, also found in nearly every small town, joined in the contest by promoting their hometown teams and denigrating rivals. This promotion was aided by new technologies that emerged in the late 1800s. According to historian Seymour, "a multitude of new inventions, many of them unknown or unimportant before 1880–like the telephone, bicycle, trolley car, camera, typewriter, phonograph, and linotype machine–poured forth in the next two decades in time to have a direct or indirect effect on the baseball business."[25]

This robust semi-pro market was not only in keeping with Spalding's "public sport" proclamation, but it was also good for a town's reputation and–most importantly, in the age of the great industrialists —good for business, since it was positive marketing for the town, attracted spectators from rival towns who would spend money at the town's stores and restaurants, and helped enable civic leaders to attract new businesses which would attract and employ even more workers.

The baseball business, such as it was, did not generally work in favor of the players. Even when paying players, baseball management tended to downplay the player's risks, burdens and base motivations (like safety and wages). As in the case of miners, factory workers and other laborers, management tended to promote less controversial motivations, such as the virtuous goals of family and home, goals that sought to unite labor and management, and discourage labor unions. Management tended to believe unionization led to labor unrest, as demonstrated by violent incidents like occurred at the Chicago Haymarket in 1886, where at least eleven were killed, including seven police officers, and dozens wounded, amidst an organized protest advocating an eight-hour workday. Management tended to promote the belief that labor was "the creator of human progress and happiness" and was "noble and holy."[26] These motivations were pursued to appeal to laborers, even as they largely ignored the simple facts that working conditions for too many tended to be unsafe and wages tended to be too low.

By the late 1880s, the baseball business was popular throughout the country, although that did not necessarily translate into financial security for the teams or sure-fire professional baseball careers for the players. "In those days every town that had a thousand people in it had a baseball team," explained former major leaguer Paul Waner. "That's not true anymore. But in those days there were so many teams along there in the Middle States, and so few scouts, that the chances of a good player being 'discovered' and getting a chance to go into organized ball were one in a million. Good young players were a dime a dozen all over the country then."[27]

Many a young man dreamed of escaping the drudgery of the factory or the mine by earning a living playing ball, but even for so-called professionals, playing ball was still an escapist pastime, not a reliable profession. Professional players had to continually compete to keep their spots, even though, similar to their mining and factory counterparts, they were generally paid little and had few labor rights.

"I enjoyed playing ball," recalled Stan Coveleski, "but it's a tough racket. There's always someone sitting on the bench just itching to get in there and take your place. Thinks he can do better. Wants your job in the worst way: back to the coal mines for you, pal! The pressure never lets up. Doesn't matter what you did yesterday. That's history. It's tomorrow that counts. So you worry all the time. It never ends. Lord, baseball is a worrying thing."[28]

Near the end of the 1880s, Waverly found itself in a position to be a local baseball powerhouse, not only due to its position as an emerging giant in railroad transportation, but also because of events that had taken place two decades earlier and halfway across the country, during one of the darkest days of the Civil War.

CHAPTER 2

Lawrence, Kansas

E arly in the morning of August 21, 1863, the men, women, and children of Lawrence, Kansas, were comfortably asleep. The battles of Gettysburg and Vicksburg had been waged about two months earlier over 1,000 and 650 miles away, respectively. The great armies waging those battles seemed to be at a safe distance.

The Civil War along the Kansas-Missouri border, however, was not like the war being fought back east. Here, historian James McPherson noted, "There occurred the tragedy of a civil war within the Civil War, of neighbor against neighbor and sometimes literally brother against brother, of an armed conflict along the Kansas border that went back to 1854 and had never really stopped, of ugly, vicious no-holds-barred bushwhacking that constituted pretty much a total war in fact as well as in theory."[29]

While none of them were on the scale of Gettysburg, the Kansas-Missouri border had seen its share of battles, and Lawrence was considered the stronghold of anti-slavery forces in Kansas. Hundreds of its citizens had relocated to Kansas from northeastern states specifically to prevent a pro-slavery takeover. Lawrence's citizens were therefore prepared and ready for conflict. Nonetheless, it was far from the Civil War's front lines and forty miles from Kansas City–a long ride even for Ohio native Captain William Quantrill and his motley band of Confederate raiders.

Described as "pathological killers" by McPherson,[30] Quantrill and his raiders, including "Bloody Bill" Anderson and future infamous bank robbers Frank and Jesse James, were guerilla ambushers, mail thieves, and bandits who spread havoc in an attempt to drive pro-Union civilians, many of whom were rabid abolitionists, out of Kansas.

Born in Ohio in 1837 the oldest of twelve children and employed as a teacher there and then in Illinois and Indiana, Quantrill first arrived in Kansas in 1857 as an opportunist. He begged, borrowed, and stole whatever he needed to make his mark and was as likely to ally with runaway slaves and abolitionists as with slave catchers. In fact, under the alias Charley Hart, Quantrill sometimes earned money from both sides in the same slave-catching transactions, collecting protection money from the fugitive slave's handlers and then collecting a bounty from the slave catcher in exchange for double-crossing the handlers and disclosing the fugitive's whereabouts.

It was as Charley Hart that Quantrill registered as a "farmer" in the 1860 census while living in a Lawrence hotel. His double-dealing and associations with multiple crimes eventually caught up with him when the county attorney indicted him for kidnapping, burglary, larceny and arson, and the federal government charged him with horse stealing. When Lawrence sheriff Sam Walker pounded on his door seeking to arrest him, Quantrill fled the city and hid out with fellow border ruffians in Missouri, not far from the Kansas border where they disrupted Union and abolitionist activities.[31] Once the wider Civil War erupted, Quantrill and his gang stepped firmly into league with the Confederacy, earning a measure of respect when they were formally incorporated into the Confederate forces. Quantrill even earned a Confederate field commission as Captain of a Partisan Ranger Company in August of 1862.[32]

In an effort to block Quantrill's guerillas from incursions into Kansas, Union General Thomas Ewing, Jr., set up security posts every few miles along the border. It was common knowledge that Quantrill's guerillas were "better fed, equipped, and clothed than most regular Confederate units," because they could count on the assistance of the local populace for supplies.[33] To deter this kind of aid, in August of 1863, General Ewing ordered the detention of any civilians who helped the guerillas, and he specifically targeted the guerillas' known family members. This order led to the arrest of seventeen female relatives, including teenagers, who were detained at a makeshift jail in Kansas City until they could be transported to a more permanent prison back east.

The imprisonment of the young women outraged Quantrill's men. As rough as the border robberies and revenge killings had been, both sides generally refrained from directly involving women and girls.

On August 14, the building housing the jail collapsed, killing four of the women and seriously injuring the others. Among the dead was Josephine Anderson, sister of "Bloody Bill," one of Quantrill's chief lieutenants. Although subsequent research found the building's collapse to have been accidental, the guerillas believed at the time that the building collapse was intentional and vowed revenge.[34]

Two days later, Quantrill gathered his leaders and let them know they would avenge the girls by attacking Lawrence, where "We can get more revenge and more money" than anywhere else in Kansas.[35] Whether the impending attack was indeed direct retribution for the deaths of relatives or had been planned long in advance, the jail's collapse gave the guerillas a vicious and edgy intensity that ensured there would be little—or no—mercy granted to Lawrence's civilians.

As day broke on the blistering hot morning of August 21, Quantrill and as many as 450 guerillas briefly rested outside Lawrence and observed the sleeping city. They had just ridden for thirty-six dusty hours from their Missouri headquarters near Blue Springs, and they were tired. Although they had been observed by Federal troops, those troops were too far behind to stop them. Still, some of Quantrill's men were hesitant. This would be their largest raid by far. Quantrill, however, was more adamant than ever. He sent Bill Gregg, a trusted lieutenant, to scout the town while the larger force waited. Once Gregg reported the coast was clear, Quantrill ordered his men to "Kill every man big enough to carry a gun."[36]

Within minutes, the guerillas descended on Lawrence and roved from house to house, systematically capturing, torturing, and killing as many men and boys as possible. They dragged many out of their houses so as to execute them in front of their families. They were especially focused on finding and killing all of those on Quantrill's "Death List," which was comprised of the city's most notorious anti-slavery Jayhawker leaders, namely those the guerillas considered most responsible for a variety of Union actions, including an 1861 raid on Osceola, Missouri, that led to the execution of at least nine Confederate sympathizers and the aforementioned deaths of the four women in the Kansas City jail. Among all the executions, the raiders also set fire to the city's buildings, including the headquarters of the city's most staunchly pro-Union newspaper, *The Kansas State Journal*. Along with destroying the *State Journal*'s facilities, the guerillas sought out the newspaper's co-owner, Josiah C. Trask, and shot him to death.[37]

Trask's business partner at the *State Journal*, co-owner and editor, Hovey Lowman, hid under a blanket in his family's cellar with his pregnant wife Harriet and their four young children (ages one, two, three, and five), while their black servant hid behind the house in an ash barrel. Lowman was well-armed in case the cellar was breached, vowing to not be taken without a fight.[38] Lowman and his family had immigrated to Kansas from Chemung County, New York, at the beginning of the war, and his pro-Union editorials for the *State Journal* had earned him special enmity among the region's pro-slavery populace. Just two weeks earlier, Lowman had taunted Quantrill in the *State Journal*, writing, "We invite any number of Border Ruffians to visit any part of our State. The nearer they come to Lawrence the better."[39]

Now the Lowman family hid in the cellar and listened to Quantrill's guerillas ransack the house above and set fire to their beds. Within a few hundred feet, neighbors were brutally beaten and murdered, while another target at the top of Quantrill's list, pro-Union firebrand Senator James H. Lane, was chased out of his house and frantically ran into a cornfield in his nightshirt, barely escaping.[40]

Destruction of Lawrence, Kansas, on August 21, 1863.
From the Library of Congress.

Miraculously, the guerillas failed to identify that the Lowman house had a cellar and left to attack elsewhere, figuring the house would burn to the ground like all the others. When the coast was clear, the Lowmans' servant emerged from the barrel and put out the fires and the family lifted the blanket and climbed out of the cellar to see that their house had been destroyed. They would eventually find that about 150 men and boys, ranging from fourteen to ninety years of age, were killed in the raid, and that many others were injured.[41] Many of the corpses were so charred from house fires that the victims were initially thought to have been black men.[42]

"One saw the dead everywhere," noted the Reverend Richard Cordley, "on the sidewalks, in the streets, among the weeds in the gardens."[43]

Quantrill and company left the city by nine a.m., and although Lowman joined a small posse of surviving militia in an unsuccessful attempt to chase them down and inflict retribution, the results of the attack were striking, one-sided, and unprecedented. It looked like the city had been struck by an earthquake. All told, seventy-five buildings in the business district were destroyed, along with more than one hundred houses.[44]

Quantrill would have more formal run-ins with Union forces before the war was over, but Lawrence was his most infamous raid. Over the next few weeks, he and his raiders were under intense pursuit and eventually headed to Mineral Wells, Texas, as Union forces crawled all over the Missouri border counties, burning crops and evicting families suspected of being Southern sympathizers.

Frank and Jesse James would rise again to criminal fame in the 1870s, while Quantrill would be killed in an ambush near Louisville, Kentucky, at the end of the Civil War in 1865. Within weeks of the Lawrence raid, Lowman would resurrect his newspaper and return to his pro-Union editorializing.

"Your letter of today inviting me to reinstate *The Kansas State Journal*, and pledging to me your hearty cooperation in the enterprise is before me," Lowman wrote to a group of leading surviving citizens on August 24. "I hasten to reply, I will with the encouragement of your valued friendship re-establish the *Journal* as complete in all its appointments as it was before Capt. Quantrill and company visited our unhappy city."[45]

In February, still living in Lawrence, Harriet successfully gave birth to a healthy boy, whom they named Nathan Bristol Lowman, in honor of Harriet's father, Nathan Bristol, a former New York state senator and successful lumberman in the small town of Waverly, New York. Ironically, Bristol had been a staunch Andrew Jackson Democrat, a "Copperhead" Southern sympathizer. Bristol's Southern sympathies were so well known that he was once burned in effigy by his fellow Waverly townspeople. He eventually moved from Waverly back to his original hometown of Point Jervis, New York.[46]

The opportunities for fame and fortune the Lowmans thought they would find in Kansas did not materialize, especially after Quantrill destroyed Lowman's newspaper investment. Within months of resurrecting the paper, Lowman and his growing family moved east to Flint, Michigan, to try the lumber trade with Lowman's brother, John.[47] Unfortunately, the Michigan lumber trade was not all it was promised to be either, and after just a few months, Lowman decided to return to newspaper work in Kansas, but was undecided whether the entire family should venture back west with him. The Lowmans had heard from friends and family that good things were happening in Waverly: the railroads were bringing new business opportunities, the coal and manufacturing businesses were booming, and the school system was strong—maybe moving back would be best for the children.

So, by 1870, while Lowman was the editor of the *Leavenworth Daily Times*, Harriet and the children were safely back in Waverly, right in the middle of a coal-mining boom to the south and a manufacturing boom to the east and west.

Lowman, "Broken in health, worn and fatigued with the exciting events he had passed through," returned home to Waverly to be with his family on September 22, 1872, but five days later, he was dead at age forty-four.[48] He left behind one of the most authoritative early written accounts of the Lawrence Massacre.

Nathan Bristol "Nat" Lowman, too young to remember his Kansas roots in the wake of Quantrill's fiery band of murderers and fatherless at the tender age of eight, attended Waverly schools, worked for the Lehigh Valley Railroad, and eventually became a railroad engineer in Buffalo.[49] Before becoming an engineer, though, young Lowman was a popular and successful student athlete. In fact, he was one of the fastest and most effective baseball hurlers that the Southern Tier had ever seen, and his skill drew special attention to Waverly's ability to field a highly competitive amateur team.

CHAPTER 3

Tioga County, 1886

I n 1886, Tioga County's largest villages–Waverly and Owego—
were competing for commercial advantages, and sporting
activity was an indicator of success. Both villages had amateur
baseball teams, and at the time, these teams were sponsored by
their respective local fire departments. The teams were in fact
extensions of the fire departments.

The use of volunteer fire departments as a basis for sporting
clubs was common among the urban working class. "Members
of street gangs and volunteer fire departments were particularly prominent members of the antebellum sporting fraternity,"
explained historian Riess. "Working class volunteer firemen typically had boring jobs. But at the firehouse they could drink and
play cards with their buddies and look forward to the excitement
of the fire alarm ringing, when they would run breathlessly to
the scene of a fire."[50]

CORNER BROAD AND FULTON STREETS, WAVERLY, N. Y.

*Downtown Waverly and its iconic town clock, at the corner of Broad
and Fulton Streets. The Opera House is the building to the left
of the clock's building and the Tioga House hotel is next,
on the corner of Elizabeth and Fulton.*

The Spaulding Hose Company—a fire department named
after Waverly pioneer Owen Spaulding, who had donated the real
estate required to build much of the village's infrastructure and
was, coincidentally, a distant cousin of baseball magnate Albert
"Al" Goodwill Spalding—sponsored Waverly's team.[51] The Susquehanna Engine Company, a fire department named after the Susquehanna River that runs along Owego's southern border, sponsored
Owego's team. Thus, the battle for Tioga County's bragging rights
was pushed squarely onto the baseball diamond in '86, as both
the Susquehannas and the Spauldings fielded competitive teams.

The Susquehannas featured Fred Gould, who worked at the
local drillworks, and Edward J. Ward, who worked at the foundry.
The locals considered Ward and Gould to be baseball players
"par excellence," who spent parts of the 1884 and 1885 summers
playing for amateur and professional teams in Binghamton, Lock
Haven and Allentown. In 1886, they alternated between the roles

of pitcher and catcher during the season. Other locals playing for the Susquehannas included outfielder Herbert Smith and infielders J. Sweeney, Eugene Barton, George Faulkner, M. Madigan, Harry Wallis, Bikley, Mabee, and printer Tom Ringrose. Young local attorneys Harry Platt and Frank Tracy were also considered strong players, though they were unable to make some games due to work conflicts.[52]

Harry Platt was also known around town as Henry Barstow Platt, the local attorney. He was the son of prominent Republican senator and New York state political boss for the party, Thomas C. Platt; a former star baseball player at Yale; and an 1882 inductee into Yale's secretive Skull and Bones society. He only played for the Susquehannas when his political and legal activities allowed.[53] Harry and his older brother, Frank, would earn a reputation in later years as strongmen in their father's political pursuits.

Frank Tracy was also a local attorney, and was also the son of a prominent national political figure. In Tracy's case, the famous father was retired Civil War General Benjamin F. Tracy, who within two years would be named Secretary of the Navy by President Benjamin Harrison.

Meanwhile, the Spauldings of Waverly featured a number of promising stars, most notably third baseman Archie Cole and first baseman Patrick Sheahan. Catcher Harry Hall, Edward Kennedy, Tom Moore, John Smith, John Touhey, John Daniels, Andy Harsh, Fred Seely, and Charles Simmons rounded out the squad.[54]

Twenty-two-year-old Archie Burton Cole was born in New York State and worked as a cigar-maker in Waverly. Like many local laborers at the time, Cole's father, Andrew, was lured to a railroad position, where he worked in 1870, but by 1880, was a farmer and vine keeper in Hammondsport, New York.[55]

Twenty-six-year-old first baseman Patrick J. Sheahan was born in New York of Irish parents, Mary and Patrick, who also worked for the railroad, in his case as foreman. The younger Sheahan was a railroad laborer as well, and an active leader of the Spaulding Hose Company.[56]

It was the starting pitcher, Nat Lowman, however, around whom the team was built. Lowman had built a sterling athletic reputation since childhood. Waverly spectators saw him rise from being a talented schoolboy player to become an outstanding pitcher for the Spauldings. In an era when effective pitching often meant the difference between winning and losing, having a hometown pitcher like Lowman meant the Spauldings never needed to import or pay for an extra hurler. He was so good, in fact, that the best area ball players were drawn from other towns to Waverly, and even professional teams from outside the area took an interest in him. This made a big difference in local baseball circles, and it gave Waverly a decisive sporting edge over its neighbors.

RAGS-TO-RICHES TALES WERE AS POPULAR THEN AS THEY ARE today, and many players dreamed of being discovered–even in the rural pastures of western New York.

"Baseball attracted all sorts of people," explained an old-time ballplayer, Davy Jones, who was born in Cambria, Wisconsin, in 1880, and played in the major leagues from 1901 to 1918. "We had stupid guys, smart guys, tough guys, mild guys, crazy guys, college men, sliders from the city, hicks from the country. And back then a country kid was likely to really be a country kid. We'd call them hayseeds or rubes."[57]

Although average players might not have had their choice of teams and good players might not be noticed by scouts, it was a buyer's market for towns looking to put together teams. The size of the town barely mattered, provided it had a good location near a railroad line and an audience willing to pay to watch. Towns competed aggressively for the best players. Stan Coveleski, for example, was reportedly pulled from a theater in the middle of a movie to be asked to sign with Lancaster, Pennsylvania, in the Tri-State League.

"Well, the semi-pro team heard about me being so good throwing stones at tin cans and they asked me if I'd like to pitch for them," he explained, noting that having an older brother already in the major leagues probably "Had something to do with it, too."[58]

The lines between amateur and professional baseball were not as clear in 1886 as they are today, but even back then, local teams were aware of the fact that the ability to pay out-of-towners gave a town team an advantage that blurred the sporting nature of inter-town rivalries. Whether this constituted an unfair advantage was the subject of much debate in local newspapers and organizations, with the result that agreements between town teams to play one another often included a written list of the eligible players on each side, so that an out-of-towner could not be added to the roster at the last minute. This was particularly important when townspeople were making relatively large side wagers on the games.

Moreover, it was at this semi-professional level where balancing the acquisition of talent and its requisite ability to attract revenue with its cost was most evident in baseball. In order to attract the largest crowd, the team's management or ownership needed to promote the games. This cost money and any additional payment to players cost even more money. The team manager or owner was reluctant to do this, but how else would the best players be attracted?

Thus the baseball industry, like the entertainment industry, was in the position of needing to manage its labor cost while simultaneously needing to promote its laborers. Unlike factory work, there was no easy way to automate or otherwise minimize this labor cost.

"Deskilling these workers, if it were possible at all," explained historian Robert Ross, "would cut labor costs but also destroy the means by which the industry attracts its customers."[59]

As a result, managers and owners tended to resort to artificial limitations, such as gentlemen's agreements on salary

caps, reserve rules, even changes to game rules, all in an effort
to balance labor promotion with labor expense. The net result
was tremendous instability, as throughout the 19th century
only 25 percent of professional baseball teams lasted longer
than two years.[60]

We will see later that such arrangements and instability
among major league ownership had a profound impact on the
development of the professional game and its players.

IN 1886, LOWMAN AGREED TO PITCH FOR THE HOMETOWN
amateur Spauldings, which significantly improved Waverly's competitiveness. He also pitched for the professional Canastota team
in the tiny Central New York League. In addition to Canastota,
the Central New York League consisted of teams from Little Falls,
Oneida, and Norwich–villages closer to the Erie Canal than to
the Southern Tier. They were also villages with very passionate
crowds and rivalries.

In 1886, Lowman's battery mate for both the Spauldings and
Canastota was fiery catcher Charles "Harry" Hall. That season,
Hall earned a reputation as one of the Central League's most notorious "kickers," frequently arguing the umpire's calls, and his antics
earned him special enmity from opposing players and fans.

Canastota also featured another Tioga County player–the
tall and lanky nineteen-year-old Harry Leonard Taylor. Taylor
grew up on a farm in Halsey Valley, New York, just eighteen
miles north of Waverly in prime farming country, and played
summer baseball to earn money while attending nearby Cornell University. By 1887, Halsey Valley was populated by about
170 families, two churches ("Christian" and "Methodist"), one
schoolhouse, one post office, three stores, two blacksmith
shops, two cooper shops, and two physicians.[61] Taylor's parents,
Fred and Hannah, had also been born in New York, and their
rural neighborhood was composed of similar families: white,

Nathan Lowman (right) with brothers Charles (left) and Henry.
Courtesy of the Chemung County Historical Society.

native-born farmers. Taylor went to local schools in Spencer and Ithaca and, like Harry Platt, was an Ivy League baseball star, serving as both captain of the baseball team and president of his class at Cornell.[62] The Taylors were very successful farmers and entrepreneurs in the area. Fred's brother (Harry's Uncle) George, for instance, was Halsey Valley's finest cooper, a skill that would prove extremely useful in the early 1880s when he partnered with his son (Harry's cousin) Walter to purchase vineyards about fifty miles northwest on the shore of Keuka Lake, and start what eventually became the Taylor Wine Company.[63]

Canastota's games had a reputation for liveliness. On July 1, 1886, for instance, Canastota hosted Oneida at a game with hundreds of passionate spectators from both towns. With Canastota leading 7-5 in the ninth, Oneida catcher John Messitt aggressively slid across home plate on an infield hit. As Messitt rose from his slide, Hall angrily alleged that Messitt "attempted to imbed his spikes into Hall's leg," and a fracas ensued. According to the story, Hall struck at Messitt, but did not appear to land the blow. Meanwhile, Oneida pitcher John O'Brien grabbed a bat and started toward Hall. This led six-foot-tall, two-hundred-pound "giant" Canastota first baseman "Jolly" Vince Dailey to intercept O'Brien, pick him up "like a bag of popcorn," and carry him away from the gathering crowd of angry players.

"The police here stepped in," recalled local reporter George Geer with an evident flair for creative hyperbole, "and the fracas was stopped. The game was then finished with no killed or wounded. As was natural, after the close of the game there was much talk of renewing hostilities among the players of the two clubs, and there were exciting moments about the hotel of the Oneida delegation. The police flaunted visions of the calaboose before the Oneidan's eyes, and matters quieted down." The violence averted, the Oneida contingent enjoyed a good supper, chartered hacks and carryalls, and headed home.

Meanwhile, false reports reached Oneida, just six and one-half miles away, that the Oneida players and many prominent

Harry L. Taylor from Halsey Valley, NY.

citizens had been arrested and were in the Canastota jail. The news created "tremendous excitement" in Oneida, and a "band of gallant rescuers" chartered a train, demanded the engineer put on all steam, and "sped to Canastota and glory." Their plan was to dismantle the jail, free the prisoners, burn down the ballpark's grandstand and fences, and wreak as much havoc as they could.

The posse arrived in Canastota just after their fellow townsmen had left. The Canastota townsmen had been tipped off to the posse, possibly by telegraphers associated with the railroad, and so summoned a team of local firemen to greet the posse at the station with a loaded fire hose. Whether they actually sprayed the posse with the hose was not said, but according to Greer, the Oneida band quickly returned to the train "amid the howls of derision of half the population of Canastota."[64]

The two clubs met again on July 17 in Oneida. This time, the Oneida partisans thought they had Canastota's number, having paid off the umpire and imported two advanced players from Meriden, Connecticut's, team in the Eastern League–pitcher Michael Doyle and catcher George Stone, described as a "$250 battery." Unfortunately for the Oneida crowd, "the game was not close enough to be interesting, the Oneidas being no match for their visitors." Lowman held the Oneidas to just two runs and earned Canastota an easy 14-2 victory. Hall, again the catcher, clouted two doubles and scored three runs, and Taylor manned second base, batted third, smacked two singles, and scored a run. Doyle and Stone, among the top professional prospects in the Eastern League, only earned one hit apiece against Lowman, and the paid-off umpire acknowledged he was unable to swing the game Oneida's way. "Gentlemen, I have given you one run," he said, "but I could not give you the game. Canastota is too much for you." [65]

Three weeks later, Canastota faced yet another near riot, this time in a game against Little Falls. Tempers were so furious both on the field and in the stands regarding close calls on the bases that the umpire "retired" in the fourth inning, leaving the teams to argue among themselves whether and how to continue the game. Lowman was not pitching that day, so he was "volunteered" to serve as umpire. Under his supervision, the game continued without further incident, with Canastota ultimately winning 6-4.

The "rowdyism, profanity, obscenity and indecent howling and wrangling as emanated from some of the spectators was not only uncalled for, but deserved arrests and severe punishment," the *Little Falls Evening Times* reported. "People who cannot restrain their passions and prejudices should remain away from such gatherings."[66]

Lowman made dedicated efforts all season to pitch for both the Spauldings and Canastota, but occasionally needed a break, as seen in early August, when he and Hall were the battery in a 12-2 Spauldings victory over Athens on August 9 and then faced Little Falls with Canastota on August 10. For the Little Falls contest, Backer pitched, and Lowman played leftfield, while Dailey started at catcher, and Hall rotated between the infield and outfield.

Unfortunately, the tall Dailey was not used to catching and did not accurately account for his height behind the plate. He also squatted much too closely behind the batter, and the very first batter's swing inadvertently struck him on the head. The sound could be heard throughout the park, and although Dailey gamely went on for two more innings, newspaper accounts reported that the blood running down his face became too much of an obstacle for him to be able to continue.[67]

Harry Taylor played infield for most of the summer and had many clutch hits, but he was also occasionally called on to pitch. On August 17, he held Little Falls hitless in the eighth and ninth, but it was not enough, as Little Falls maintained its 7-5 lead for the win.[68]

The Susquehannas and Spauldings met three times during the season, with the Spauldings winning two of those three games, the last a 13-0 shutout on September 6 on Waverly's Elm Street grounds.[69] Archie Cole pitched for Waverly that night, and not a single Susquehanna player reached second base, while Kennedy and Smith each scored three runs.[70]

After a few days of consideration, the Susquehannas requested a post-season rematch, presumably for a time when all of their best players would be available. The date was fixed for October 7, 1886, in Owego. The team's rosters were fixed in advance, and $200 was promised to the winning team, along with the gate receipts. It was determined that Lowman would pitch for the Spauldings and Gould for the Susquehannas. Kennedy, Cole, and Hall would all be playing for the Spauldings, and the Susquehannas would see the return of Platt and Tracy.[71]

A "large audience" of "about one thousand spectators" witnessed the game. Cole led off with a walk for the Spauldings. Then, Kennedy reached base on an error by first baseman Platt, and with that, the floodgates opened and the Spauldings soon took a 3-0 lead. The Susquehannas scored once in their half of the first inning, but were overly aggressive on the base paths, as both Gould and Ward were thrown out while trying to steal bases. The Spauldings scored once more in the second inning and three more times in the seventh, going into the ninth with a 7-1 lead. Lowman had grown tired by then and allowed runs to Tracy and Gould, but he still held on for a 7-3 win. It was a brisk affair, lasting only one hour and forty-five minutes.

Platt and Tracy turned out to be very mediocre against Lowman, registering no hits and just one run between them. Platt also chipped in two errors at first.

Following the victory, Waverly's players and fans barely escaped Owego unscathed; unhappy locals attacked them as they made their way back through town. "A crowd of hoodlums and gamins disgraced themselves and their town by throwing rotten eggs, tomatoes, stones, etc. at the Waverly party," the *Waverly Advocate* reported. "It was an outrageous proceeding and those who engaged in it should yet be arrested and severely dealt with."[72]

The *Owego Daily Blade* was more measured, merely noting, "The Waverly people carried away quite a sum of money aside from the winnings of the club, and made the streets lively while they remained in town."[73]

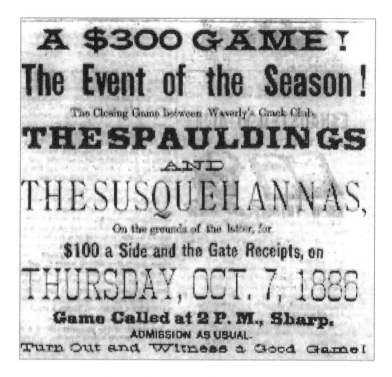

Game advertisement from the Owego
Blade on October 6, 1886.

Once safely back in Waverly, the team was met by the citizen's band, fireworks, and bonfires. "The enthusiasm was unbounded."[74] Whereas the official victory receipts were reportedly in the $300 range, rumor had it that hundreds of dollars had also been won and lost in side wagers, which likely animated the celebration.

This appears to have been Harry Platt's last season of baseball in Owego. He remained a proud member of the Susquehanna Engine Company,[75] but his legal, political, and business activities led him to spend more time elsewhere.

The Spauldings won the Tioga County championship in 1886, but Canastota, in first place as of July 21, wound up losing the Central New York pennant to arch-rival Oneida. The experiences of both teams predicted a good foundation for Waverly in 1887.

CHAPTER 4

Honest John Clapp

E ager to show its neighbors that it was the equal of the biggest towns in the Southern Tier, in 1887, Waverly looked to take advantage of its central location, star pitcher, and busy railroad stations to start a semi-professional baseball team.

The Spauldings had done a credible job as an amateur team in '86, but Waverly was looking for something more. The village fathers wanted a team that could not only compete with Owego, but could also step up and go toe-to-toe with Elmira and Binghamton. Waverly's baseball proponents were looking for a leader who understood the local environment, but also had enough national and league background to know what it took to get the town to the next level. They believed they had found just the right man in one of baseball's biggest names, thirty-five-year-old former big-league catcher and manager "Honest John" Clapp.

Born and raised in nearby Ithaca, New York, Clapp played amateur ball as a teenager for local teams (such as Owego in 1870) and got his start in professional baseball in 1872 at the age of twenty with the Middletown, Ohio, Mansfields. His teammates there included the twenty-one-year-old future Hall-of-Famer Jim O'Rourke. Clapp spent the next three seasons with the Philadelphia Athletics, where his teammates included a young Adrian "Cap" Anson, not only a future Hall-of-Famer, but

John Clapp with the 1874 Philadelphia Athletics.
From the New York Public Library.

also someone considered to be one of nineteenth century baseball's most influential personalities, both on and off the field. That
team also included first baseman and outfielder Tim Murnane,
who would go on to become a prominent baseball writer in
Boston and be honored by the Hall of Fame with a J.G. Taylor
Spink Award for his journalism work.[76]

As members of the Athletics, Clapp, Anson, and Murnane
participated in one of baseball's early overseas trips–an exhibition trip planned by Boston pitcher Al Spalding that involved the
Philadelphia and Boston teams travelling to England from July
to September of 1874. The purpose was to introduce the Brits
to American baseball, as well as play cricket with English clubs.
At the time, cricket was nearly as popular in the United States
as baseball, so the American teams were not only competitive
with each other in their baseball games, but also competed well
against the English cricket clubs.

The Boston and Philadelphia teams featured some of baseball's biggest stars; in addition to Spalding, Clapp, Anson, and
Murnane, were Harry, Sam, and George Wright, Jim O'Rourke,
Andy Leonard, and Harry Schaefer. Unfortunately, attendance
at the baseball games was meager, and the tour was a financial
failure.[77]

When the National League was formed two years later in
1876, Clapp joined the St. Louis franchise. At 5'7" and 190
pounds, Clapp was stocky and strong, and he spent the next
several seasons as one of the game's best fielding catchers, with
stints in Indianapolis, Cincinnati, Buffalo, and Cleveland. It was
in Cleveland in 1881 that Clapp earned his nickname, "Honest
John," for turning in a bookmaker who had offered him $5,000
to commit passed balls at strategic times. At the time, this was a
sum that far exceeded all but the most prominent players' annual
salaries.[78]

Clapp was a catcher in an era when pitching was still tightly
regulated, and catching equipment was in its infancy. Only
below-the-hips tosses were allowed, varying from full underhand

to low sidearm, and some of the fastest twirlers were extremely challenging to catch. This was especially true since the official pitching distance was only fifty feet (where it would remain until 1893).

Among the first fastball pitchers was the legendary Jim Creighton, who pitched for the Brooklyn Excelsiors from 1860 to 1862. Like other New York City baseball clubs at the time, the players on the Excelsiors tended to be from the artisan class. Before Creighton, the arm and wrist were kept stiff and the pitches tended to be slow and flat, perfect for the sporting gentry. Creighton's pitches instead rose quickly from the ground to the shoulders, inflicting damage to batting averages and inciting complaints. He was the first to combine speed and control, and thus single-handedly changed how players approached the game. Without him, wrote historian Tim Wendel, "we would have had no Bob Gibson or Sandy Koufax a century later."[79] A fellow player, John "Jack" Chapman, said Creighton "had wonderful speed, and, with it, splendid control. He was fairly unhittable."[80]

Tragically, Creighton died at the age of twenty-one in October of 1862 after hitting a home run and allegedly rupturing an inguinal hernia. Chapman witnessed the game and said he heard a snap following the hit that, at the time, he attributed to Creighton's belt.[81] Creighton's death at such an early age shocked the sporting world and further fueled his legendary status.

Once Creighton set the standard, other pitchers began striving for both speed and control. In 1867, Candy Cummings further raised the bar by perfecting the curve ball, a feat that caused baseball writer Henry Chadwick to declare him the nation's most outstanding player.[82] By the time Cummings joined the fully professional ranks in the early 1870s, pitching had become more important than ever.

Good pitchers needed competent catchers, and Clapp was considered one of the very best. Among the young fastball pitchers who benefited from Clapp's catching skill were Dick McBride, for whom Clapp caught from 1873 to 1875; George Washington

Bradley, for whom Clapp caught in 1876 and '77; and James "Pud" Galvin, for whom Clapp caught in 1879 while with Buffalo.

Dick McBride won an impressive 101 games in the three seasons Clapp was his catcher on the Athletics. Bradley, at only twenty-three years old, won forty-five games with Clapp in 1876 and eighteen more in 1877. On July 15, 1876, Bradley threw the first major league no-hitter–with Clapp as his catcher. In 1879, Galvin was only twenty-two years old, but he won thirty-seven games with Clapp as his battery mate and was already on his way to a Hall-of-Fame-worthy career.

In 1877, Clapp was again part of catching history when he was stuck in the face by a foul ball, and, depending on whose story one believes, became among the very first major league catchers to regularly wear a newly invented protective mask. Fortunately, this made it more acceptable for other catchers to wear masks, as, up to that time, they had to endure teasing and insults for donning such overtly protective gear.[83]

From 1877 through 1882, one of the National League's chief deficiencies was that it had no team based in New York City. Instead, New York teams found they could make more money by remaining independent of the League, and luring League teams to play them at the Polo Grounds, then located just north of Central Park, as their schedules allowed. Clapp was one of the key players for the last of these rebel teams, the 1882 New York Metropolitans, or Mets. Clapp and pitcher Jack Lynch formed a powerful and popular Mets battery that extended into business, as they opened a saloon (variously named Clapp & Lynch, Old Club, The Club and the Exchange) at 1980 Third Avenue not far from the Polo Grounds. The Club was a regular hangout for players and fans, and it kept patrons and passersby updated on the latest scores by receiving updates via telegraph and posting them on large indoor and outdoor blackboards.[84] Clapp and Lynch would frequently welcome players after games, whereby "they lit their cigars, and by-gone games were played over until a late hour."[85]

The Club not only attracted players and fans, but members of the rival sporting media. The *Chicago Tribune*, for instance, likened The Club to the "Wigwam at Spalding's in Chicago," and the Boston Globe was impressed with the exhibition of seventy Mets winning baseballs in The Club's window.[86] To further encourage the media, Clapp and Lynch designed a reading room in the back of the saloon, "where the sporting journals of the country are placed on file."[87]

"Returning from the Polo Grounds," wrote the *St. Louis Post-Dispatch*, "a person can drop in at Clapp & Lynch's and find the result of the principal games played elsewhere, already bulletined."[88]

The New York City atmosphere was ripe for real major league baseball, and the next season (1883), both the National League and the newly created rival American Association invited the Mets to join their league. The Mets owners accepted both, and to facilitate stocking the two teams, acquired the Troy (NY) franchise and turned it into a new Gothams (eventually Giants) team for the National League. The Mets franchise then went to the American Association, also known as the "beer and whisky league" for its promotion of lively play on the field and alcohol sales in the stands.

Clapp went with the National League squad, and served as the Gotham's player-manager. At thirty-one, he was the veteran on the team, and his line-up featured future Hall-of-Famers Roger Connor, Buck Ewing, Tip O'Neill, Mickey Welch, and John Montgomery Ward, all of whom were under the age of twenty-six. His battery and saloon partner, Lynch, stayed with the Mets.

New York League Base Ball Club.

Player-Manager John Clapp and the 1883 New York Gothams, soon to be renamed the Giants. Back row L-R: Ewing, Hankinson, Dorgan and Ward. Center row L-R: Gillespie, O'Neill, Clapp, Caskin and Connor. Front row, L-R: Welch and Troy.

Clapp's young team was beset by cliques, and as a manger he had a hard time keeping them focused. As a player, he injured his hand and wound up batting just .178, far below his respectable career average of .283. Twenty-five-year-old Connor, meanwhile, led the team with a .357 average. Twenty-three-year-old John Ward, who would be the team's manager within two seasons, batted just .255 and went 16-13 as a pitcher in '83, but also began his studies at Columbia School of Law that year, marking the beginning of his rise to prominence not only on the diamond, but as an outspoken advocate for players' rights.

The idea that ball players should have similar rights as other laborers was new for the game at the time, and the New York team of Clapp, Ward and the other young players was its primary incubator. When major league owners first devised a reserve system following the 1879 season (whereby each team reserved a certain number of current players each season, preventing them from signing with a rival club), Clapp and Ward were two of just thirty players reserved (five players per team). The owners' intent was to slow down the movement of players from one team to another and to keep salaries low.

Even at that early stage, the reserve system had its angry critics. Oliver Perry Caylor of the *Cincinnati Enquirer* in August of 1880, for example, declared the system an "outrage," and said it was especially unfair to "such men" as Clapp.[89]

The number of players reserved per team each year jumped quickly from five in 1880 to eleven in 1883 to twelve in 1885. The owners clearly felt they had the upper hand, so they went for even more control, and following the 1885 season announced an annual salary cap of two thousand dollars per player.

Within five days of the announcement, Ward, brandishing his new law degree, with his New York teammates launched The Brotherhood of Professional Baseball Players, the purpose of which was to "protect and benefit its members, promote a high standard of professional conduct, and advance the interests of the national game." Although Ward was careful not to characterize the Brotherhood as a "union," preferring to promote its value to the sport as a whole, it was clearly a labor union in structure and represented the world's first for professional sports.[90]

Like Clapp, Ward was a native of the Twin Tiers, born in the small central Pennsylvania town of Bellefonte in 1860. His mother Ruth was an admired schoolteacher in town and his father James was a small business owner.[91] Ward was a very bright youngster who attended Penn State University at 13 before both of his parents died suddenly. Ward then quit school and supported himself as a traveling salesman before discovering semi-pro baseball.[92] From the beginning, Ward strived to be as highly skilled as possible, and looked at baseball as a craft as well as a sport. Among his early professional journeys was a stint with Binghamton in 1878 when he was eighteen.

"I had already seen that base-ball was lucrative only to players in the first class," he said, "and I concluded that if I could not get into that I would quit altogether."[93]

Ward's creation of the first player's union as a means to improve the perception of the players' roles as skilled craftsmen was successful in at least one important respect in that within a year it had signed up 107 players in the National League and American Association. This membership included close to 90 percent of the National League's players.[94] Among other things, the union earned the enmity of the National League's owners. It was not a typical union, but baseball was also not a typical industry. In addition to this labor activity, Ward wrote books and articles promoting baseball skills training to the public, consistent with his aim to improve the sport's standing as a craft.

Clapp, meanwhile, had slowed down considerably compared to his young stars, and he did not return to the Gothams/Giants as player or manager following the 1883 season. Based on media accounts, he appears at a minimum to have been in social contact with Lynch and the other Mets during the 1884-1886 period, and perhaps assisted as a coach while running his and Lynch's saloon. Some media accounts alluded to him being ill, but did not specify the illness.[95] His retirement from active play coincided with the end of the game's underhand pitching era; his last documented season was the first in which overhand pitching was allowed.

In addition to operating the saloon and possibly assisting with the Mets, the retired Clapp, when healthy, kept his baseball chops in shape as an umpire for the National and International Leagues. His International League stint was rocky, and he was removed from their umpiring staff in mid-1886 following allegations of favoritism in a series between Utica and Toronto, where his "peculiar umpiring reached the highest pinnacle of eccentricity," and the Toronto media reported that he "fraternized with the visiting club."[96]

In the midst of these activities, Clapp accepted Waverly's call to return to the diamond as a player and coach for the 1887 season. He arrived in Waverly in mid-May of 1887 and worked with non-playing manager John C. Shear to build a club that would be "one of the best in this part of the state."[97]

With Clapp as the catcher, the rest of the Waverly line-up featured a core of talented players from the 1886 Spauldings. This included star pitcher Nat Lowman; third baseman Archie Cole; first basemen Pat Sheahan and Tom Moore; outfielders Ed Kennedy, Johnny Smith, and John Daniels; and catcher Charlie "Harry" Hall. Among those Clapp and Lowman attracted to the team were Harry Taylor from the 1886 Canastota club and local banker Percy Lang.

Twenty-six-year-old shortstop Percy Lyford Lang was born in Waverly in 1861, had graduated from Yale University in 1885, and worked in a hardware business before working as a teller and then as an assistant cashier (and eventually Vice President) at the First National Bank in Waverly. His father, Andrew Jackson Lang, a graduate of Union College, came to Waverly from Maine in 1857 and was the first principal of the town's new private preparatory school, Waverly Academy.[98] While at Yale, Lang played shortstop for the freshman baseball team, wrestled and played football as an upperclassman. He was likely a member of the 1885 Yale football team that finished 7-1 and outscored its opponents by a combined score of 366-21. Among the other players on that squad were future Football-Hall-of-Fame coaches George Woodruff and Amos Alonzo Stagg.[99]

As the 1887 season began, Taylor was wrapping up his junior year at Cornell, Hall was working in Elmira, Lowman was a clerk in the Lehigh Valley Railroad's front office in Waverly, and all three looked forward to playing with a bona fide major leaguer. With at least two college boys, Waverly's team matched up well with the 1886 Owego squad's Platt and Tracy. Taylor's presence on the Waverly squad represented what was becoming a trend, as with the increase in popularity of college baseball in the 1880s, an increasing number of college players sought summer work as ball players, even though relatively few thought of baseball as a career due to its relatively low pay and low status. This was changing, however, and Taylor would become one of the best examples. According to historian Steven Riess, just two percent of 1880s major league ballplayers had college experience, but in the 1890s, the percent of major leaguers with college experience climbed to eight percent.[100] By comparison, the general working population lagged these figures, since as of 1900, only 1.9 percent of the U.S. population under age twenty-four had earned Bachelor's degrees.[101]

Clapp and the Waverly boys put together their first victory of the season on May 30 in an impressive 25-5 drubbing of Painted Post's team before a "very large" crowd at its home field on the Elm Street grounds.

Three days later, they traveled to Elmira and suffered an 8-4 defeat at Elmira's Maple Avenue Park, near the location where Dunn Field would eventually be. In reporting the game, the *Elmira Gazette* noted, "Waverly has a strong team and they are gentlemanly and well behaved. The battery they played yesterday is an unusually strong one. Lowman throws a very swift ball and Johnnie Clapp still does admirable work behind the bat. The fact that ten of the Elmira players were left on bases yesterday shows that Lowman, the Waverly pitcher, has a cool head which is not turned in an emergency."

Despite the loss, Waverly's populace was excited, and local businessmen were eager to take advantage of the team's marketability. For future road games, Joseph O. Rezeau set up a blackboard at his saloon on 209 Broad Street to post scores for Waverly citizens and workers as soon as the telegraph office reported them[102]–reminiscent of Clapp's old saloon in Manhattan.

The day after their victory, Elmira traveled to Waverly's Elm Street grounds for a rematch, and this time, Waverly won 6-5 in an "interesting" contest. In each case, there were questions regarding the home umpire's bias, which was a recurring theme in nearly all baseball games at the time. In defeating Elmira, Waverly had to come from behind with three runs in the ninth—a difficult feat, to be sure.

Like Waverly, Elmira's team was not part of a formal league. They put together a schedule based on other non-affiliated teams' availability, and they likely paid some but not all of the players.. Regional minor leagues were becoming increasingly common, but it was very difficult to find the right group of cities to make such a league work. Successful arrangements, like the New York Central League's, were rare. The schedule had to be demanding enough to maintain the attention of players and fans, but not so demanding that fans lost interest and ceased coming to the ballpark. This was long before teams had figured out how to earn significant income from ancillary businesses, like advertising, souvenirs, food, and media, so it was common for teams and entire leagues to fold mid-season due to lack of income.

Other local towns with teams included Susquehanna, Watkins Glen, Owego, and Bradford. Each team's motive was different. Some played for community pride or simply entertainment. Very few thought of it as a profit-making enterprise, but they did not want to lose money either, which generally meant relying on local talent more than paying for out-of-town talent. Elmira's line-up, while not featuring a former major league out-of-towner like John Clapp, included several strong local players, most notably John F. Doran from Athens and William C. "Bill" Heine from Elmira.

Pitcher John F. Doran was born in Athens, Pennsylvania, in August 1861 to Irish immigrants Michael B. Doran and Mary Mullins. He had two brothers (Michael, or "Mickey," and Patrick) and four sisters (Elizabeth, Anna, Helen, and Mary). Michael, Senior, was a blacksmith, and, according to *Sporting Life*, much of John's "effectiveness is due to his terrific speed, which comes from a pair of arms which are as finely developed as one could wish. He can thank he early work as an iron molder in Athens, Pa., for his fine muscles." [103]

In the 1880 census, the Dorans lived in the Athens Borough, and both John and Mickey worked in a "Bridge Shop," likely the

Kellogg and Maurice Bridge Company, a bridge manufacturer. Like many immigrant families who moved to the area for work, they tended to live amongst other immigrants. Among the Doran's neighbors were the Moore family, headed by John, who was also born in Ireland, and the Ronne family, headed by James, who was born in Denmark. Both John Moore and James Ronne worked in a "Furniture Shop." Many of the other immigrant families in the neighborhood also had workers in the furniture or bridge shop, like the Doran boys.

The Doran's family home burned down in July 1871, when John was less than ten years old,[104] and his younger brother Patrick drowned in the Susquehanna less than a month later.[105] These tragedies must have traumatized the young family, and could have contributed to some of the behavioral problems both John and his older brother Mickey exhibited as they grew older. Mickey, for instance, was allegedly connected with a local "hoodlum" group called the "White Caps."[106]

Although a relatively old prospect at twenty-six, Doran's first documented semi-professional baseball experience was with Elmira in 1887. A stocky 5'4" and 160 pounds,[107] he likely played undocumented amateur or semi-professional ball before that when not working as a blacksmith or at the bridge shop. At a time when baseball was played during the light of day, it was especially challenging for working-class boys to play, since their families depended on their reliable wages.[108]

Catcher William Charles "Bill" Heine, meanwhile, was born in the German province of Hanover in 1868. His parents, Henry and Johanna, brought Bill to the U.S. when he was eight months old and settled in the Elmira area, where they had three more sons–Henry, George, and Charles. The senior Henry ran a saloon at 165 Baldwin Street near the Lyceum theater.

Young Bill Heine played as the catcher for Elmira School Number 1 prior to joining the village's 1887 squad. Like Doran, he also likely played undocumented amateur ball in the area prior to joining the semi-pro team and was also likely counted on to help support his family.

With both Doran and Heine on hand, Elmira's semi-professional team defeated the Owego Susquehannas 11-4 on May 24. Doran and Heine combined scored five of Elmira's eleven runs, and Burns pitched for Elmira with Heine as his catcher. Owego's line-up featured many players from the '86 team, including Ringrose, Ward, Madigan, and Gould. A new player, Lincoln Roberts, pitched and scored two of the Owego runs.

Umpires in these games had a very tough challenge. Not only did they have to keep the players and crowds as calm as possible, but they had to cover the entire field, as rarely was more than one umpire used each game. Typically, the home team would use someone who was respected and had playing experience. Elmira, for instance, used William Bally, a traveling salesman and thirty-year-old son of a prominent local watchmaker from Switzerland. Bally had organized and played for the Elmira Actives as a teenager in 1874, so was very familiar with the rules and with getting around the field.

Unfortunately, for Bally, however, opposing teams considered him to be heavily biased in favor of the home team, and such was the case with this contest. "It is customary for the vanquished, in any contest, to excuse their defeat," the *Owego Record* reported, "and it must be urged that several, three or four, at least, of the decisions against our boys were openly laughed at and derided by the fair-minded audience of Elmira people, while none of [Bally's] decisions against Elmira were called in question."

The two teams met again two weeks later on June 7 at Owego, and Elmira won again, this time 14-9. Doran was again among the team's hitting leaders. Gould caught for Owego and was the victim of "violent contact" with Elmira base runner Shay in the eighth inning, when Shay collided with him just as a throw arrived. Gould "was knocked down and lost sight of the ball, so that the bases were cleared before he recovered the missing sphere." Gould "raised the objection that the base runner was in fault, but Umpire Mabee decided that Gould was in the line and the scores counted."

The Owego Record noted that "threatening" weather kept attendance down and complained about spectators who stood outside the grounds and failed to pay the admission fee. "The usual large crowd of Johns patronized the board piles, adjacent to the grounds, and during the evening kicked as vigorously over the mistakes of the club as if they had ever invested a cent in the support of the club."

Elmira, Owego, and Waverly each had its share of successes and failures that summer. On June 15, Waverly hosted Owego, with Roberts as the starting pitcher for Owego and batting fourth. It was a much-anticipated contest. Waverly took a 4-3 lead after the first inning and never looked back, ultimately winning 23-7. Harry Taylor led Waverly's scoring attack with five runs, and the rest of Waverly's line-up was not far behind, as everyone scored at least once.

Owego and Waverly met again on June 22, this time on Owego's grounds. Waverly again took an early lead—3-1 in the first inning. Owego came back to pull ahead in the third inning, and the teams then traded leads until Waverly took a slim 8-7 lead in the fifth and held it for the next two innings. In the eighth, Owego got Wallis and Gould on base, and then Ringrose hit a long fly ball. Unfortunately for Waverly, Hall and Kennedy collided while attempting to catch it, and the ball fell to the ground, allowing both runners and Ringrose to score. Owego pulled ahead again with a 10-8 lead.

"The accident was quite severe and Hall was knocked out for some time," the *Owego Record* reported, but after doctors treated him with a "strong 'sniffler,'" which must have been a contemporary nickname for smelling salts, the game resumed.

Waverly's next game was on June 30 at home against the tough Lockport club. The crowd size was disappointing, due, the *Waverly Free Press* surmised, to the "extreme heat," and Waverly again had trouble holding a lead, this time allowing four runs in the ninth to tie the game at 10-10 and go into extra innings. In these days before electric lights on the field, extra innings were difficult to play and watch, but Waverly scored in the tenth to secure the win.

As July rolled around, and the weather became hot and humid, interest in local professional baseball contests declined. "Waverly has one of the best home clubs in Western New York," reported the *Waverly Free Press*, "and should receive better encouragement. It costs considerable to secure attendance of first-class clubs, as a guarantee has to be given, and unless the attendance is good, many times the boys have to make up the amount from their own pockets. If it is desirable to maintain a good club here, and but few will say it is not, a more liberal patronage should be given." [109]

In an editorial entitled "Baseball Bluster," published on July 8, the *Owego Record* explained its town's situation similarly: "The lack of support given the club has made formation of a stock company, which could purchase the entire 'plant,' lease of grounds, fence, grand stand, uniforms, masks, bats, etc., a good idea and one which could be done to advantage," the *Record* wrote. "If twenty, forty or a hundred men had stock in a base ball club, the interest would be greater and the games better patronized. Owego has a good club, but to play such teams as Waverly, Elmira and Lockports have, we need strengthening."

The Waverly and Elmira teams continued to play one another in early July. For the July 12 game in Elmira, the Waverly team was almost short a player when Pat Sheahan missed the train from Waverly to Elmira. Fortunately, Sheahan, the "fancy first baseman," lived not far from the train station and raced after the train on his horse, Nick. "He was only trying to overtake a passenger train that contained the balance of the club who were bound for Elmira," the *Waverly Free Press* explained. "He succeeded. The horse still lives, likewise the popular first baseman." Still, despite Sheahan's heroic effort, Waverly lost 11-5.

Fortunately, Waverly had an immediate opportunity for redemption–they were hosting Elmira the very next day. Once again, the umpiring was in question, as Elmira disputed Harry Thatcher's calls for Waverly. "We would like to see an umpire that would suit the Elmira kickers," the *Waverly Free Press* chided. "The Elmira club has the reputation of being the best mouth ball players in this part of the state, and they are justly entitled to that honor. They could beat Detroit or Chicago nine games out of ten, if they could secure an umpire to suit their fancy, but when they get an umpire that they can't work, then trouble begins."

Waverly took a first-inning 1-0 lead in the game, extended that lead to 3-1 by the sixth inning, and held Elmira off in the end to win 3-2 in a contest the *Waverly Free Press* called "The finest game ever played on the grounds." Despite the excellent baseball, however, the crowd was still not as large as had been hoped.

Waverly expected financial and athletic success on the diamond in large part because it was experiencing overall commercial success. The shops, stores, and factories on Broad Street in Waverly had been humming all summer with busy commerce and the trappings of wealth and boom times. On the evening of June 29th, for example, Waverly's business streets were the first in the county to be lighted by electricity. "They give a steady dazzling light which penetrates into the gloom," the *Waverly Free Press* reported. "The lights were greatly admired, and all seem to favor their adoption for lighting the main business streets. Speak it loud and plain that Waverly is on the high road to prosperity."[110]

Boom times for companies did not necessarily mean boom times for laborers, however. Throughout the country, factory and mine owners were adopting increasingly sophisticated methods to squeeze as much revenue out of their businesses, as possible, included those intended to reduce labor expense. Long hours, six-day work weeks and unsafe working conditions led to the United States having one of the highest industrial accident rates in the Western world, as from 1880 to 1900, 35,000 workers were killed annually in work-related accidents and another 536,000 were injured.[111] In an effort to help counter this trend, state governments initiated regulatory reforms aimed at some of the most significant labor challenges, especially workplace safety.

Waverly's largest employer, the Hall & Lyon Novelty Works, experienced this new regulatory environment first hand in 1887, when New York State first inspected it. Hall & Lyon employed 120 men and boys, and, among the items cited by the Factory Inspectors, was the fact that it had just one bathroom for all of its workers.

The inspectors faced criticism and resistance from business owners, but insisted that the "same fundamental principle of law which protects the millionaire from the depredations of the highwayman, and punishes at the expense of the State the forger of a capitalist's note, should surely reach out and save the child from the clutches of the avaricious, and insist that the life and limbs of the citizen shall be as sacred as the capitalist's signature." [112]

*Hall & Lyon Novelty Works at the corner of Broad
and Spaulding Streets in Waverly.*

Hall & Lyon imported wood from Canada to make its furniture, and they attracted workers from across the region. Business was booming at the factory during the mid-1880s, obliging many workers to work nights to keep up with orders.[113] One of the factory's first products was a $100 Bible stand (equivalent to over $2,600 in 2018) made of "maple, hand carved, and veneered with ash root."[114]

Many of the factory workers were of the same post-Civil War generation as the village's ball players. Some, like Vernie Aldrich, were also athletes, but lacked the skill or work schedule flexibility required to play on the baseball team on weekday afternoons. Aldrich, born in 1867, worked at the factory with his father, Samuel, and was one of the leaders of the Waverly Athletic Club.

Many other Hall & Lyon workers of that generation grew up on farms around the region, like Henry McKibbon from Brees-port, Augustus Smith from Baldwin, Lynn Congdon from Troy, William Dobell from Van Etten, and Reuben Genung from Danby. Many of these young men would remain in Waverly or Sayre for years to come and work for the railroad or related industries.[115]

One local farm boy, Earl Burgess from Marathon, worked at Hall & Lyon for a time, but was better known as an usher at Waverly's Opera House.[116] It was there that he caught the show-business bug, went on to work at Barnum & Bailey's Circus, and eventually became a successful Vaudeville producer. Up until the movies replaced Vaudeville in the 1920s, Burgess regularly brought top-notch variety shows to Waverly and other local stages across New York and Pennsylvania.

A fair number of recent immigrants worked as the factory as well, including the Krist brothers: Joseph, born in 1861 in Baden, one of the coalition states that would eventually form the German Empire, and Fred, born in 1869 after the family emigrated to Oswego County. The Krist brothers lived on Park Place, within earshot of and easy walking distance to both the factory and the ball grounds.

The men and boys at the factory were like a large extended family. Factory events like shutdowns, fires, and accidents were documented in the local newspapers, and family events like weddings and funerals were occasions of special interest to managers and co-workers alike. "I wish to extend my heartfelt thanks to all those who assisted me during the sickness and burial of my husband," wrote one aggrieved widow at the time, "and especially to his fellow workmen in the Novelty works."[117]

HALL & LYON WAS ONE OF MANY WAVERLY BUSINESSES THAT hoped to benefit from a successful local baseball team, but success at the factory and shop was not translating to success on the ball field. Echoing the financial concerns of many ball teams throughout the region, on July 23, the *Waverly Free Press* reported that the "Waverly base ball club has cancelled all engagements for the present" and that even the popular Lockport baseball team was disbanding because "it was not a financial success."

Despite the baseball season's early conclusion, Waverly's young players benefited from John Clapp's tutelage. Years later, Harry Taylor described his own work ethic in a manner that transcended the game and harkened back to lessons learned as a young player: "I made up my mind years ago that disposition was a strong factor in the makeup of a ball player; in fact, in a winning team you will notice that there are lots of willing workers, players who have the interest of the team at heart; never slacken their vim and play ball with heart and soul."[118]

Taylor and two other Waverly players–Hall and Cole–would go on to join Doran and Heine on a professional team in Elmira in 1888. Taylor and Cole both played for many more years: Taylor eventually became a major leaguer and played a prominent role in professional baseball's future, while Cole moved first to Chicago to play minor league ball, and then kept heading west until eventually settling in Seattle.[119]

ªNat Lowman's professional baseball activity seemed to have ceased after 1887, as no further such news was found in local newsapapers. By 1891, at the age of twenty-seven, he had moved to Buffalo, where he progressed in his railroad career, and was eventually listed in the census and city directories as an engineer. He passed away in Buffalo in 1936.

For John Clapp, a teammate of some of the greatest baseball players in history, it was a humble end to his professional career. According to the *Waverly Free Press*, following his season as Waverly's "first professional player," Clapp returned to Ithaca and "again took up his trade, that of painter." He reportedly played on occasion for a local amateur team in Ithaca, and he also worked as a police officer, becoming particularly well known on the Cornell campus. He died in 1904 while on duty "assisting a policeman in making an arrest."[120]

While Clapp remained in Ithaca following his retirement from baseball, his younger brother Aaron, also a former major leaguer, moved to Sayre to be a painter and eventual foreman at the Lehigh Valley Shops before passing away in 1914 in Sayre.[121]

John and Aaron Clapp represented the generation of ballplayers born before the Civil War who were in their prime when the National League was formed in 1876. By the late 1880s, though, only a few of these players, such as John Ward and Cap Anson, were still prominent major league players. Most, like Clapp, were either on the fringes of the game or were out altogether.

Talented young men from immigrant families, like Doran or Heine, were fortunate that baseball opportunities were plentiful in New York State. The playing field was a great equalizer, a place where they could momentarily wipe away the pressures of immigrant life. Playing alongside young Ivy League-educated men from long-time American families, like the Platts and the Taylors, these sons of immigrants felt that the differences among them were not so stark as they had previously thought. They too could aspire to a formal education and social elevation beyond the working class, if not for themselves then for their children. It was a true melting pot, an American dream.

However, this was not true for young men of color who were perceived to be at the bottom most insecure level of the working class. Even in the relatively tolerant northern states, these kinds of opportunities were simply not open to them. The ability to integrate and associate with male white craftsmen was very limited, even when not restricted legally. This limitation belied the notions of commonality and unity that were otherwise said by industrialists to be available to all those who had talent and worked hard.

In the face of this trend, professional baseball club owners in New York and its environs tried something radical in the late 1880s, adding several top African-American players to their previously all-white teams. Since these players were at least as talented as their white counterparts, adding them helped their teams win and thus improved their ability to draw crowds. The need to balance this goal against any possible backlash was obviously on the owners' minds. To them, this dilemma was similar to that between attracting the "reputable class" of patron who admired the game for its skill, sportsmanship and science, and the "hoodlum element" who loved noisy coaching, gambling, kicking against umpires and similar exciting disputes.[122] Nonetheless, it was a courageous move that resulted in increased crowds in some places, but also predictably bred controversy. It also led to some of the most competitive professional baseball the Southern Tier would ever see.

PART TWO

Skill and Labor

Baseball Around the Region (1887-1895)

"Aggressiveness is the main thing in baseball."[123]

—JOHN J. McGRAW

CHAPTER 5

A Sliver of Justice

J ack Chapman, born in Brooklyn in 1843, was a decade older than John Clapp and represented the generation of ballplayers who were in their prime during the Civil War. They largely preceded the National League or entered it as seasoned veterans and managers.

In fact, when Chapman began playing left field for the Brooklyn Atlantics in 1861, the same era in which he played against the legendary Jim Creighton, the Civil War was just starting up and professional baseball was in its infancy. Most of the professional baseball world centered on New York City and its environs (Elysian Fields in Hoboken, New Jersey, for example), and baseball was considered a game to be played and watched by gentlemen.

Baseball was played in camp and parade grounds wherever the young soldiers were stationed during the Civil War, and rules became standardized as players from different parts of the country exchanged ideas and reached consensus, allowing for rapid expansion once the war was over.

Throughout the 1860s and 1870s, Chapman played for the powerful Atlantics, which was "mainly composed of Irish, Catholic food-industry employees with strong Democratic Party ties."[124] Among his teammates was the fiery five-foot-three-and-a-half-inch sparkplug Richard J. "Dickey" Pearce. A Brooklyn native like Chapman, Pearce was born in 1836, seven years before Chapman, and was a fierce competitor who joined Creighton as one of the very first recognized stars to be paid to play baseball. "His pudgy, ungainly physique ruled out good running speed," noted his biographer Frank V. Phelps, "but he compensated with extremely able judgment, anticipation, competitiveness, unflappable coolness and mastery of the playing rules."[125]

While many of their contemporaries went off to battle in the Civil War, Chapman and Pearce remained in the New York City area to play baseball, and they were pioneers in the game's post-war evolution. Pearce was the first to play the shortstop position between second and third base, where it has remained ever since. Originally, the position was treated similar to a roving short fielder in softball, but the three infielders at the time played much closer to their bases than they do today, and Pearce decided he was more valuable plugging the gap between second and third. As a catcher, he was among the first to signal pitches, and he was the very first to intentionally use the bunt as a hitting tactic. This led to refinements in the sacrifice bunt, squeeze play, fair-foul hit, and place hitting, all of which would be further developed by later generations.[126]

Chapman and Pearce both played important roles in the Atlantics' thrilling extra-inning 8-7 victory over Cincinnati on June 14, 1870. It was said to be the greatest baseball game ever played up to that time, and it broke Cincinnati's unprecedented eighty-four-game winning streak. Pearce played shortstop and batted leadoff, while Chapman played left field and batted cleanup.[127]

Upon formation of the National League in 1876, Chapman was named player-manager of the Louisville franchise. He went on to manage major league teams in Milwaukee, Worcester, Detroit, and Buffalo. When Buffalo's franchise disbanded in the midst of financial trouble in 1885, Chapman stayed in the city to manage Buffalo's new minor league franchise in the International League.

Pearce not only played alongside Chapman, but in 1876, at the age of forty, he joined George Bradley and John Clapp in St. Louis, where he mentored the twenty-four-year-old Clapp on inside baseball tactics that the young catcher would later pass on to his Waverly players. Pearce partnered with Clapp for two years in St. Louis before returning to Brooklyn, where, in 1881, he opened a bar at 7 Boerum Street called Atlantic Shades, which featured baseball memorabilia and other trappings akin to today's sports bars.[128] This preceded Clapp's own Manhattan tavern by just a year or so, and it marked both men as pioneers in bringing baseball celebrity to other forms of urban entertainment.

By the late 1880s, Jack Chapman had become one of the top managers in organized baseball, mentoring dozens of the best players and some of the most influential baseball leaders in history. As the manager of the Buffalo franchise, Chapman was one of the top figures in the International League's 1887 season, organized baseball's top minor league. He had a keen eye for talent and was an advocate for including "colored" players on his roster.

"Probably no other man has brought out so many players as I have," he wrote in 1900, "mainly because I always have made it a point to be on the lookout for new blood by means of which I could improve my team… I think I may claim without anyone gainsaying my assertion, that I have turned out and sold to the National and other leagues more players who have proved to be crackerjacks than any other man living." [129]

In 1877, one year after the National League was formed, there were only four other professional baseball leagues, but by 1887, that number had ballooned to twenty-eight, two at the major league level (the National League and the American Association), and the rest at the minor league level. Just below the two major leagues was the International League, which in 1887, featured teams from twelve different cities: six from New York (Binghamton, Buffalo, Oswego, Rochester, Syracuse, and Utica), two from New Jersey (Jersey City and Newark), two from Pennsylvania (Scranton and Wilkes-Barre), and two from Canada (Toronto and Hamilton).

The caliber of baseball in the International League was very high. Overall, according to the Society for American Baseball Research (SABR), there were 240 documented roster spots in the International League during the 1887 season, and 163 of these, or 68 percent, were filled with players who either had played or would later play in the major leagues. These percentages shrink significantly when we look at the lower minor leagues though, like New York's Central and Western Leagues.

Naturally, nearly all players aspired to compete at the highest levels, and to earn enough income to make a living. Even at the highest levels, it was common for teams to begin a season with large crowds and full coffers, but fail to sustain these through the summer's dog days, and ultimately fall apart, leaving their players high and dry. As mentioned previously, only 25 percent of 19th century teams lasted over two years. Without a paycheck, players were forced to find other teams or return to alternative employment, such as working in mines, farms, and factories.

While Waverly, Elmira, and Owego toiled in the very low minor leagues or in the non-affiliated, semi-professional world outside of "organized baseball," their rival Southern Tier city, Binghamton, nicknamed "The Parlor City" for its thriving cigar industry, was already reaping the benefits of being a part of a top baseball league.

Binghamton's 1887 team featured one of the boldest, most talented, and most controversial ball players of the nineteenth century: twenty-nine-year-old John "Bud" Fowler. Fowler was not only a great player, but also an experienced team organizer, manager, businessman, and barber. Arguably, the fact that he was African American was the only thing that kept him out of the major leagues.

Fowler was actually born John W. Jackson, Jr., on March 16, 1858, in Fort Plain, New York. By 1860, his family had moved to Cooperstown, thirty miles away, where John, Jr., grew up and first played baseball. In the 1860 census, his father, John, Sr., was listed as a twenty-six-year-old barber born in New York, and his mother, Mary, as a twenty-two-year-old, also born in New York. A sheriff's family lived on one side of the Jacksons, and a surveyor's on the other. Other tradesmen in the neighborhood included a printer, a laborer, a blacksmith, and a milliner. It was a steady working-class neighborhood.

By the age of twenty, John, Jr., was playing baseball under the name of Fowler, rather than Jackson, though his rationale for the name change is unknown. He was working as a barber, like his father, as well as a ballplayer, and it has been speculated that he changed his baseball identity to hide it from his parents. In the late 1870s, he pitched for teams in Chelsea, Lynn, and Malden, Massachusetts, including at least one exhibition game against a major league team. In practically every case, Fowler was the lone "colored" player on his team–and oftentimes, in his entire league.

By the early 1880s, Fowler was working with others to form a national colored league, an effort that nearly succeeded in late 1886 with the formation of the League of Colored Base Ball Players. Unfortunately, it collapsed after just ten days due to lack of financial backing.[130]

1885 Keokuk, Iowa, team picture. Bud Fowler back row center.
Courtesy of the National Baseball Hall of Fame.

By the time Fowler signed with Binghamton in 1887, he was well known throughout the country, not only as an organizer, but also for having had productive stints as a barber/ballplayer in such wide-ranging locales as Ontario, Louisiana, Virginia, Iowa, Kansas, and Colorado. A right-handed batter and thrower at 5'7" and 155 pounds, Fowler was "A good player, very versatile, a fast runner, and a slick fielder at second base, which became his primary position."[131]

At the time of his signing, Binghamton team officials humorously told *Sporting Life*, "Fowler is a dandy in every respect. Some say that Fowler is a colored man, but we account for his dark complexion by the fact that he is no record player, and in chasing after balls has become tanned from constant and careless exposure to the sun." He was eager to join the team and was one of the first to begin pre-season workouts.[132]

Fowler was not the sole African-American player in the

International League in 1887. In fact, the league had seven "colored" players during the season, an unprecedented number. Not surprisingly, given that they would likely have been in the major leagues if not for their skin color, these players were extremely talented compared to their white teammates. Each of them was among the very best players on his team: Randolph (or Randall) Jackson with Oswego, Robert "Bob" Higgins with Syracuse, George Stovey and Moses Fleetwood "Fleet" Walker with Newark, Fowler and William Renfro with Binghamton, and Ulysses Franklin "Frank" Grant with Buffalo. Stovey, a strong left-handed pitcher, was so well thought of that John Ward repeatedly asked New York Giants' owner John Day to sign him, "but when other owners and players complained, Day backed off."[133]

At twenty-one, Grant was among the youngest of this group, but he was already considered one of the most talented second basemen in the game, earning the nickname "The Colored Dunlap," intended to be a flattering comparison to flashy white major league second baseman Fred Dunlap, baseball's highest paid player from 1886 through 1889.[134] As a second baseman, Grant had such "extraordinary range and rifle arm" that opposing newspapers frequently put down his spectacular fielding as a "circus act," but it also drew tremendous interest and acclaim.[135]

Grant was born on August 1, 1865, in Pittsfield, Massachusetts, the youngest of seven children of Franklin and Frances Grant, both of whom were born in Massachusetts. In the 1860 census, the family was living in Dalton, Massachusetts. Franklin was listed as a thirty-six-year old black farm laborer, and Frances was listed as black and twenty-seven years old. Their neighbors were white, and most worked at the local paper mill. By 1870, when Frank was five, his father had passed away, Frances headed the family as a "Restaurant Keeper" in Williamstown, and the family was listed as mulatto, rather than black. Their immediate neighbors were a boarding house of white college students on one side and a white family, the Perrys, headed by a college professor, on the other.

The family's situation was similar in 1880, with Frank's oldest sister, Amelia, running a bakery. All told, young Frank Grant grew up in an intellectual collegiate predominantly white environment, playing baseball with his older brother, the Perry boys, and other white boys in town. By May of 1886, he was playing with Michael Doyle and George Stone for Meridian, Connecticut, in the Eastern League, where he batted .316 in forty-four games. He also played forty-nine games for Buffalo in the International League that year under manager Jack Chapman and batted .344. His performance for Buffalo was notable for its high skill and energy.

One of the Perry boys, Bliss Perry, went on to become a notable English professor and eventually editor of *The Atlantic* magazine. His 1895 fictional portrayal of Grant in *The Plated City* celebrated Grant's aggressive and exciting brand of baseball:

> The runner checked himself by a violent effort, his black eyes fastened upon the ball. The catcher made a feint of throwing to third, and then tossed the ball deliberately to the pitcher. And alas for him, he tossed it too deliberately, for certainly the ball had not left his hand before Tom Beaulieu [Frank Grant] with a cat-like bound, darted for the plate! Ten yards to run and five to slide, before the pitcher could return the ball! The grand stand leaped to its feet as one man, as the frantic pitcher seized the ball–it seemed like forever before it would reach him–and hurled it back with a throw that was perfection itself. Man and ball seemed to reach the plate together in a cloud of dust; but as it settled, it disclosed Beaulieu lying at full length across the plate, while the catcher, upset by that tremendous slide, lay on his back a yard away. The umpire waved his hand impressively. He could have been heard if he had whispered, so hushed was the crowd. "That man is safe," he said. The catcher sat up and flung down his mask with

a curse; Beaulieu leaped to his feet, wiping his forehead
with his brown forearm; then Bedlam broke loose, and
the game was over.[136]

Grant, Fowler, and the other African-American players were
pioneers in professional interracial sports at the very moment
in history when racial boundaries were hardening, especially
in the south where Reconstruction had broken down in the late
1870s and segregation laws popular prior to Reconstruction
were being reintroduced without Northern interference. These
laws, popularly known as "Jim Crow" laws after the stereotypical "plantation rustic" character of blackface minstrel shows (as
opposed to "Zip Coon," the "urban dandy" character)[137] would
by the 1890s evolve to the point where ten of the eleven former
Confederate states enacted new Constitutions or Amendments
to severely restrict African-Americans and some poor whites
from voting.

Although such legal segregation was uncommon in the
North, significant racial discrimination existed for African
Americans in the North, and the root causes and nuances
were complex. Some was undoubtedly tied to perceptions
of economic class and security on the working class ladder.
Some was also undoubtedly tied to culture and the stereotypes
popularized by such entertainments as the aforementioned
blackface minstrelsy, which had its roots in a complex mixture
of circus clowns, burlesque, exciting African-based music and
dance, cultural expropriation, and disguise (not unlike the
patriots who dressed like slaves and native Americans during
the Boston Tea Party).

Blackface minstrel shows, in fact, were the most popular
working class entertainment in the 19th century.[138] They were
common in large cities and small towns, and the main feature
was white male entertainers who covered themselves in black
burnt cork, told pun-filled jokes and stories, and sang and danced
to stereotypical African-American songs. Among the acts were

dances like "cakewalks" and "coon runs" where participants demonstrated colorful dance moves to syncopated polyrhythms and sometimes competed for prizes.

Blackface minstrels both exploited and honored their characters, depending on their shifting motivations and those of their audiences, and they earned the enmity of critics like Frederick Douglass, who called them "filthy scum," as well as the patronage of beloved cultural touch points like Walt Whitman, Abraham Lincoln and Samuel Clemens.[139] Defenders commonly cited their celebration of African-American culture, but this ignored the obvious stereotypes and lapses in quality that could easily be manipulated for purposes beyond entertainment.

"On the one side there is a disdain for 'mass'-cultural domination, the incorporation of black culture fashioned to racist uses;" explained Professor Eric Lott in his landmark study *Love and Theft*, "on the other a celebration of an authentic people's culture, the dissemination of black arts with potentially liberating results." Lott argued that there were elements of both in early minstrelsy, thus contributing to the moral complexity and making simple analysis obsolete.[140]

It was onto this complex cultural landscape that Fowler, Grant and the other African-American pioneers stepped at the beginning of the 1887 season. Despite the challenge, they were among the smartest and most talented players in the league, and they were eager to show their stuff.

Of the seven African Americans in the International League, only Walker, with Newark, had spent any time in the major leagues during a regular season, as he and his younger brother, "Weldy," had played one season three years earlier with the American Association's Toledo franchise. Fleet Walker had played forty-two games and batted .263, while Weldy Walker played in five games and batted .222. Neither received another shot in Toledo. After that, Fleet played minor league seasons in Waterbury and Cleveland before arriving in Newark, while Weldy played in Cleveland and Akron.

The 1887 International League season presented a unique opportunity for the races to compete directly with and against one another at a high level on the same ball field. The teams were centered in upstate New York and Canada–far from the Deep South–so there was hope among the ownership that the right number of minority players would generate excitement, attract more fans, both minority and white, and bring in more revenue.

Although there were a number of players that year who had previously played in Southern League teams, the International League only had one player who was from the formerly Confederate Deep South: pitcher Douglas "Dug" Crothers, who was born on November 16, 1859, in Natchez, Mississippi. Crothers was of fairly small-to-average size (5'9" and 140 lbs.), but was durable, having gone 27-16 for Syracuse in 1886 after splitting 1885 between Memphis in the Southern League, where went 1-2, and the major league New York Metropolitans, where he went 7-11.

The Civil War was still a recent memory for Americans in 1887, having ended just twenty-two years earlier. Many war veterans from both the North and South were still in their prime working years, and they attended games when work hours allowed. In the International League alone, Syracuse manager Jim Gifford and Scranton manager Fergy Malone both had first-hand Civil War recollections, having fought with the 152nd New York and the 196th Pennsylvania, respectively.

Despite the similarities in many players' working-class backgrounds and the ideals of Northern tolerance and honorable military service to help end slavery, the 1887 season was a rough one for the seven black pioneers. Crowds, fellow players and the media were far from universally receptive, and open hostility toward African-American players was typically met by team and league ownership with an indifference that spoke more of wanting to avoid unnecessary annoyances (and the resultant financial headaches) than of promoting social justice.

Upon Oswego's signing of Jackson early in the season, for example, one *Sporting Life* reporter expressed his dismay, and no doubt that of many players, in no uncertain terms: "How far will this mania for engaging colored players go? At the present rate of progress the International might ere many moons change its title to 'Colored League.'"[141]

This comment may sound over-the-top to today's readers, especially given that the percentage of African-American players in the League was still very low. Nevertheless, it was an example of the passion many in both the North and South felt regarding race relations. Fortunately for the seven pioneers, International League owners and management, at least at the beginning of the season, were willing to pursue the "mania."

An early test of integrated play occurred during Buffalo's 1887 exhibition season, which preceded the regular International League schedule. Due in part to Chapman's strong connections throughout organized baseball, Buffalo played a heavy schedule of major league teams in April of 1887, including trips to Pittsburgh, Baltimore, Washington, DC, Philadelphia, and Boston. Notably missing from the schedule was any game against Cap Anson's Chicago club, as Anson was notoriously opposed to competing with or against African-American players.

Buffalo competed poorly against the major leaguers, but Chapman saw it as a valuable tune-up for the regular season, as a unique opportunity to get his pitchers and hitters prepared for high-caliber play, and as a showcase for his young star second baseman.

"Had the weather been good on Monday," *Sporting Life* reported regarding early games in Pittsburgh, "the attendance would have been as large again just to see Grant play second base, in which position he has no equal."[142] A week later, *Sporting Life* was just as effusive about Grant's performance: "The second base play of the colored lad Grant [is] winning commendation wherever Buffalo goes."[143]

In Baltimore on April 5, Buffalo struggled through the "intense cold" to lose "easily." Grant had a walk, a stolen base, and a run against Oriole starter Matt Kilroy, who would go on to win a league-leading forty-six games during the 1887 regular season.

Grant was in the line-up again the next day for a rematch, this time against Oriole pitcher Ed Knouff. Buffalo kept the score closer, as the Orioles "had to work to win," but it was still a loss.[144]

The following week, Buffalo played Pittsburgh, and the *Daily Post* reported that local "dusky" residents were very taken by Grant's speed and skill. "Ain't he a combusticator!" was cited as one sample remark, "whatever that meant."[145]

1887 Buffalo team. Top row (L/R): Chapman, Remsen, Easterday, Zell and Galligan; Middle row: Lehane, Hamburg, Roeschle, Reidy, Purvis and Calihan; Front row: Walsh, Fanning, Grant and O'Neill. Courtesy of the National Baseball Hall of Fame.

Grant's exploits drew notice in the national media, prompting at least one reporter to declare the youngster, "A hero with the colored population of every city where his club appears."[146]

Although there were likely many racially charged incidents during Grant's April journey through the exhibition major leagues, especially in the relatively southern cities of Baltimore and Washington, DC, very few specifics were recorded in the national sporting press. *The Glens Falls Times*, however, a paper located near Grant's then-hometown of Plattsburgh, New York, reported that things became heated when Buffalo faced Philadelphia on April 16.

Philadelphia's starting pitcher for that April 16 game was Ed Daily, a twenty-four-year-old right-handed pitcher and outfielder from Providence, Rhode Island, who showed tremendous skill and potential. In his rookie season of 1885, he won twenty-six games and lost twenty-three, with an earned run average (ERA) of just 2.21. One particular area of concern for him though was that he led the league in wild pitches, with a total of forty. In the 1886 season, he won sixteen games and lost nine, and although his ERA grew to (a still-respectable) 3.06, he significantly reduced his wild pitches to nineteen. He had not played as often in '86 and was hoping to return to top form in '87. His brother, Con, was also a major leaguer.

As Daily faced the Buffalo team that day, he reportedly let his teammates know that he would have fun with "that nigger," Grant. To make fun of Grant while on the field, Daily reportedly sang or whistled the popular minstrel song "There's a New Coon in Town," whenever he was within Grant's earshot.

The reaction of Daily's and Grant's teammates to the insult was not recorded in press accounts, nor was Grant's initial or exact reaction. One imagines laughter and guffaws among the Philadelphia players, the spectators and perhaps even some of Grant's teammates. One sees Grant digging in confidently against the smirking young pitcher in the midst of the insult, well aware that all eyes were on him and how he would react.

While posterity did not record these details, the baseball results were clear and dramatic: Daily threw the pitch and Grant "got square by knocking the ball out of the lot for a clean home run," and "Daily's opinion of him changed."[147]

The home run shook up Daily so much that Jim Devlin replaced him on the mound. Although Philadelphia wound up winning the game, Grant's home run was the big story.

Ed Daily. From the Library of Congress.

"Grant, the colored second baseman, was the lion of the afternoon," wrote *Sporting Life* of that day's game. "His exhibition was unusually brilliant."[148]

As for Daily, the *New York National Police Gazette* reported that, "When Daily, of the Philadelphias, hears any one whistle 'There's a new coon in town,' he turns livid and trembles like a leaf. Grant, the 'colored Dunlap' is still fresh in his memory."[149] It was a sliver of justice that likely raised the young African-American slugger's hopes.

Buffalo got off to a strong start when the International League's regular season opened, and Grant was its star. In describing an early loss in Utica, the *Utica Herald* reported, "The great player of the afternoon was Grant, the colored second baseman of the visitors. He seemed to hit everything, steal everything (no reflection) and catch and stop everything within a radius of a hundred feet around his position."[150] Even the *Sporting News'* Binghamton correspondent complemented Grant, while chiding the team, saying, "The Buffalos are not doing as well as was expected. Grant seems to be doing most of the playing."[151]

The start of Binghamton's baseball season was slightly delayed due to the fact that, as of late April, "the grounds at Riverside Park" were "under six feet of water" on account of the cold, wet spring.[152] The team's 1887 regular season began on May 3, with an 8-2 victory over Utica, followed by a 26-8 win the following day. This set them up for one of the best contests of the era: a long-awaited two-game set with Chapman's Buffalo team starting on May 7, where arguably the two greatest African-American ballplayers of the century—second basemen Frank Grant and Bud Fowler—would match up against one another on a level playing field with white players.

On the afternoon of Monday, May 7, the two teams squared off in Binghamton. Fowler was at second base and batting cleanup for the home team, while Grant was at second and batting fifth for Buffalo. Binghamton took a 4-0 lead in the first inning, and held the lead throughout the first seven innings. Buffalo picked up a run in the bottom of the seventh to pull within 7-3, but when Binghamton scored an insurance run in the top of the ninth to make it 8-3, it seemed like the game was over.

At 5'5" and 126 pounds, Binghamton pitcher Tony Madigan would not strike modern-day fans as having the typical build of a workhorse, but in this case, he held Buffalo to just three runs for the first eight innings, and he had done so efficiently. The game's running time was about ninety minutes when the final half-inning began, and the hometown cranks were eager to close the game out.

Frank Grant and his teammates had other ideas, though. Grant cracked a double to ignite a ninth inning rally that brought Buffalo to within one run. Ultimately, though, Madigan held onto the win, finishing 8-7.[153]

During the game, Grant and Fowler each held their own: Fowler landed three hits and one run, and Grant landed two hits, including that ninth-inning double, and one run.

Two afternoons later, May 9, the two teams squared off again, this time Bones Ely pitched for Binghamton and Mickey Walsh for Buffalo. Fowler was moved down a spot in the batting order to fifth, and started again at second base, as did Grant. It was not as exciting as the prior match, however, as Binghamton scored eight runs in the top of the first inning and never looked back, ultimately trouncing Buffalo, 16-9. Fowler again had three hits and one run, and Grant again had two hits (including another double) and one run.[154]

The next two-game Fowler-Grant match-up followed on June 14 in Buffalo. Two New Jersey natives, twenty-year-old Bill Husted for Buffalo and twenty-seven-year-old Ed Green for Binghamton, were the starting pitchers. Fowler and Grant were each in the same roles as before—batting fifth and playing second base—and, once again, Fowler's team took an early insurmountable lead. They picked up two runs in the first inning, four in the third, and five in the fifth to take a commanding 11-0 lead en route to a 21-3 win. Grant hit a single and scored one run, while Fowler picked up four hits and scored four times. In the three contests between the two, Binghamton now had a decisive 3-0 edge.

Fortunately, the next day, Wednesday June 15, Buffalo had another shot. Walsh for Buffalo and Madigan for Binghamton were the starters. Walsh had given up sixteen runs the last time he faced Binghamton, so he was due for a better day. Fortunately for Buffalo, Charlie Hamburg returned as a starting outfielder for this series. Hamburg was a twenty-three-year-old slick-fielding six-footer from Louisville, Kentucky.

Hamburg was new to the Buffalo club in 1887. He was born Charles M. Hambrick in Louisville on November 22, 1863, the fifth of eight children of German immigrants Maximillian and Theresa Hess Hambrick. Max was himself born Max Haubrich in Frankfurt around 1832 and immigrated to the U.S. in 1848. He passed through the Port of New Orleans on May 18, 1848, and settled in Louisville as a saddle maker before Americanizing his surname, marrying Theresa, and starting their family. The 1870 census found Max working as a "Harness Maker" and Charlie's eldest brother, John, then sixteen, working in a rope factory. Among their Louisville neighbors were a cabinetmaker, a machinist, a cigar maker, a milliner, a bartender, a streetcar driver, a blacksmith, a laundress, and two teamsters. Practically all were from Germany; so pervasive was the German influence in the area that the census listed the family heads by their German province (for example: Bayern, Hesse Damstadt, Baden, and Hanover).

Hamburg started his organized baseball career as an eighteen-year-old in Columbus, Georgia, with the Southern League, batting just .196 in ninety games. In 1886, he found himself in Bridgeport, Connecticut, in the Eastern League, where he improved to .243 in ninety-two games and showed sufficient potential that Jack Chapman added him to the Buffalo roster for 1887.

According to Louisville baseball manager Billy Reccius, whose younger brothers John and Phil both played in the major leagues, Hamburg was a local boy who stepped up and made the best of his baseball prospects:

Hamburg … was working in a Main Street saddlery-shop. I had arranged to play two exhibition games in Evansville, and Hamburg asked me to give him a trial with the Eclipse Club, which team I was managing. I had never seen him play, but I took chances on him and let him go to Evansville. It was a caution to see him hit that ball. He knocked it so far that they never saw it again, and he also led the team in fielding. Soon after that I got him an engagement in Columbus, Ga., along with Hub Collins and Leve Shreve, and since then he has developed into one of the best fielders in the country. He is strictly temperate in his habits, and that makes him all the more desirable.

Hamburg played right field and batted second in the Buffalo lineup on June 15. This time, it was Buffalo who took the early lead, with Madigan giving up one run in the first inning and four in the third. Binghamton scored four in the sixth to pull close at 5-4, but failed to keep pace in the late innings and wound up losing 8-7. Fowler had a triple and a single, and Grant, a double and a single. Grant and Hamburg each scored two runs, helping Buffalo to their first victory of the season over Binghamton. They were not scheduled to meet again until early July, giving both teams plenty of time to consider their successes and failures.

According to press reports at the time, these first Binghamton-Buffalo contests appeared to be played honestly and competitively. "With all these players performing creditably (and some of them brilliantly) in 1887," wrote historian Robert Peterson, "there was reason to hope that more and more Negroes would enter organized white leagues."[155] However, prejudice against them was strong. On May 25, for example, just weeks after the first Fowler-Grant match-up, Syracuse played at Toronto, where nineteen-year-old Robert "Bob" Higgins, Syracuse's "new colored pitcher" started. Unlike Fowler and Grant, Higgins was a child of the south, having been born and raised in Memphis,

Charlie Hamburg from Louisville, KY.

and was therefore not as accustomed to playing with whites on an integrated team. It would be an understatement to say his team-mates failed to support him. The final score was a "disgraceful" 23-8, largely due to Syracuse's fourteen errors, many of which were likely committed on purpose. Only seven of Toronto's twenty-three runs were earned against Higgins, but he largely took the blame. It didn't help that, in an 8-3 loss to Hamilton just one day earlier, with fellow (white) southerner Dug Crothers on the mound, the Syracuse fielders made only four errors. The disproportionate quality of the fielding support in favor of Crothers was so obvious that even the national media remarked on it.

"There is said to be a clique in the Syracuse Club against the colored pitcher Higgins," reported *Sporting Life* on June 1. "The wretched work of last Wednesday seems to bear the rumors out."[156]

Media discussion of Syracuse's "clique" was fueled by the fact that although Crothers and Higgins were the only Syracuse players born in the deep south, seven of the team's seventeen white players, including Crothers, had recently played in the Southern League for white Nashville, Memphis or Atlanta clubs, and the perception was that their displeasure with Syracuse management was broader than just Higgins, and included how the team was managed.

The split on the team was further confirmed by a story in the *Sporting News* on June 4, where it reported allegations that Harry Jacoby, a Philadelphia native on the Syracuse team and not one of the Southern League contingent (although he did play for at time with Norfolk in the Eastern League), was part of the anti-Higgins clique. "Jacoby is doing good work every day," the *Sporting News* said. "If it is true that he is a member of the [Syracuse team's] Ku-Klux-Klan to kill off Higgins, the negro, he has made a mistake. His friends did not expect this."[157] The *Sporting News* spelled out the "Multitude of Cliques" in detail, noting that union Civil War veteran Gifford allowed the "Ku-Klux coterie from the South" to run things, thus compelling team management to replace him with Joe Simmons. Simmons was perceived to be more of a disciplinarian, and this was much less to the Southerners' liking.[158]

The *Sporting News* references to the KKK and killing off Higgins were very likely intended to be hyperbole referring to the Southern League contingent's desire to remove Higgins from the team, but the intensity of the language reflected the intense feelings below the surface. Within a week of these reports, tensions among the Syracuse players broke into open and violent warfare. Crothers and outfielder Hank Simon, a native of Hawkinsville, New York, refused to pose for the Syracuse team picture with Higgins. When manager Simmons confronted Crothers for failing to pose, Crothers had "imprudent" words with the manger and was suspended. Later that same day, Simmons told Crothers not to bother joining the club for an upcoming road trip, whereupon the two argued again, and Crothers struck him in the breast before the two were separated.[159] Although there was some question as to whether the suspension would be permanent, Crothers was released by the end of the month and returned to St. Louis. By 1888, he would be playing and managing with Dallas in the Texas State League.

"A new trouble has just arisen in the affairs of certain baseball associations," noted a *Sporting News* editorial in response to these events:

> It seems to have done more damage to the International Association than to any other we know of. We refer to the importation of colored players into the ranks of that body. At Syracuse an open revolt has followed the signing of Higgins, the colored pitcher of that club. At first certain of the Syracuse players tried to queer him by refusing to support him as well as they were able to. Later they took other means but Higgins appears to have held his own throughout. The climax came, however, when Manager Simmons asked his player to sit beside Higgins while a group portrait was being taken of that team. Crothers the

St. Louis boy and Simon the Stars great left fielder begged
to be excused from taking part in such a proceeding. The
manager insisted and Crothers responded by banging the
manager one. The latter then suspended Crothers. Simon's
fate still hangs in the balance, and in the meanwhile there
is no peace nor quiet in all Syracuse.[160]

From all reports, Higgins was playing well. "He is a fine fielder,
strong batter and fast runner," the *Sporting News* reported.[161]

Crothers, for his part, insisted that he had been misunder-
stood, and that his real problem was with the manager, Simmons.
Moreover, although his remarks show he was clearly prejudiced
against Higgins' race, he said his disagreements with Higgins
were not personal. It was a cultural thing. "I don't know as people
in the North can appreciate my feelings on the subject," he told
the *Syracuse Standard*. "I am a Southerner by birth, and I tell
you I would have my heart out before I would consent to having
my picture appear in that group. I could tell you a very sad story
of injuries done my family, but it is personal history. My father
would have kicked me out of the house had I allowed my picture
to be taken in that group."

The Standard later reported an encounter between Higgins
and Crothers, in which Higgins confirmed that Crothers had
been "kind and friendly" and had given Higgins "points on the
players" and "what kind of balls to pitch."

"You see," Crothers continued to the reporter, following the
encounter, "I was willing to be on the same nine with Higgins,
to be civil to him and to help him. But I couldn't appear in the
same group with him. As to the 'scrap' this evening, now that I
think over the circumstances, I believe that Manager Simmons
led me on purposely."[162]

Outfielder Hank Simon, for his part, stayed with the team,
and a team photo of individual portraits was eventually produced.
Simon's portrait is right next to Higgins', though Crothers' portrait is missing altogether.

By mid-June, Buffalo's success on the field led the players "to jubilate in honor of their victories," according to the *New York Sun*, but their jubilation quickly got out of hand after their game on June 12. "Their celebration began with weiss beer and ended in a fracas, in which a knife is said to have been used," the *Sun* reported.[163] Grant and outfielder John Gallagan were each fined twenty-five dollars, and catcher James Purvis was fined fifty dollars and suspended. Whether race had anything to do with the episode was not reported.

Meanwhile, according to the *Toronto World*, "A number of colored players are in the International League, and to put it mildly their presence is distasteful to the other players." *The Sporting News* also reported that the league's black players were frequently the targets of opposing players: "Fowler used to play second base with the lower part of his legs encased in wooden guards. He knew that about every player that came down to second base on a steal had it in for him and would, if possible, throw the spikes into him."

On June 27, Binghamton players Buck West and Joe Dilworth requested that they play in place of Fowler and Renfro. Nine other players joined them in signing a petition to team management, demanding Fowler and Renfro be released. The fact that Fowler and Renfro were arguably the team's two best players did not dissuade the petitioners.

Although the Binghamton ownership fined the petitioners fifty dollars each, Fowler was fed up. After two more games, he requested his own release, finishing his 1887 Binghamton season with a .350 batting average. He immediately headed east to finish the season first with the Jersey Blues and then with Montpelier (Vermont), where he was a fan favorite and the first black captain of an integrated team.[164]

The Vermont Watchman consistently provided effusive praise for Fowler while he was with Montpelier and questioned the motives of those he left behind in the International League: "Captain Fowler of the Montpeliers is a colored man and a first-class ball-tosser in every respect…Considering his superiority as a base-ballist, it is reasonable to suppose that jealousy and not prejudice against color influenced the weak fellows of the Binghamton club." When the Montpelier team folded at the end of August, Fowler, ever resourceful, joined the team in Laconia, New Hampshire.

The Binghamton club never recovered from the loss of its most valuable player and folded before the season ended.

The team's petition against Fowler and Renfro was a precursor to even more heavy-handed treatment of black players in the International League as the '87 season wore on. Most famously, on July 15, John Clapp's old teammate, Cap Anson of the Chicago National League club, refused to play an exhibition against Newark if Fleet Walker or George Stovey played. This was a continuation of Anson's ongoing opposition to minority players in general and to Walker in particular. Newark benched the two, and the game proceeded, with a 9-4 victory for Newark.[165]

That same day, the International League agreed to prohibit the signing of any additional "colored" players. Fowler, Renfro and Jackson had been released and were no longer on their team's rosters. Those on rosters and already signed—Grant, Walker, Stovey, and Higgins—could remain, but that was it.[166]

In a story describing the meeting, which featured the subtitle, "The Color Line," *Sporting Life* explained: "Several representatives declared that many of the best players in the League were anxious to leave on account of the colored element, and the board finally directed Secretary White to approve of no more contracts with colored men."[167]

The move to limit "colored" players was repeated in other organized leagues that year as well, both in the Union North and the Confederate South. The formation of the new Ohio League at the end of 1887, for instance, included this proviso: "On motion of E.G. Taylor of the Kalamazoo team, the constitution was amended so that colored players will not be signed by this league."[168]

The League's owners willingly reduced their labor pool and sacrificed the quality of their product—in terms of talent, competitiveness, and revenue—for the sake of jealousy, racial prejudice, and the perception that associating with African-American players relegated other players to a lower rung on the working class ladder. It was a move backward that would take more than six decades to reverse, and it helped make the "separate but equal" mindset that was emblematic of Jim Crow America more acceptable. Setting aside the question of justice, had the League considered issues of performance or economics alone, it would have expanded the number of "colored" players, especially given the example of Grant in Buffalo. Buffalo was the league's "best drawing city," Grant was Buffalo's best player, and, according to the *Buffalo Express*, he was the most popular man on the club with the fans.[169] In fact, Grant finished the 1887 season as arguably the best player in the International League, and Buffalo finished the season just behind Toronto in a tight International League pennant race.

The national media was clearly impressed with him. Grant "is a very accurate thrower, and withal swift," reported *Sporting Life*'s Buffalo correspondent. "He is exceedingly hard to fool at the bat, as his average of .366 will testify, and his shots are generally long. He led the League in matter of extra hits last season, having twenty-seven two-base hits, ten three-base hits and eleven home runs. He also led the Buffalo club in base-stealing. With all due credit to the ability of Hardis Richardson and Jim O'Rourke, I think I can say that Grant is the best all-round player Buffalo ever had." [170]

Heading into 1888, just three black players remained in the International League: Higgins, Walker and Grant. Higgins would play one more season for Syracuse before returning to Memphis to work as a barber. He would not reemerge in organized ball after 1888, but was among those listed on a Bud Fowler pre-season barnstorming roster for 1895. Walker would move to Syracuse and remain for two more seasons before retiring as the last International League African-American until Jackie Robinson starred for Montreal in 1946.

Grant had another excellent season in 1888. In addition to his consistently fine fielding, Grant hit an average of .346, with eleven home runs and ninety-five runs scored in eighty-four games for Buffalo in 1888–superlative numbers in almost every area. He even faced Ed Daily again in the April exhibition season–this time in Washington, DC–and ripped a double.[171] The author was unable to discover any more details of this encounter, for instance whether Daily again attempted to bait Grant with racist shenanigans.

The other pioneers who did not make it to 1888 played only sparingly after the 1887 season, according to available records. Stovey went to the Cuban Giants in 1889 and played there several years before becoming a prominent umpire in the Williamsport area. According to SABR records, neither Renfro nor Jackson played organized professional baseball again after 1887.

"Some of the finest ball players in the country are colored men," the *Detroit Free News* editorialized after the 1887 season. "These men would prove a boon to some of the weak clubs of the League and Association, but if there is one thing the white ball player insists on doing it is drawing the color line very rigidly. And thus distracted managers cannot employ the strong material which would be so welcome."[172]

Despite his on-field success in 1888, Grant was not fully accepted by his teammates, and he found himself caught between two baseball worlds: the white baseball world where he had excelled for the majority of his life, and the black baseball world of travel teams like the Cuban Giants, a team not altogether different from the Harlem Globetrotters of today. Although they were called "Cuban" Giants, they were predominantly made up of African-American players. The "Cuban" moniker was used in an effort to lessen the prejudice they would face.[173] These kinds of teams displayed a high level of skill and competitiveness, but they were also known for their clowning entertainment. For the serious Grant, neither world was ideal.

His position between these two worlds was clearly evident in a game near the end of the '88 season on September 28, when Buffalo hosted the Cuban Giants. A "half-frozen crowd of 800"– roughly half of whom were "gentlemen of color"– attended. According to the *Buffalo Courier*, they were highly entertained, as the Giants "kept the spectators in a constant roar."

"Some of the Giants have the 'cake walk' and 'coon run' down to perfection," the *Courier* reported. "It's fun to see and hear them. When they got mad because the umpire called a strike on them, they would throw down their bat and walk around the plate a couple of times."

It was not recorded how Grant responded to the Giants' clowning, but the *Courier* described other antics and how some of the Buffalo players joined in: "The coaching of the Giants was funny, very funny. [Buffalo second baseman Henry] Bittman entered right into the spirit of the thing, and with the assistance of [Buffalo third baseman John] Reidy and [Buffalo first baseman Mike] Lehane, gave it to the Cubans as hot as they sent it. [Clarence] Williams, the catcher, [Ben] Boyd and [Arthur] Thomas were a show all by themselves. 'Couldn't hit a box car,' 'git off dat base,' 'put it out de lot,' were some of the Cubans' merry salutations."

Buffalo took the lead in the first when Hamburg scored on Lehane's double. This brought Grant to the plate, which resulted, according to the *Courier*, in "considerable amusement," as Grant reached first on an error and was then picked off by what the Buffalo players claimed was a balk move by Giants pitcher Whyte. Grant, "a quiet, modest and unassuming man" who "never argued on the diamond,"[174] must have been especially annoyed to have been picked off and called out on such a controversial call. Fortunately for him, Buffalo would score five more runs in the second to take a commanding 6-0 lead; a lead pitcher Jack

Fanning held on to for an 8-2 victory.[175]

As masterfully as Grant played and as much as the Buffalo media liked him, many of the Buffalo players were not happy with his presence. Chapman, an advocate for Grant, tried to keep the peace, but, as with Syracuse the prior year, several players refused to take a team picture with Grant. The '87 team picture is the only known photograph of Grant with his white teammates, as no such picture appears to have been taken of the '88 team.

"The only reason why we didn't have our pictures taken last year was on account of that nigger," one anonymous Buffalo player told the *Buffalo Courier* in early 1889. "Chapman wanted us to come around and be photographed, but one of the boys said: 'Not if the nig is in the picture,' and we all backed him up."[176]

Following the '88 season, Grant requested a contract to continue to earn $250 a month to remain with Buffalo in '89. Although this was the same salary he earned in '88, it was perceived as being too much, especially by Grant's resentful white teammates, most of whom reportedly made less.[177] Instead of returning to Buffalo for less money in '89, Grant joined the same Cuban Giants he had played against at the end of '88.

"The feeling is pretty general among professional ball players that colored men should not play with white men," the *Courier* reported. "'He's where he belongs now, with the Cuban Giants,' said one of the players, 'and I hope he stays there, for I won't play with Buffalo if he does.' This is rather hard on Grant. The boys acknowledge that he is a good player, but don't like to travel with him."[178]

Although Grant played the 1889 season with the Cuban Giants, he would return to integrated professional baseball in 1890, a season where there were three major leagues, his best opportunity to make it to the top.

CHAPTER 6

Elmira, 1888

J ust as workers and towns battled for economic advantages, corporations battled for advantages as well, seeking efficiency and ways to save money everywhere they could. To battle the corporations' efforts to minimize wages, labor union leaders attempted to organize workers to improve negotiating power. In the process, the unions embraced immigrant laborers from southern and eastern Europe when labor demand was high (and the immigrants could take the lower-paying jobs leaving the higher-paying jobs to native-born laborers), but advocated restrictions on immigrant labor when labor demand was low (so that immigrant laborers would not take scarce jobs from native-born laborers).

Organized baseball had a degree of labor strife as well, as evidenced by John Ward's new Brotherhood organization, but it was minor compared to the larger labor troubles throughout the nation. In Pennsylvania coal country, in particular, mine laborers felt industrialists were taking unfair advantage of them, and that working conditions in the decades since the Civil War had progressively worsened.

"Since 1877, the men have been reduced I supposed about 25 per cent, on their wages from that time," explained W. H. Hines, an attorney and former miner from Wilkes-Barre to U.S. House of Representatives investigators in 1888. "The miner today is forced to do double work now for what he did at that time for a less price."[179]

This timeframe was no mystery, as it coincided with an increase in industrialist monopoly control over both anthracite coal production and anthracite coal transportation. The Pennsylvania and Reading Railroad alone, for example, since 1870 had taken possession of the primary local canals and one-third of the Lehigh Valley coal fields in addition to its 1,700 miles of railroad track. With this monopoly power, the owners were able to manipulate coal prices by managing supply and costs with only minimal regard for true market supply and demand.

To help manage labor cost the anthracite owners retained a surplus supply of laborers who rented company-owned housing, purchased food and supplies at company-owned stores, and (when necessary) saw company-endorsed doctors. Since they were only paid when they worked, and work could be intermittent and unpredictable, they were often left without cash and in arrears to the company once the "dockage" was accounted for.

To make matters worse, the mine workers' wages were typically based on the future price of the extracted coal at the time it was sold, not on an agreed-upon-in-advance rate like most other laborers. As a result, the owners kept their workers in continuous suspense and at competitive odds with one another.

Given these circumstances, the Knights of Labor and other unions began to make deeper inroads into the mining community, much to the chagrin of the owners. In response to the immediate problems in the anthracite region, the union leaders formed a committee in mid-1887 to petition the owners to negotiate better terms. Among the committee members was forty-eight-year old James Broderick, a miner from the Lattimer and Milnesville collieries.

"We had been considering the matter [of wages and other terms] for years past and we found our condition was getting worse continually," Broderick told investigators. "We were reduced in pay and could not live."[180]

Ownership ignored the petition, and refused to negotiate. "We would not negotiate with them at all," seventy-seven-year-old Lattimer mine operator Ario Pardee said. "We have always been willing to deal with our own employees or a committee of our own employees, but we will not deal with the officers of their associations."

"I look upon the leaders of these associations," Pardee went on, "as meddlers."[181]

Given the impasse, the miner workers commenced a strike on September 10, 1887. When mine owners like Pardee found a need to operate any of their collieries during the strike, they relied on replacement workers from the surplus labor pool. Tensions within the mining communities increased, and to protect the replacement workers, owners hired special coal and iron police, who far outnumbered the local police.

Such were the circumstances in the afternoon of February 3, 1888, on the outskirts of the small mining town of Shenandoah, when a group of alleged strikers brandishing snowballs, rocks and pieces of picket fence confronted a group of coal and iron police who were escorting several replacement workers home after work. During the melee, members of the coal and iron police fired into the crowd, wounding six, including a young ballplayer named Michael Heffron, who was shot in the mouth and seriously injured.[182] It was not clear whether Heffron was taking sides in the melee, or was simply an innocent bystander. The bullet removed part of the roof of his mouth, knocked out four teeth and resulted in a face that "was disfigured for life." [183]

Heffron, a twenty-four-year-old pitcher with great potential, was signed to play for New Orleans in the Southern League in the 1888 season. New Orleans was a team on the rise, having lured numerous northern veterans, such as former Clapp teammate George Bradley and young prospects like Heffron, fellow Pennsylvanian native Abner Powell, and Detroit native Charles "Count" Campau.

Fortunately, Heffron was eventually healthy enough to return to baseball. He pitched one game for New Orleans in 1888, went eight innings, walked four, struck out two, scattered five hits, gave up just three unearned runs and was charged with a loss. According to BaseballReference.com, it was his only organized professional baseball outing. He was listed among third basemen looking for a professional tryout in early 1889, and was recorded as being released by Muskegon in the Michigan State League in 1890. In early 1892, he was listed among several "gentlemen" in the Shenandoah coal country working on the creation of a new Anthracite League.

Heffron's example was an especially dramatic one of how the baseball and mining worlds sometimes collided, revealing the harsh circumstances of working people. In both baseball and mining, the stakes were high, competition was intense, and mistakes were costly.

The strike continued for several months, and pro-union advocates throughout the Twin Tiers encouraged citizens to donate to funds set up to assist the striking families.

The *Elmira Telegram* took up the cause in a special appeal to its readers in early 1888:

"Let every man who loves liberty and hates tyranny subscribe towards the men of the Lehigh region who are now four months in suffering and want, and who are fighting against the most heartless monopoly the world has ever seen, and who are fighting for liberty guaranteed them by the constitution of our land, but which monopoly treats with the meanest contempt."[184]

ELMIRA'S BUSINESS COMMUNITY WAS LOOKING TO UPGRADE its baseball team to a fully professional league in 1888, and it was a challenge to get enough financial backers on board in the midst of the labor turmoil. Baseball was not only competing for attention with the everyday realities of work; it was also competing with other sports and entertainment. Leisure time was still relatively new to working class Americans. Prior to post-Civil War industrialization, according to historian Dubofsky, when farm life was more typical "life and work seem to flow together, as they grow out of the necessities of nature and the traditional norms of the cultural order."[185] Industrialization brought more regimentation and division between time and life, and the sports and entertainment pages of the 1880s were at least as dominated by horse racing, boxing, and other field sports as by baseball. Run- and walk-racing, in fact, were two of the nation's most popular sports. Long-distance walk-racing, also known as pedestrianism, was so popular throughout the country in the 1870s that even Samuel Clemens and a friend in 1874 attempted to walk the one hundred miles from Hartford to Boston, before giving up after ten miles and taking a train the rest of the way.[186]

Pedestrianism's popularity was bolstered in the 1860s and 1870s by the design and building of large indoor spaces, typically exposition or agricultural halls, within which activities like roller skating and pedestrian races could take place under the watchful, paying and gambling eyes of thousands of spectators. Among the most prominent of these spaces were Madison Square Garden in New York City and the Interstate Exposition Building in Chicago. International races involving prominent walkers like long-distance pioneer Edward Payson Weston, Irish-American Dan O'Leary, African-American Frank Hart, and Charles Rowell from Britain commanded worldwide attention.

According to historian Matthew Algeo, pedestrianism's national popularity, eventually dragged down by allegations of race-fixing and increasingly challenged by organized baseball and competitive bicycle racing, peaked in 1881.[187] Nevertheless, races with big purses continued throughout the 1880s. Each race was set up with its own rules regarding distance, time and style. One race might declare the first person to reach a certain mileage (500 miles, for example) the winner, whereas another might declare the person with the most mileage after a certain period of time (hours or days) the winner. A "go-as-you-please" race was literally a free-style race where the racers could walk or run, whereas a "walking" contest meant no running was allowed.

In Elmira, the Burns brothers, Daniel and Felix, were better known for their racing prowess than for their periodic scrapes with the police, although both were the subjects of frequent news stories. As early as the 1870s, Daniel Burns was considered one of the top champion walk-racers in the country, frequently training with the "colored" racer Frank Hart, and winning pedestrian races throughout the region, many of which carried substantial purses.

At a match in Cortland, New York, in October, 1879, Daniel walked 118 miles by the ending time of 9:30 pm.[188] This was likely a race of between one and two days, as the six-day record at the end of 1880 was 566 miles, or just over 93 miles per day.[189] A little less than a year later, he won a match against both men and horses in Chicago, where he covered 578 miles, while the fastest horse, Betsey Baker, only covered 568 during the race period.[190] Sadly, the horse died following the race.

At the same time as Daniel was beating a horse in Chicago, his younger brother, Felix, was being arrested back home for stoning Erie Railroad cars.[191] There did not seem to be any purpose to Felix's hooliganism. Staying out of trouble was a constant challenge for him, but he had enough talent as a walk-racer to be at least somewhat aligned with his older brother. The two were billed together in late 1885 at a "Great 50 Hour Pedestrian Contest" in Oswego that promised to be the "event of the season" and was scheduled to run from December 17 to December 19. The billing stressed that "300 miles must be covered to entitle contestants to a prize." First prize was $200 and second $150 out of a total purse of $450[192]–excellent compensation for a couple days of walking, especially when the average daily wage for U.S. workers was just $1.50.[193]

The Burns brothers frequently raced against Hart, O'Leary and fellow Elmiran Jerry Cronin, and commonly traveled to venues as obscure as local tents and fairgrounds and as famous as Madison Square Garden. In Elmira, the races were typically held at a tent on the lot behind the Lyceum Theater on Carroll Street or in the Stancliff Hall on Baldwin Street, which at the time was a theater with a circular gallery.[194] The tent was likely made of canvas and large enough to resemble a "Big Top" circus tent, with a center pole, side walls and quarter poles. Throughout the 1880s, the Burns brothers competed in races and had their fair share of success. The newspapers covered their races just as they covered the action at local horse tracks and boxing rings.

So, as the spring of 1888 beckoned, baseball found itself competing for the attention of Elmira's spectators. The sport had at least two prominent local enthusiasts in writer and humorist Samuel Clemens and his close friend the Reverend Thomas K. Beecher. Beecher was a prominent Congregational preacher whose sister, Harriet, wrote *Uncle Tom's Cabin*, the second best-selling book of the nineteenth century (behind only the Bible). The two were scheduled to umpire a contest between local businessmen the previous July. Ultimately, however, despite Clemens' stated willingness to "perish in a good cause," he and Beecher decided not to risk spending too much time in the hot sun as umpires and instead watched the game from the grandstand. Clemens battled the heat throughout the game by shaking a "big fan in a vigorous manner" and was glad to "encourage the players by his presence."[195] Clemens summered at nearby Quarry Farm and was known to frequent the local drinking establishments, especially Charles Klapproth's tavern on lower Lake Street, located near the mansion of Clemens's in-laws (the Langdons) at the corner of Church and Main Streets.

Elmira's baseball challenge was a common one at the time. Unlike an individual sport like boxing or racing, a team sport like baseball required greater organization and capital. When it came to putting together a professional baseball team, towns scrambled to pick their optimal approach. If a town team was going to be part of a league, the town wanted to be in a league where it would be competitive enough to build interest, but not so competitive that it would fail to win. Attracting crowds was a tricky challenge, and there were few templates to follow. Getting on a losing streak and failing to bring in enough crowds to meet expenses was a recipe for disaster that could negatively impact the entire town's economy, especially if local businesses were the team's primary investor. Thus, teams were better off cutting their losses and folding early than playing out a losing season.

After folding early in 1887, Binghamton joined the Central League in 1888, as did another former International League city, Newark. Other cities in the Central League were Allentown, Easton, Hazleton, Jersey City, Scranton, and Wilkes-Barre.

Elmira also eagerly joined the Central League that year, making a huge jump from its semi-pro status the previous year. This new league put it on par with its rival, Binghamton. Although the Central League was not as elite a league as the International, town organizers expected that the games would attract even more loyal spectators.

At the time, Elmira had a reputation for punching above its weight in terms of raising good ballplayers–Elmira native Danny Richardson, for example, had been a star player with the New York Giants since 1884–so expectations for those in the 1888 Elmira club were high. In fact, the season began with the hope that the city might eventually be successful enough to lure a major league franchise. According to a *Sporting Life* correspondent, "Elmira has the best grounds in the State, and should have a good club and a winner. It has a population of 30,000 and would make a good stopping off place for many of the League and Association teams."[196]

Manager W. Charles Smith, a city police commissioner, pulled the team together on April 9, with an initial core that featured outfielders Albert Fowler, "Bert" Kenney, Thomas Bowen, and John Dougherty; infielders Frank Shugart, John Rembe, Hobart Van Alstine, and David Beadle; catcher James Allison; and pitchers Charles Lohr and Joseph Punch.[197] Within one week,

Lohr, Punch, and Dougherty were out, and Herb Goodall from
Mansfield was in. A week later, following an opening season exhibition game against Cornell—which played without an ill Harry
Taylor—resulting in a 15-4 victory for Elmira, "Jumbo" Latham
from Utica joined the squad.[198] Herman Pitz from Brooklyn
joined the team as catcher soon thereafter and was a regular by
mid-May.[199] Among the future stars that would also soon join the
1888 Elmira roster were Bill Heine and John Doran from the '87
team and Harry Taylor from Cornell and the '87 Waverly team.

*1888 Elmira players. Front row L-R: J. Burns, W. Charles "Spooney"
Smith, J.C. Velder, Charles Hall. Back row L-R: J. Chamberlain,
Vince "Jolly" Dailey, Harry Taylor, E.M. "Babe" Shay,
Hobart Van Alstine, Albert "Bert" Kenney,
G. Backer, and Bill Heine.*

The team did not get off to a fast start; in fact, as of May 20,
Elmira's record was 5-9, and its recent 15-7 loss to Easton "was
a loosely played game throughout, and the 500 spectators were
able to work up but little enthusiasm." [200]

By the end of June, the Elmira players had changed again,
though the situation had not. On June 30, Elmira lost to the
"peanut vendors" from Allentown, 6-2, and by then, Doran, Heine,

and Taylor were all in the regular line-up. In that game against Allentown, Heine caught Doran's three strikeouts, but also had three passed balls. Meanwhile, Phil Tomney, who had played in Binghamton in '87, played shortstop for Allentown and managed a double, single, and two runs for the victors.[201]

As of July 1, Elmira was in seventh place in the eight-team league, with a 10-29 record. Newark led the league with a record of 36-6, followed by Jersey City at 32-8. One consolation for the Elmirans was that they were over three games ahead of their bitter rivals in Binghamton, who trailed the rest of the league at 6-32.

Overall league attendance was lower than expectations, and manager Smith believed the entire Central League was on the verge of collapsing. Nevertheless, he sought to encourage local crowds, vowing that his team would continue through the season, "league or no league." This bluster was in spite of economic realities, since, according to the *Elmira Telegram*, even in Elmira "the attendance is not heavy enough. At the game Friday there were present not much more than 100 or 150 persons," which was due in part to stormy weather.[202]

On July 14, Doran held Wilkes-Barre to just one run through the first eight innings, but Elmira was being shut out. Then, in the eighth, right fielder McCarthy hit a single, and Shugart sent a double over the Wilkes-Barre right fielder's head to drive in the tying run. Then, in the tenth, shortstop Heine reached first on a grounder that the second baseman fumbled, made a "daring steal" of second, and then scored a go-ahead run on a Shugart triple. Doran held Wilkes-Barre scoreless to earn Elmira a 2-1 victory in the tenth inning.

"It was a great game throughout and the fair sized crowd of spectators present got excited, depressed and finally jubilant by turns," the *Telegram* reported. The victory brought Elmira's season record up to 15-36–still in seventh place and now only two and one-half games ahead of Binghamton.[203]

In early August, Binghamton folded for the second straight year, and it was up to a replacement team in Hazleton, Pennsylvania, to compete with Elmira for the cellar. The season that had begun with so much promise ended with little excitement or fanfare. As of September 2, Elmira was solidly in seventh place at 26-57. Newark remained comfortably in first at 69-18. The gap seemed too far to bridge, even when looking ahead to 1889 or 1890. How long would locals support a team with such a losing record?

On September 15, the Elmirans had one last strong game for the year, riding Doran's hot pitching to a 7-2 victory over Allentown. "Doran made monkeys of them in nine well played innings," the *Telegram* said. "The sluggers from the wilds of Pennsylvania with the exception of [shortstop Norris 'Tip'] O'Neil, could do nothing with him." Shugart led the Elmira hitters, landing two singles and scored two runs. The team ended the season still comfortably in seventh place, with a record of 31-62.

ONE OF ELMIRA'S VETERAN PLAYERS WAS BERT KENNEY, WHO had been born in rural Truxton, New York, in 1861. He was the son of Oscar and Mitty Kenney, who were native-born farmers. Their 1870 neighborhood was comprised of farmers like themselves, with a few farmers and laborers from Wales, England, Ireland, and Germany.

Bert Kenney's Truxton of the mid-1880s was a village of about 400 people just eleven miles northeast of Cortland and ninety minutes by train from Syracuse. It consisted of a main street, rutted roads, wooden sidewalks, Jerry O'Connor's general store, Mary Goddard's two-story wood-framed hotel, a smaller inn, a bank, a one-room schoolhouse, and three churches–Catholic, Methodist, and Baptist. About one-fifth of the town's residents were foreign-born.[204]

In addition to playing for Elmira, by the late 1880s, Kenney was also managing the Truxton town team. It was Kenney that a fifteen-year-old John McGraw—also a Truxton native–

approached for help with his ball playing. Unbeknownst to
Kenney or the rest of the Elmira squad, those lazy summer
afternoons he spent tutoring young McGraw were to be among
the most significant in baseball history.

Young John McGraw's father, also John (though spelled
"McGrath"), was born in Ireland, emigrated to the U.S. in time
to serve in the Union Army during the Civil War, and moved
to Truxton as a widower with a young daughter in 1871. At
Truxton, he helped build the railroad line that would become
the Elmira, Cortland, & Northern (EC&N), connecting Elmira
with Canastota on the main New York Central Line, and stayed
on as a maintenance worker tending the roadbed and track. He
soon married a local Catholic girl, Ellen Comerfort, and they
settled in a rented house on West Hill, two miles from the center
of town. There, they had eight children, the first of whom was
John Joseph, born on April 7, 1873.[205]

"If it was a period when poor people basically had to fend for
themselves," wrote historian and biographer Charles Alexander,
"it was also one in which children usually looked after their own
recreations and entertainments, uninhibited by organizing and
supervising adults. And it was a period when, across the United
States, in little places like Truxton and big cities as well, boys
loved to get together and throw and catch and knock around
a baseball."[206]

From the age of seven, young John McGraw was never without
his baseball, "not even when he served at mass for the itinerant
priests who drove eleven miles from Cortland winter and summer
to hold services and hear confession," recalled his wife, Blanche.
He could be identified "not only by the incongruous lump at the
rear just below his white blouse, but also by the red stockings that
his mother had knitted for the weekly service as an altar boy."

"He looked like a person afflicted with permanent tumor of
the buttock," recalled one Truxton neighbor, "which was not
strange for a boy on the street or in school, but he was the only
one who 'wore his tumor' at the church altar!"[207]

Day after day, little John gathered with other local boys on the school green to play. Then, after all the others had dwindled away, he would draw a chalk circle on the carriage shed behind the Methodist Church and practice his pitching. "Townspeople soon became used to the sight and sound of the pint-sized McGraw boy hurling his ball against the shed," Alexander wrote.[208]

Sadly for the McGraw family, the Truxton area was hit with a diphtheria epidemic in the winter of 1884-85, which killed John's mother, Ellen, and four of his siblings. Neighbors convinced the elder John to move the remaining family closer to town, which he did, moving in right across Main Street from Mary Goddard's hotel. John had a difficult time looking after all of his children on his own, and repeated beatings prompted young John, at age twelve, to move out of the house and into the hotel with the Goddards. The night he left, he brought his entire library, which consisted of five books–*DeWitt's Base Ball Guide for 1875, DeWitt's Base Ball Guide for 1876, Spalding's Constitution and Playing Rules for 1877, Beadle's Dime Base-Ball Player for 1877,* and *Our Boy's Base Ball Rules for 1877,* in a sack.[209]

Young John worked at the hotel to earn money, and he eventually obtained work in Cortland as a delivery boy for the *Elmira Telegram's* Cortland edition. "Money was always needed, but especially in the spring when the baseball playing season neared," wrote his widow, Blanche. "It wasn't only for new base-balls; rule books had to be bought. Luckily John got his *1886 Reach Guide* early. He was one of the first in Truxton to know that the pitcher's box was lengthened to seven feet, placed fifty feet from home base instead of forty-five, and that the pitcher could now raise his arm above his shoulder and throw overhand!"[210]

McGraw wasn't Truxton's only baseball expert, however. Bert Kenney, already a veteran ball player, was also aware of the changes. At the age of nineteen in the 1880 census, Kenney lived at home with his parents and worked at the local saw mill. A few years later, in 1887, Kenney was managing the town team while fourteen-year-old John played for the school team. John also participated in the local brass band, helping carry the bass drum in all the parades. The band usually played concerts before every baseball game, and John never missed a concert or a game.[211]

Making money was extremely important to young John, and during the next season, in 1888, he found an excellent source of income on the EC&N Railroad as a butcher boy, or "butch," as this type of vendor was often called. His widow described the job:

> He walked through the swaying wooden cars with a basket containing bananas, magazine, 'O.K.' gum, loose candy, small candies in glass pistols, and many of the tempting articles sold by Union News butchers today. The basket was almost as big as he and often weighed a third as much, as his weight when he was sixteen totaled only 105 pounds.[212]
>
> He caught the accommodation train on its southbound trip in the morning, and sold his wares between Cortland and Elmira, which he reached before noon. With about three hours of layover time on his hands in Elmira, he found his way to some baseball competition, and played hard until just before time to leave on the northbound journey at 3:00 p.m.[213]

It was during these breaks that Kenney spent time coaching and mentoring young McGraw. They worked on refining all of his skills–pitching, fielding, and hitting–as well as discussing the more subtle ways to take advantage of the rules. Other Elmira players, like Heine, Doran, Shugart, and Taylor, may have participated in these coaching sessions as well. For baseball-crazed McGraw, associating with professional ballplayers at such a young age had a tremendous impact.

"John McGraw was one of the millions of youngsters, Irish or whatever, who not only fantasized about playing baseball professionally but practiced endlessly, and played as often as they could in the hope that somehow, some kind of opportunity would come along," wrote historian Charles Alexander. "In a period long before big-time ball clubs used paid scouts or even held regular tryouts for prospects, getting that opportunity was usually a matter of chance, of knowing somebody who was both interested and able to help. In young McGraw's case that man was Bert Kenney," and McGraw never forgot it.[214]

IN 1889, ELMIRA SWITCHED FROM THE CENTRAL LEAGUE TO the New York State League (NYSL), which included Auburn, Oneida, Seneca Falls, and Utica. Many of the '88 Elmirans stayed on board, including Goodall, Pitz, Shugart, and Taylor, though several others moved on to other organizations. Bill Heine and Bert Kenney, for example, moved to nearby Canandaigua, also in the NYSL, where Kenney had a particularly strong season, batting .290 in forty-nine games.

CHAPTER 7

1890
The Chaotic Season

T he 1890 season was very unusual for professional baseball, in that there were three major leagues, which created unprecedented opportunities for players to rise from the lowest rungs of the minors. It was also a confusing and important season. As a result, this chapter contains four separate stories from 1890 that involve prior and future Waverly players, mentors, mentees and opponents: the "World Tour and Players' League" (Ned Hanlon, Frank Shugart and John Ward), the Louisville "Cyclones" of the American Association (Harry Taylor, Jack Chapman and Charlie Hamburg), the Olean club of the New York and Pennsylvania League (Bill Heine, Bert Kenney and John McGraw), and the New Haven and Harrisburg clubs of the Atlantic Association (John Doran, Frank Grant and Hughie Jennings). Although there are some linkages among these stories that become more apparent in subsequent years, we will address each separately as of 1890.

World Tour and Players' League

Major league owners continued to stress the game's international potential and aimed to promote it abroad. In fact, following the 1888 season, Al Spalding and other major league magnates sponsored a world baseball tour. The tour started out from San Francisco in October and visited Hawaii, Australia, and Egypt, before touring Europe and ending up in the British Isles.

Having learned their lesson in England in 1874, Spalding and Anson were more careful with finances this time, but they were still unable to generate sufficient revenue to cover their expenses. Nonetheless, the trip wound up being an advertising success for Spalding. Already the world's leading sporting-goods manufacturer—in addition to being the owner of the Chicago National League team—the long-term advertising value of the trip was priceless.[215] By the 1890s, Spalding "nearly monopolized all aspects of the sporting goods industry."[216]

Although the stated purpose of the tour was to promote baseball in foreign countries, Spalding had an alternative motive: wanting to get Brotherhood activists like John Ward and Ned Hanlon out of the country long enough to enact a plan "to classify players by their presumed abilities, then cap their salaries within those classifications."[217] Since its creation in 1885, Ward's Brotherhood had had some success negotiating with ownership over limitations to the reserve system, including an agreement not to reserve players whose salary would be cut.[218] The owners were dissatisfied with this agreement and eager to scrap it.

When, while on tour, Ward heard about the new player salary cap classification system that the baseball magnates planned to implement, he threatened to leave the tour early, but Spalding persuaded him to stay. Ward would instead have to wait until after the tour to fight the plan.

Clearly, although major league owners were largely successful in getting the National League and American Association organized, they were not as successful as they would like in minimizing

JOHN M. WARD.
ALLEN & GINTER'S
RICHMOND. Cigarettes VIRGINIA.

John Montgomery Ward. From the Library of Congress.

their labor expenses and maximizing their profits. This business dynamic was a reflection of American industry at large. By 1890, U.S. capitalism was extremely productive: U.S. steel production climbed from 1,643 tons in 1867 to over seven million tons in 1900; U.S. oil production rose from 2,000 barrels in 1859 to sixty million barrels in 1900; iron and steel exports increased from six million dollars per year before the Civil War to over one hundred twenty one million dollars in 1900; and, one of the primary drivers of all this productivity, railroad building, increased its total U.S. mileage from 30,636 miles of track in 1860 to 193,346 miles of track in 1900.

In order to organize this economic activity, industrialists embraced new accounting standards and very limited regulation, but bristled at the idea of robust government regulation or at granting concessions to organized labor, even as the public grew increasingly concerned about the combinations, trusts and monopolies that emerged.

"Capitalism without regulation and regulators is inherently unstable," explained historian John Steele Gordon, "as people will usually put their short-term self-interests ahead of the interests of the system as a whole, and either chaos or plutocracy will result."[219]

Thus was baseball's economic environment rippling between chaos and plutocracy as the sport completed its international tour. Despite the Brotherhood's disagreement with ownership's new classification plan, the touring team returned to the United States in the spring of 1889 to a flurry of adulation and excitement. "Enthusiasm ran riot," upon the entourage's arrival in New York. "Everyone hugged everybody else and everybody had something to say to someone else."[220]

On April 8, two days after their arrival, the city of New York celebrated the team with a huge dinner at luxurious Delmonico's Restaurant in lower Manhattan. *The Clipper* declared the dinner to be "a brilliant success" that "will long be remembered by every participant."[221] The entertainment included "a full orchestra" that "played 'Yankee Doodle' from a balcony festooned with flags and bunting."[222] Among the celebrants were author and humorist

Samuel Clemens, prominent attorney and politician Chauncey Depew, famous actor DeWolf Hopper, and thirty-year-old Civil Service Commissioner Theodore Roosevelt. Owego's Senator Thomas Platt may also have been on-hand.

Roosevelt, only recently returned to New York from his Dakota ranch following the deaths of his wife and mother, was not known as a baseball fan. He preferred more "manly" sports,[223] but as a young and ambitious bureaucrat undoubtedly felt he needed to be in attendance at such a prominent event.

Clemens, on the other hand, had a generous perspective on the game and gave a speech at the dinner wherein he lauded the touring team and noted that baseball was "the very symbol, the outward and visible expression of all the drive and push and struggle of the raging, tearing, booming nineteenth century." Clemens toasted them, saying, "I drink long life to the boys who ploughed a new equator round the globe, stealing bases on their bellies!"[224]

Ward may have been persuaded to stay on the tour, but once back in the U.S., he was eager to renegotiate the new classification system.[225] Under the new system, major league salaries would be capped at $2,500 per year. Veteran stars like Ward, whose salary was $4,250, and Fred Dunlap, whose salary was at the very top of the scale ($5,000), would be grandfathered, but the next generation of stars would be capped.

When the magnates refused to negotiate, Ward hatched a scheme with his Brotherhood allies to create a new major league, one where players' rights would be observed. His new Players' League, operating without a reserve rule, officially began in 1890.

Fellow tour veterans Ward and Ned Hanlon were among the very first to put the Players' League together, luring as many players from the National League and the American Association as possible. It was a radical gambit to compete directly with the industrialists at their own level. They were very successful in attracting top players, including Elmira infielder Frank Shugart. In fact, the quality of the Players' League was so good that over half of the future Hall-of-Famers who were playing in the major leagues in 1890 (seventeen out of thirty-one) opted for the Players' League, compared to twelve in the National League and two in the American Association.

Unfortunately, as with labor unions in the U.S. as a whole, off the field the players were more fragmented and less capable of organizing their own league than they thought. Although many players, like Ward and Hanlon, had the means to invest their own capital and to take partial financial interests in their teams, the total capital needed to build and run an entire league required the players to solicit their own set of industrialists, which they did, securing teams, investors and space to build or renovate ballparks in Boston, Brooklyn, New York, Chicago, Philadelphia, Pittsburgh, Cleveland and Buffalo.

Moreover, although the Players' League purported to be a unique player-managed organization, its business practices wound up differing relatively little from its major league competitors, or from big business in general. An early indication of this was that it "did not consistently attempt to hire unionized workers"[226] to build its ball parks and perform other off-the-field labor necessary to run a league of teams.

"That we receive larger salaries and that our hours are shorter leaves us none the less workingmen," Ward explained. "We are hired men, skilled in a particular employment, who work not only for the profit, but the amusement as well of our employers."[227]

According to historian Robert Ross, Ward's positioning of the players as both owners and laborers "allowed the Players' League to both discursively align itself with working-class people and to share the game's profits only with its partner investors,"[228] thus differentiating the players from the very workers they hoped to attract as fans, and likely sowing the oats of discontent that would ultimately, other than avoiding the salary cap and reserve rule, lead the league to being little different from the National.

At the major league level, there were now three major leagues: the National League, the American Association, and the Players' League.

Louisville "Cyclones" of the American Association

Meanwhile, old Elmira teammates Harry Taylor and Herb Goodall were playing key roles in the major leagues in 1890 for Louisville in the American Association. Their timing was perfect, because 1890 was a miraculous year for the Louisville club. It had finished 1889 with the worst record in the league–a tragic 27 wins and 111 losses—but manager Jack Chapman, who had moved from Buffalo after the 1888 season to manage Syracuse before moving again to Louisville in 1889, fully took over at Louisville in 1890, and turned the Louisville roster upside down in an effort to reverse the team's fortunes. Besides Goodall and Taylor, Chapman's 1890 Louisville line-up also included former Buffalo stars Charlie Hamburg and Henry Easterday and former Binghamton nemesis (and Allentown shortstop), Phil Tomney.

The spring of 1890 had begun auspiciously in Louisville, with one of the most violent and damaging storms in the city's history. On the evening of March 27, a tornado swept through the center of town, destroyed dozens of properties and killed over one hundred people within five minutes. The baseball team was at a local theater not far from the tornado's path, enjoying a show, when it hit. The next day, team members helped pull bodies from the rubble and clean up the wreckage. They subsequently took the nickname "the Cyclones" and swept through the Association's competitors.

"President Parsons and Jack Chapman have a team around them which always plays a game for all there is in it, and this fact, whether they win or lose, serves to attract patrons who had sworn off forever," *Sporting Life* reported. "Every man in the club, I am gratified to say, plays with encouraging vim and interest, and it is pleasing to see them."[229]

Hamburg was himself pleased to be rejoining Chapman. Following the '89 season, Buffalo had released Hamburg, despite his having hit a solid .281 with forty stolen bases. In leading up to

Louisville Manager Jack Chapman.

the 1890 season, Hamburg had to decide whether to keep playing ball or to return to his family's saddlery business.

Fortunately, the creation of the Players' League in 1890 was a prime opportunity for players to move up to the major leagues, since the number of teams and jobs was increasing. Several prominent players on Hamburg's hometown Louisville team jumped ship in favor of the new Players' League, opening up spots on the club. In addition, the fact that Jack Chapman, who had led the Buffalo club, was now at the helm in Louisville made the arrangement even more ideal.

Hamburg settled in well with the Cyclones, playing a solid outfield and hitting .272 with three home runs and seventy-seven runs batted in. In comparison, his ex-Buffalo teammate Easterday played in a mere seven games before earning his release.

Meanwhile, former Elmira players Taylor and Goodall and former Binghamtonian Tomney also had strong 1890 seasons in Louisville. Taylor batted .306 with forty-five stolen bases. Goodall went 8-5 with a 3.39 earned run average. Tomney hit .277 and played solid shortstop.

"Louisville, the jay team of the American Association, has, through the efforts of Manager Chapman, become the best drawing city this year," the *Sporting News* reported in July. "Its tail end team of last season now looms up as an almost certain pennant winner."[230]

"If there is a happier and more contented manager than Jack Chapman, we have yet to see him," *Sporting Life* reported. "Without fuss or feathers he laid his lines and now everything is coming his way."[231]

At the end of August, Chapman surprised many observers when he signed pitcher Ed Daily, Frank Grant's old nemesis. Since his breakout rookie season, Daily was having trouble maintaining form as a pitcher and was having at least as much success as an outfielder and heavy hitter. Chapman was betting a change of scenery would help Daily turn the corner.

"The signing of Daily was considered a master stroke," wrote the *Sporting Life's* Louisville correspondent, "as some of our strongest rivals for the pennant were after him. He made his debut with the Louisvilles in one of the games played at Rochester, and though the game was lost by us, Daily did very well." [232]

As the end of the 1890 season approached, Louisville was poised to win the league championship, what would be the first "worst-to-first" in major league baseball history. The showdown game that would was scheduled for October 6 against Columbus. A win, coupled with a St. Louis loss in its game, would clinch it for Louisville.

Chapman selected Scott Stratton to start at pitcher for the Cyclones, while Hank Gastright started for Columbus. Louisville scored right away in the first inning when Taylor, leading off and playing first base, walked, advanced to second on a bunt by third baseman Harry Raymond, and then raced for home from second on Farmer Weaver's line single to center. The throw was too late to catch him, putting Louisville on top 1-0. Weaver then took second on the throw.

The Cyclone clean-up hitter, right fielder Jimmy "Chicken" Wolf, was next. Wolf led the Association with a .363 batting average, and he hit a sacrifice fly to right field, advancing Weaver to third. This brought up Hamburg, batting fifth and playing leftfield.

Hamburg, a reliable right-handed batter, dug his tall frame into the batter's box. He had an excellent eye, having led the team in walks during the season. With one out, a runner on third, and a run already home, this was a good chance for a big inning. Gastright went into his delivery and gave Hamburg a pitch he couldn't resist. He sent it into left field and right past leftfielder Spud Johnson, allowing Weaver to score and putting the Cyclones up 2-0.

The score remained 2-0 the rest of the way. Louisville second baseman Tim Shinnick was particularly busy, with nine assists and three put-outs. The game ended when Columbus shortstop Jack Doyle hit a long fly ball to leftfield that Hamburg ran down to secure the victory and the American Association pennant.

"If anyone at the beginning of the season had foretold the result he would have been laughed at," wrote *Sporting Life* of Louisville's season victory. "It has been accomplished by good behavior and hard work on the part of the players, and by good management."[233]

Among the Cyclone players receiving special media complements following the championship win was first baseman Harry Taylor. "One of the players who did much toward winning the Association pennant is Taylor, the young college first baseman who went to the team and asked for a trial early last spring," wrote *Sporting Life*. "He is a good all-around player." [234]

Compared to the drama of the American Association championship, the 1890 World Series against National League pennant-winner Brooklyn was anticlimactic. Cold weather kept the crowds down–attendance dwindled for each game–and whole thing was called after six games as a 3-3 tie. Louisville's "worst-to-first" season was over.

Overall, 1890 was a confusing season for major league spectators, who had a hard time rooting for teams when their favorite players kept switching sides. "As it unfolded, the 1890 campaign was one of all-out war" between baseball clubs and leagues, both on and off the field, explained historian John Thorn, "with inflated attendance figures, contract jumping, player raiding, bribes to players and press, lawsuits, lowered ticket prices, and self-destructive head-to-head scheduling in cities with a club in each league."[235]

The chaos helped lead the industrialist owners of the Players' League to find more in common with their counterpart owners in the National League and the American Association than with their player patrons. Ward hoped that the labor rights enjoyed in the Players' League could be salvaged as part of negotiations over how to distribute the franchises and their assets, but the owners instead insisted that the future of baseball be decided "on a purely business basis."[236] As a result, labor considerations were absent, and "Spalding cut the brotherhood out of the negotiation, insisting that talks be conducted between the money men alone."[237] Ultimately, the Boston and Philadelphia franchises joined the American Association and the Brooklyn, New York, Chicago and Pittsburgh franchises merged with the National League, and players who had invested were offered fifty percent of the value of their stock.[238] The players were back to dealing with the reserve clause and potential salary caps. Moreover, the sudden reduction in major league teams meant fewer opportunities for those players still climbing the professional baseball ladder.

"The cause of the Players' League trouble," said Ward in a statement, "can be summed up in three words: stupidity, avarice and treachery."[239]

It was a bitter reminder that the owners still controlled the game, and the players would have to wait for a better and more incremental opportunity to re-organize.

Confused fans and sportswriters who preferred to see more action on the field and fewer shenanigans off were satisfied to return to a less tempestuous season in 1891. "Were it possible," *Sporting Life* lamented, "the real friends of the national game would wipe the season of 1890 out of memory. May we never see its like again."[240]

Olean of the New York and Pennsylvania League

Below the major league level in 1890, there were three primary northeastern minor leagues: the International, the Atlantic, and the Eastern Interstate, in order of importance. As of mid-summer, the Atlantic Association cities were Baltimore, Hartford, Newark, New Haven, Washington, DC, Wilmington, and Worcester; and the Eastern Interstate League cities were Harrisburg, Altoona, Easton, Lancaster, Lebanon, and York. All three of the minor leagues ranked higher than the Southern

Tier leagues, such as the New York and Pennsylvania League and the Western New York League.

For local players from Waverly, Elmira, and the rest of the Southern Tier, taking a step up in status to a higher league was uniquely exciting. While Taylor, Goodall and Shugart were competing in the major leagues, Bill Heine, Bert Kenney, and John McGraw soon moved west to Olean in the newly formed New York and Pennsylvania League, and Jack Doran moved east to New Haven in the Atlantic Association.

1890 Olean team. John McGraw is in the front row on the left and Bill Heine is next to him in the center. Bert Kenney is in the middle row second from the right. From the New York Public Library.

Kenney owned a boardinghouse in Truxton, and had saved up enough money to become an investor in the Olean team. He named himself Captain and brought along his eager mentee McGraw, having signed the teenager (who did not turn seventeen until April 7) to a contract at forty dollars per month.[241] He also brought his former Elmira teammate Bill Heine. Other teams in Olean's league were Jamestown, Bradford, Erie (PA), Dunkirk, and Meadville. *The Olean Democrat* stated that Kenney would be "one of the strongest players in the team, and will occupy center field." Heine, reported the *Democrat*, would be a "strong batter" and "has a great reputation as a catcher." McGraw, the *Democrat* said, is "an amateur player with bright prospects" and "comes highly recommended by the new manager, Kenney, and there is no doubt but that he will fill the bill."[242]

Heine and McGraw began the season with high hopes. In their second game of the season—a 13-0 victory over Allegany College (soon to be renamed St. Bonaventure College) on May 5— both were in the starting line-up with Kenney and played well. Heine hit a single, scored two runs, and started at catcher; Kenney hit a single and scored four runs; and McGraw hit a single and scored a run.[243]

A few days later, Olean traveled to Bradford for a double-header, where they lost 8-0 in the first game and 10-9 in the second. McGraw had two errors in the first game, another in the second, and no hits. Heine and Kenney each had single hit in each game, and Heine's hit in the second game a home run. "Heine covered himself and Olean with glory by knocking the sphere over the fence in the second inning," the *Democrat* reported.[244]

Bradford returned the favor with a visit to Olean on Monday, May 12. There, before a crowd of six hundred people, Bradford defeated Olean in twelve innings, 9-8. Heine and Kenney each had hits again, while McGraw again had an error and went hit-less, but did manage a walk and a run.

The next day, the two teams met again, and this time, Olean won 1-0 in an abbreviated four and one-half innings due to rain. In the third inning, McGraw walked, made "an elegant steal" of second, and advanced to third on a sacrifice fly, only to be stranded when Heine struck out. Olean finally scored in the fourth on an error, a stolen base, and another error, giving them a victory without a single base hit.[245]

On May 18, Olean faced Erie, and McGraw had a disastrous game. On the first ball hit to him, a slow grounder, he said, "For the life of me, I could not run in to get it. It seemed like an age before I had the ball in my hands and then, as I looked over to first, it seemed like the longest throw I ever had to make. The first baseman was the tallest in the league, but I threw the ball far over his head."[246] McGraw would make seven more errors that day, with only one hit.

Olean soon lost six straight games, and spectators ceased coming to the ballpark. McGraw found himself on the bench, and Kenney had no choice but to release him, though he did give the young man a seventy-dollar loan. "I was quite a bust in my start as a third baseman," McGraw later wrote. "I was benched–and [by] my friend from Truxton, too! I was certainly heartbroken. That benching, though, was the making of me, and often I have thanked Mr. Kenney from the bottom of my heart. I didn't then, though."[247]

Rather than go home to Truxton following his release, McGraw moved down a level and headed east to Wellsville in the Western New York League. Meanwhile, the Olean team was having little success on the field or at the box office, so Kenney was bought out by the other investors prior to season's end and given his release. Kenney and Heine would each eventually join McGraw in Wellsville to finish out the 1890 season.

Among the other young players in Wellsville by the end of the season was twenty-one-year-old Alfred William "Al" Lawson. Lawson was born in London, England, immigrated to Canada and then to the U.S. as a child, and grew up in Detroit, the son of a carpet maker. Lawson's 1890 experience reflected the season's chaotic nature, spanning from the low minors in Wellsville and the middle minors in Wilmington and Harrisburg, all the way to pitching three major league games for the National League's Boston and Pittsburgh franchises, losing all three. In the midst of all this baseball activity, Lawson distinguished himself more for his potential as a promoter than as a player, and he was particularly impressed with the young and energetic McGraw.

New Haven and Harrisburg of the Atlantic Association

Meanwhile, John Doran was faring so well with New Haven in the 1890 Atlantic Association that the majors appeared to be within easy reach. He was among the biggest stars in the Association and was coveted by multiple major league teams. "New Haven's great left-handed pitcher, Doran, has been doubtless as uniformly successful this season as any other pitcher in the game to-day, and this is largely due to his having control of the ball, a characteristic he has acquired this year," *Sporting Life* reported.[248]

John Doran from Athens, PA.

Doran's exploits made him a hero in his home town of Athens, particularly following his break-through fourteen-inning shutout performance against Baltimore on Memorial Day, a scoreless game the *Associated Press* termed "the finest game that has ever occurred" in New Haven. "Fully 7,500 people went crazy as the innings piled up, and the immense crowd will not be in its normal mental condition for a week," the *AP* concluded. "Doran and Baker both did grand work."[249]

"Mr. Doran, our popular townsman," the *Athens Daily News* reported, "is pitcher for the New Haven club, and has earned the reputation of being one of the best players in the country. It is doubtful if he has a superior in any of the associations or leagues."[250]

In addition to Doran, New Haven also had two other strong pitchers, southpaw Jack Horner and Louis Gilliland. "New Haven's pitching trio–Horner, Gilliland and Doran," said *Sporting Life*, "are the men who have held that team up to the front."[251]

Among the best hitters of 1890—in any league—was Harrisburg second baseman Frank Grant, still hanging onto his professional dreams. Despite stellar International League performances for Buffalo in 1886-1888, Grant had failed to make any organized baseball roster the subsequent season and instead played with the traveling Cuban Giants in 1889. As one of the very last African-American stars to play integrated professional baseball before Jackie Robinson, Grant was both beloved and loathed by spectators, depending on which team they supported.

Grant began 1890 by signing with York (PA), as it was a fully "colored" team that competed against whites. Before playing for York, though, he switched to Harrisburg, which was an integrated team. Although this was a demotion from Buffalo, it was still on the path to the majors. York attempted to block Grant from signing with Harrisburg, and the case went to court. Grant argued that he was entitled to sign with whichever club he wished, and the Court ruled in his favor.[252]

When he joined Harrisburg, Grant and Clarence Williams, the hard-hitting catcher from the Cuban Giants, were the only two "colored" men on the team's roster. Harrisburg was highly successful in the Eastern Interstate League, winning games and drawing spectators. Grant's aggressive and flamboyant style of play was by then well-known in baseball circles, and Harrisburg's followers enthusiastically welcomed him. Many even stood outside the ballpark upon his initial arrival to town in anticipation of seeing "the most famous colored ballplayer in the business."[253]

Despite Grant's drawing power, the Eastern Interstate League was teetering on the brink of financial failure by mid-July, and Harrisburg petitioned to move up to the Atlantic Association as a replacement for the Jersey City franchise, which had been struggling financially. Atlantic Association officials were in favor of bringing Harrisburg into the Atlantic, but only on the condition that Harrisburg release Grant and Williams, its two star "colored" players.

Sporting Life commented:

> One of the anomalies of professional baseball patronage is the objection of the bleaching board occupants to the playing of colored men in the teams. Hence a case in point. The Atlantic Association is in distress. Their Jersey City Club is bankrupt. The Harrisburg Club is anxious to take its place in the Atlantic arena. There is only one obstacle in its way. The immaculate teams of Baltimore, Wilmington, Washington, and Newark, and of New Haven, Hartford, and Worcester–says the *New York Sun*–object to the playing of colored men in the Atlantic Association.[254]
>
> The glorious inconsistency of objecting to a gentlemanly colored man in a team, while making no objection to the presence of so many white 'toughs,' 'roughs' and drunkards who have been allowed for years to bring disgrace on the fraternity, is one of the absurdities of the existing condition of things in the base ball world. I hope to see the Atlantic Association show some common sense in this matter.[255]

Harrisburg compromised, releasing Williams, who rejoined the Cuban Giants, but retaining Grant.[256] With that, the Atlantic Association agreed to accept Harrisburg with Grant, who became the sole black player in the League. It was another opportunity for Grant to show that he belonged at the highest level of baseball.

Once in the Atlantic, Harrisburg and Grant were eager to compete with the League's best teams and players, including New Haven and Doran. "The crowds have been immense and everything possible is being done by the management to strengthen and build up the team," *Sporting Life*'s Harrisburg correspondent explained. "The Atlantic Association [teams] now know why Harrisburg fought so desperately to retain the services of Frank Grant. Wait until he gets up before some of those crack pitchers in the Atlantic Association, and they will wish they never had seen him. He is a great hitter, and is an entire infield himself."[257]

Harrisburg's first few games in the Atlantic were uneventful. On August 4 and 5, they hosted New Haven for the first time. Horner and Gilliland pitched for the visitors, with New Haven taking the first game 8-7, and Harrisburg, the second 6-1. Gilliland struck out fourteen batters in the second game, though New Haven still lost, and Grant "did some remarkable fielding" in addition to picking up two hits in each game.[258]

Harrisburg and Grant held their own against Baltimore and Newark over the next two weeks. On August 18, "Grant's phenomenal stop in the ninth inning" preserved a 1-0 victory for Harrisburg.[259] Two days later, Harrisburg visited New Haven for the first time, and this time Gilliland shut them out 2-0. "Grant showed up in good shape, both in the field and at the bat," picking up a double.[260]

Grant was not universally well received, however, especially in the south. "[Pop] Tate, [Mike] O'Rourke, and Reddy Mack, of Baltimore, all Southerners, are making a lively kick against playing with Harrisburg while Grant, the colored man, is connected with the Pennsylvania club," *Sporting Life* explained.[261]

On August 26, Harrisburg defeated Wilmington at home 16-2, a huge victory for the home crowd. Leadoff hitter Bill Eagan had four hits and five stolen bases, while Grant had three hits, including a double, and scored four runs.[262]

This victory set up Harrisburg's hometown fans for another big contest the next day, a showdown against New Haven and their ace pitcher, Doran. "The work that John Doran has been doing in the pitcher's box for the New Haven base ball team this season has commanded the attention and admiration of all the base ball cranks all over the country," reported the *Elmira Telegram*. "He has done remarkably good work ever since the season opened and as a result, several of the teams of the larger leagues have tried to buy or steal him from New Haven."[263]

The media frenzy around Doran was reaching what was— for those days— a fever pitch. National and local newspapers ran regular features and snippets about him. He was constantly rumored to be signing with one major league club or another— first Pittsburgh, then Baltimore ("Considering how his pitchers are being hit, Manager Hanlon must feel like kicking himself for letting young Doran, of New Haven, go last winter when he had him as good as signed."[264]), then [Players' League managers] "Ward [Brooklyn], Ewing [New York], Comiskey [Chicago] and Kelly [Boston] have their eyes on Doran, the star pitcher of the Atlantic Association."[265] Rochester's major league franchise in the American Association thought Doran agreed to sign with them as early as mid-July, only to be mistaken, since Doran apparently wanted to keep his options open.[266] All the leading major league teams were interested in the hot left-hander, and his future in baseball seemed assured.

"[Doran] was a country lad, and used to work at the anvil down in Athens, Pa," *Sporting Life* reported. "He pitched for an amazing team, and finally was picked up by the Jersey City Club. His work was very poor, and he was finally released to the New Haven Club. He is now wanted by nearly all of the major league clubs and he is considered so valuable a player that $1,000 is asked for his release."[267]

Sporting Life's New Haven correspondent commented:

> While the work of every man has contributed to our success, the laurel wreath belongs to Doran, "Old Bill South Paw." All previous records in the pitching depart-

ment have been wiped out. Washington and Newark, shut out without even a scratch hit in full games and the Baltimores held for two singles, one a scratch, in a fourteen-inning game, is a wonderful performance. In six consecutive games only fourteen hits were made by opposing teams. His bases on balls, quite a factor in determining the effectiveness of a pitcher, have been very low–averaging less than four per game. His work so far stamps him at least the peer of any man in the Association.[268]

Doran lived up to the hype as the August 27 Harrisburg-New Haven showdown began. Doran shut down Harrisburg's batters in each of the first four innings, though Harrisburg pitcher John Cox was similarly effective. Grant, batting clean-up, was unable to connect on Doran's pitches. Eagan, who had so thoroughly roasted Wilmington the day before, was similarly stymied.

The two teams went into the sixth tied 0-0. Doran handled Harrisburg in the top of the inning, which brought Cox back to the mound. New Haven's leadoff hitter John McKee—a Harrisburg native—hit sharply to third, where Harrisburg third baseman Frank Foulkrod touched the ball, but could not hold it. Grant raced from shortstop to pick up the ball and throw it to first, but the throw was wild and McKee reached first safely. Jim Cudworth and Pat Petee then each hit singles to knock in McKee for a 1-0 lead. After that, Cox shut New Haven out the rest of the way.

Harrisburg had three more chances against Doran, but could not score, and the final score was 1-0. Doran had nine strikeouts and gave up just two hits and three walks, while Cox gave up just three hits and one walk.[269] In four games against New Haven, Harrisburg was just 1-3.

Still, Harrisburg continued to be competitive in the weeks ahead. In early September, the Eastern Interstate League folded, and skinny catcher Hughie Jennings, formerly with the Allentown franchise, joined Grant in Harrisburg. Together, they created a powerful duo–two great young enthusiastic talents on the same club.

Jennings, a child of coal country, was born in 1869 in Pittston, Pennsylvania, the ninth of twelve children, and grew up in Moosic. His parents, James and Hannah, had been born in Ireland, and the 1880 census states that James worked as a "Tracklayer," a mining function. Hugh's older brother, Thomas, was a "Teamster," and his brothers James and Henry were both "Laborers." Their neighbors were primarily miners, headed by parents born in Ireland, Scotland, and Wales. Several teenage boys in the neighborhood were listed as "Door Boys," another mining function.

Although mining was tough work, Jennings' exuberant, fearless, and hard-working attitude, the same attitude he brought to his ball playing, led him to be more successful than most of his peers, moving up from breaker boy, to "nipper," to mule driver in a relatively short period of time.

In his autobiography, *Rounding Third*, Jennings wrote:

Many people have asked me how anyone can stand to work in the mines, but it is not so bad as you think. It is dark there, of course, but you get used to the eternal darkness. You become accustomed to the lantern light and find your way about easily. I don't think it is any hardship for the men not the mules that are used to haul the coal. I never saw a mule that seemed to mind it in the least.

Mining has its compensations. You never get soaked by rain; there are no biting winds in the winter time; you never encounter sudden changes in weather. The temperature is about even the year around, and it is a relief from the heat of summer and the cold of winter. You appreciate being down in the mines on blistering days of summer and on the bitter days in winter. It is always comfortable down there. The mines hold dangers, but you are in danger anywhere else.[270]

Hughie Jennings from Pittston, PA.
Courtesy of the National Baseball Hall of Fame.

Jennings left the mines behind in 1889 by signing with a semi-pro
team in Lehighton for five dollars a game, an unbelievable sum
compared to typical daily unskilled mining wages. This increased
to fifty dollars a month in 1890, which led to his signing with
Allentown and then joining Harrisburg when Allentown folded.

Both Grant and Jennings finished the 1890 season incon-
sistently, just like the Harrisburg team as a whole. The entire
Atlantic Association was on the brink of collapse, as it went from
eight teams in mid-August to six by the last week of August to
just four in early September. On September 8, in a game against
Newark, Grant batted fourth and had three runs and three hits,
while Jennings batted seventh and had a run, a hit, and a stolen
base. The team lost 10-9. The next day, Jennings scored the lone
run in a 2-1 loss, with Grant going hitless.[271] A week later, on
September 16, the two men led Harrisburg to a 5-1 victory over
New Haven. Jennings caught most of the game and chipped in
a stolen base. Grant had a hit and a run, and his fielding "contributed materially to the decisive victory of the home team." [272]

A few days later, however, on September 25, the two teams
met once more. Harrisburg took an early 2-0 lead in the first,
but New Haven tied it up in the third and then pulled ahead 3-2
in the fourth. This time, neither Grant nor Jennings had a hit,
and Grant had an error to go with Jennings' two passed balls.
To make matters worse, New Haven asked for the game to be
cut short in order "to catch a train." As a result, they only played
seven innings and the game only took one hour, which was not
enough time for Harrisburg to come back.[273]

In the last two games of the regular season, Lebanon swept
Harrisburg 18-11 and 1-0. Jennings and Grant each had hits in
that first game, but Grant went hitless in the second, which was
played "before a small crowd," and "lost the game for the home
team by an over-throw to first into the bleachers, the runner
making the circuit on the error."[274]

Despite their late-season swoon, club management was
optimistic about the 1891 season. "That they have been playing

good ball, and at times brilliant contests have taken place, those who have been to Island Park will agree," said *Sporting Life*.[275]

For his part, Grant finished the season with a .328 batting average–the fifth highest average in the Atlantic Association.[276] Once again, he had proven his prowess on the same competitive field as whites. "Grant, as usual, is still covering himself with honors," *Sporting Life*'s Harrisburg reporter said. "Without the least doubt he is the cleverest player that ever played ball in this city, and the title given him as the 'Colored Dunlap' is justly imposed."[277]

Although his 1890 Harrisburg season had been personally successful from a baseball standpoint, Grant had continued to experience the unpleasantness that came with being the only "colored" player on his team. This time it was not as much his teammates or opponents as the prejudice he encountered on the road. In fact, he reportedly only associated "with his fellow-players on the field,"[278] but this did not help him when he needed to find accommodations with his teammates.

In one notorious example, Grant was denied sleeping quarters with his Harrisburg teammates at the Clayton House in Wilmington, Delaware, because "the boarders protested against being obliged to eat in the same dining room with a colored man, and threatened to leave the house unless the dusky-hued player was turned out." Although his teammates stood by him and left Clayton House en masse in "high dudgeon," they were only able to find mutual accommodations in Wilmington if Grant either ate with the "colored help," or ate elsewhere. Grant decided to eat elsewhere, and the injustice certainly grated on him.[279]

While Grant continued to focus on competing in an integrated fashion in 1890, his old on-field rival, Bud Fowler, who was playing second base for the Sterling Heights club in the Illinois-Iowa League, continued to look for ways to create new opportunities for "colored" players. He requested support from *The Sporting News* for a "Colored All Americans" team that could wear the newspaper's uniform and travel through Nebraska,

Montana, and Washington, and then play in the California League. "I think I ought to know what I am talking about," he wrote to the newspaper. "I am sure it will be a drawing card. It is something new. Not a club has ever gone to the coast without making money." Fowler went on to explain that he would get "twelve of the finest colored ball players in the country," the newspaper could "print our photographs," and that that "would be about all the advertising we would want." *The Sporting News* replied that the idea "would surely be a winner," but advised Fowler to "get some millionaire to back it."[280]

Fowler's specific request did not pan out, but it was just one of many early efforts of African-American baseball players and promoters to build self-sustaining outlets for talented players, who were not going to be accepted onto white teams. African-American teams like the York Monarchs, Cuban Giants, New York Gorhams, Boston Resolutes and Pittsburgh Keystones continued to jockey one another for the best players, as well as compete (and sometimes collaborate) for limited slots in new or established minor leagues, like the Connecticut State League and the Connecticut Central League, and New York Semi-Professional League. Fortunately, a few teams, like the Cuban Giants and the Gorhams were able to make enough money to sustain themselves, particularly when they were able to schedule games in urban areas where attendance was more reliable. In 1891, for example, the Gorhams averaged 1,089 fans per game in the New York City area, but much less on the road. "Black baseball clubs, like their white counterparts," wrote historian Michael E. Lomax, "needed a large urban base to sustain their economic viability."[281]

For John Doran, fortunes were rocky at the end of the 1890 season. On the positive side, in early October he agreed to contract terms with John Ward's Brooklyn franchise. On October 3, his hometown *Athens* (PA) *Daily News* confirmed that Doran had signed a contract with the Players' League club and would draw a salary of over $2,000. "Johnnie knows how to work that 'south paw' for all there is in it," the paper said.[282]

On the negative side, however, questions about the New Haven pitching star's sobriety and fitness began to surface in the media. True, he had an amazing 1890 minor league season on the field–with thirty wins against eleven losses, six shutouts, and 240 strikeouts–but questions about his stability seeped into coverage.

On October 4, 1890, for example, *Sporting Life* carried a statement from New Haven manager Walter Burnham in which he explained that Doran was fined fifty dollars and suspended indefinitely following a series of drinking incidents that impacted his playing. In addition, Burnham alleged that Doran had a Players' League contract with Brooklyn "in his pocket" without New Haven's knowledge or consent.

"The next day he was not in condition to pitch," Burnham went on, "although I put him in the box, and on learning that he had been up the night before, matters were becoming interesting. With the musical words 'I will go to the Brotherhood if not allowed to do as I please,' filling the air, he was disciplined regardless."[283]

In the same issue, Doran explained that he threatened to jump to the new Players' League because New Haven had suspended him unjustly, saying that he was unable to pitch due to "ill health" and not due to excessive drinking, as Burnham had alleged. Moreover, Doran told reporters that there had been offers to New Haven for his release, but they were ignored.

Although *Sporting Life* reported these disagreements, a correspondent also noted that Burnham's account was "entitled to credence," and that "Doran will find [Brooklyn manager John] Ward just as rigorous as Burnham if he acts in Brooklyn as he did in New Haven." [284]

"The New Haven Club must now regret not having accepted almost any kind of offer for the swell-headed player," another *Sporting Life* reporter noted, taking into consideration both Doran's over-confidence in contract negotiation as well as his rumored propensity to over-imbibe.

Still, in the midst of this post-season chatter, positive media coverage of Doran continued to be the norm, particularly in the local newspapers of towns where he had pitched previously. The *Auburn* (NY) *Bulletin*, for instance, ran a special story on him on October 17, 1890, complete with a picture, labeling him "Speedy Pitcher Doran," noting that he was "alongside the crack twirlers of the National and Players' Leagues," and proudly reminding their readers that "his first work of note was with the Elmiras, of the Central league, two years ago."[285]

It is possible that much of this rocky coverage was due to the larger baseball war being waged off-the-field between the leagues. Unfortunately, with the demise of the Players' League weeks later, Doran would not have the opportunity to pitch for John Ward in Brooklyn, and would have to sign elsewhere with another league. Despite the strength of his season, notwithstanding the sobriety questions, the reduction in major league teams meant a reduction in his offers for 1891.

CHAPTER 8

1891
The American Association's
Last Hurrah

A t the major league level, with the Players' League out of
the way, the remaining teams in the National League and
the American Association hoped 1891 would bring more
paying spectators and better overall success at the box office.

Despite the reduction in major leagues from three to two,
there were many hot prospects throughout the minor leagues
looking to break into the big leagues in 1891. Both Grant and
Jennings, who had finished the season with a .250 average in
nine games, looked forward to 1891 with great anticipation. So
did McGraw, who had batted .365 in 107 trips to the plate for
Wellsville.

Al Lawson, meanwhile, was not interested in waiting until
the 1891 season to go after the next big idea. Whether he got
the notion from observing fans' reactions to the former Cuban
Giant great Frank Grant up close while playing briefly with him
at the end of the 1890 season in Harrisburg or he simply recalled
previous international tours, Lawson's plan was to outfit a team
of "All Stars" to travel to Florida and Cuba in January through

March of 1891, playing exhibitions and hopefully earning a profit. Impressed with McGraw's knowledge of the rules as well as his aggressiveness, Lawson asked McGraw to join his "All Stars," and McGraw accepted, traveling from Truxton to Ocala, Florida, on his own to meet up with the team. Lawson convinced several other minor and major league players to join him as well. It seemed like a harebrained scheme, as it was not nearly as well funded or organized as Spalding's world tour, but it launched McGraw–a lively, cocky, and smart player—as a national figure. It was on this trip that Cuban fans dubbed McGraw "The Yellow Monkey," due to his appearance in Lawson's yellow uniforms.

The tour made barely enough money to pay expenses, and the team returned to Gainesville, Florida, by the end of February. Some of the players returned north, but Lawson and the remaining players waited in Florida to play major league teams during spring training. It was during one of these exhibition games that McGraw's luster brightened. On March 26, 1891, for example, in an exhibition contest, he faced Cleveland pitcher Lee Viau, a major leaguer six years McGraw's senior. Viau was part of Cleveland's regular pitching rotation, trailing only Ed Beatin and twenty-three-year-old future Hall of Famer Cy Young in pitching wins in 1890. McGraw not only played flawless shortstop in the game, but also burned Viau for three doubles in five trips to the plate.[286]

It was yet another example of how due to his daring and persistent opportunism, the young teenage diminutive player with arguably only slightly above-average skills was well on his way to stardom. As a result of his performance versus Viau, McGraw said he earned twenty-eight different competing offers.

"I looked over all the offers carefully and then decided to grab the job that paid the most money, no matter where I had to go," McGraw said. "This happened to be Cedar Rapids. They offered me $125 a month, $75 advance money and transportation. I got the $75 by wire and started."[287]

McGraw used his time in Cedar Rapids to springboard to

Baltimore, which had jumped from the Atlantic Association to the American Association prior to the end of 1890. McGraw wound up splitting 1891 between Cedar Rapids in the Illinois-Iowa League (batting .276 in seventy-nine games) and Baltimore (.270 in thirty-three games).[288]

Unfortunately, McGraw's old teammate Bill Heine was not faring as well in Elmira. He injured his hand early in the 1891 season and struggled with his hitting. On August 22, *Sporting Life* reported that Heine's "hand is in shape once more, and he is now ready to take his regular turn behind the bat," but this was relatively late in the season. Heine would finish the season with a .190 batting average, and looked forward to a much healthier 1892.

Meanwhile, building on his 1890 championship, Chapman pursued and won the post-Players' League John Doran sweepstakes, signing the lefty for the 1891 season. In Louisville, Doran joined his fellow ex-Elmira teammates Taylor and Goodall, though he would have to compete with Daily and other pitchers for innings.

Chapman also looked to the 1890 Harrisburg club for talent, but not to his old superstar, Grant. Despite having managed and supported Grant in Buffalo and knowing full-well the value his skill would bring to the field, Chapman did not sign him. It is likely he understood, after working so hard and so unsuccessfully to get teammates to accept Grant in Buffalo, that he would have even less success in a Southern city like Louisville. Instead, he signed Grant's teammate, Hughie Jennings.

The Atlantic Association folded after the 1890 season, and Harrisburg did not field a team for 1891, so Jennings started the '91 season in Lehighton. According to Chapman, he discovered Jennings while reading the Philadelphia newspaper in May of 1891 and noticed Jennings' performance for Lehighton in a box score. At the time, Chapman was short a catcher, as Jack Ryan was injured, and he immediately recognized a ready back-up when he saw Jennings' line in the box score.

"Casually reading the paper the evening of my trouble I

noticed an account of a game between the Lehightons and some other team in which a young man by the name of Jennings, who caught, seemed to be the whole show. He had 15 put-outs and four-of-five hits, a home run among them. I rushed to the telegraph office and sent a hurry-up call to his home in Moosic, a little mining town six miles from Scranton, asking if he would not join my Louisville team."[289]

By the time, Jennings had joined the team in June, Jack Ryan was healed from his injury, and so Jennings waited on the bench. Then, when first baseman Taylor remained injured from a spiking suffered in Baltimore in May, Chapman asked Jennings to fill in for him. A variety of players had been substituting for Taylor during his injury, but none were doing particularly well. Chapman wanted to get the enthusiastic Jennings into the line-up, but Jennings was concerned about playing first base. According to Chapman, Jennings did so only reluctantly, remarking, "All right, I'll do the best I can."

Then, "things began to happen," Chapman recalled once Jennings was placed at first on June 7 versus Baltimore. "He tickled the crowd by the way he pulled down the high-sailers, reached for wild ones and dug balls out of the dirt. His best was amply good. I might add that I was tickled, too."[290] Louisville lost the game 4-2, but Jennings quickly established himself as a highlight of an otherwise bleak season. "He has shown that he has the making of a great ball player," wrote *Sporting Life's* correspondent. "In addition to being a good first baseman he is a fine catcher."[291]

Moving to Louisville had been a big change for young Jennings, and veteran player Harry Taylor, then twenty-five, was a huge influence. Jennings later said of him:

> I never knew a finer character and I never had a
> better friend. Nor do I owe more to any man I have
> ever known in my life than I owe to him. He was a kind
> of big brother to me when I needed one and from him
> I learned the value of right living and of regular living.

> You see, I was a young lad of 18 when I went to the
> National League [actually the American Association]. I
> had grown up on a farm, had never before seen a city
> except the nearby cities of Scranton and Wilkes-Barre.
> I had never seen very much money and overnight had
> come to be a teammate with a group of generous spend-
> ers; had come to earning a salary that made me feel like
> a millionaire and had come to living in big hotels in the
> big cities on the circuit. When we were together in the
> summer he talked education to me.[292]

The two would remain close teammates for the next three seasons, and Jennings would eventually follow Taylor—a law school stu-dent at Cornell during the off-season—to Cornell as a baseball coach and law student.

Among those in the stands watching many games at the end of Louisville's 1891 season was former Detroit star and Players' League activist Ned Hanlon, laid up with a large plaster cast as a result of knee surgery. "It was there that I saw a little fellow so full of ginger that I admired his play," Hanlon said of Jennings. "He had red hair and a smiling countenance."[293]

Meanwhile, another of Grant's and Taylor's old teammates, Charlie Hamburg, was a victim of the glut of major leaguers fol-lowing the demise of the Players' League, and he moved down to the Western League. He played ninety-seven games for St. Paul/Duluth and saw his batting average slump to .249. Former Binghamton shortstop Bones Ely joined him there.

Despite the collapse of the Atlantic Association, Harrisburg reserved Grant for 1891 with the intention of joining another league. As late as March 22, there was media speculation that Harrisburg might join New Haven and other similarly sized cities in the new Eastern Association, "provided they dispense with Grant, their colored Hercules." [294] Whether Harrisburg's owners seriously considered the option or not, they did not field a team in 1891, and Grant returned to the Cuban Giants. There he joined his old teammate Clarence Williams and other stars. The Giants started the season as the Big Gorhams in Ansonia, as part of the Connecticut State League, but when the League broke up in midsummer, the Giants returned to barnstorming.

With the Cuban Giants, Grant was immediately "the best known man" on the team, even though Williams was more prominent as the team's entertainer in part by creating "a great deal of merriment by his chattering."[295] Grant, Williams, and the Giants played in at least one prominent game over the summer, when Frederick Douglass was among the spectators at a highly anticipated contest versus a team "of picked players from the local colored teams" in Washington, D.C., on August 31. The Giants won 8-5, and Grant had a triple and two runs. "The majority of those present were colored," reported the *Washington Post*, "but there was a fair sprinkling of the regular ball patrons, who are anxiously awaiting the Senators' return. They were agreeably surprised by the really good game of ball which was put up." [296]

FROM THE BEGINNING OF THE 1891 SEASON, LOUISVILLE WAS unable to recreate its 1890 magic. Taylor had another strong year, batting .296 with eighty runs scored. Jennings was also very strong at bat, hitting .293, and he was one of the team's top hitters. However, the league's top hitter in 1890, Chicken Wolf, slumped from .363 to .256; infielder Shinnick, from .256 to .220; and the team as a whole fell from .279 to .258. They scored 819 runs in 1890 and only 698 runs in 1891.

The pitching decline was similarly pronounced, with the team's earned run average climbing from 2.57 to 4.22. They gave up 588 runs in 1890 and 873 in 1891. The aces of 1890, Stratton and Ehret, had fifty-nine combined wins in 1890, versus only nineteen in 1891. Doran performed credibly, considering he was a major league rookie, but his 5-10 record, 5.43 earned run average, and fifty-five strikeouts versus seventy-five walks were not going to set the world on fire as so many had hoped. Daily's performance was not much different from Doran's, going 4-8 with a 5.74 ERA before being released by Louisville and re-signed by Washington.

Doran's tepid performance in early 1891 was initially said to be "attributed to malaria."[297] This may have been accurate, but a month later, little if anything was mentioned of malaria, and the news media was more critical. On June 6, 1891, for example, *Sporting Life* reported that Doran's troubles were more off the field than on: "Pitcher Doran was the first Louisville player to be disciplined this season. He was fined fifty dollars and laid off ten days last week for over-indulgence. That was his besetting sin while with the New Havens. He has promised to sin no more." [298]

On another page of the same issue, *Sporting Life* confirmed that Doran had actually been released and was headed back to New Haven, after an unsuccessful trial in Cincinnati. [299] After a brief stint in the majors, Doran was back in the minors.

On June 13, Chapman also gave Daily his unconditional release. "His arm has failed," noted one newspaper.[300] Daily would remain in the majors, signing with Washington.

In the face of its significant pitching problems, Louisville finished the season at 54-83, and Chapman went from miracle worker to dunce in one year. Although he had hit the jackpot with his Jennings acquisition, his Doran and Daily experiences were dramatically unsuccessful.

One of Grant's fellow African-American pioneers in integrated professional baseball, thirty-four-year-old Moses Fleetwood Walker, earned notoriety during the 1891 season for a tragic bar fight in which he stabbed an assailant who died of the injury two days later. According to the April 11 *Sporting Life*, Walker was in Syracuse "passing through a low district" when "several men came out of a saloon and accosted him." An assailant, James Murray, "struck him in the face, when Walker drew a knife," he struck Murray in return.[301] In June, Walker was acquitted of murder charges.

"Walker is well-known throughout the country as a ball-player," reported the *Hammondsport Herald* at the time of acquittal, "but at the time of his arrest he held an important position in the railway mail service." [302]

Meanwhile, Ed Daily, a major league phenomenon at twenty-two, was, at twenty-eight, fighting for his baseball life. On June 30, freshly released from Louisville, Daily started for Washington against Boston, and "pitched a weird game, alternating bases on balls with strike-outs. The only enlivening feature of the game outside the batting of the Bostons was the 'chin music' between Ed Daily and Umpire Kerins. The umpire had all the better of the argument, and fined Daily successively $5, $10, $50 and then fired him from the field."[303]

Daily was a shell of his former self, and local sports observers were unable to explain it. "Washington folks are wondering just now what keeps Ed Daily here," wrote *Sporting Life*. "He has played bad ball, he has played worse than bad ball, and he has apparently done nothing to the team as captain to warrant his hire. He is frightfully inefficient in right field, not only fumbling balls and muffing them, but making no effort to get flies that ordinary men would catch, and altogether presenting a most pitiable spectacle of inefficiency and uselessness."[304]

It was a shockingly quick decline in a previously stellar career. By the end of July, Daily was released again and looking for work. Nothing was written about him in the national sporting press over the next two months, other than to remark that he and outfielder Paul Hines were "in Washington disengaged, but waiting for something to turn up."[305]

Hines turned up two seasons later with Sandusky in the Ohio-Michigan League, but Daily suffered a far worse fate. On October 21, 1891, less than two months after Grant and his Cuban Giants entertained Frederick Douglass and other Washington, DC, fans, Daily was found dead in that very city of what appears to have been consumption, a common name at the time for tuberculosis.[306] It was unfortunately not an uncommon disease among urban working-class men and women in the 1890s, even among professional ballplayers. In fact, Daily may have first contracted it while playing in Philadelphia, as two of his 1887 teammates, Jim Fogarty and Charlie Ferguson, also died of the disease–Fogarty in May of 1891 and Ferguson in April of 1888.[307]

Fear of consumption in the midst of rapid urbanization and a lack of awareness about how to fight it prompted a proliferation of "snake oil" cures throughout the latter part of the nineteenth century. These cures remained part of popular culture until reliable treatments became available in the middle of the twentieth century.

Unfortunately, as with many diseases, there appeared to be no rhyme or reason as to how it chose its victims. The bad luck seemed to strike completely at random. Daily, a strong athlete most of his life, was just twenty-nine. His brother, Con, a man with the same genetic and family background and in the same profession, would go on to play in the major leagues until 1896 and live until 1928, over three decades longer than his ill-fated older brother.

Unfortunately for major league players, the American Association, financially weakened after the 1890 season, would fold after 1891, leaving the National League as the only remaining major league. The National League's monopoly coupled with the poor economic conditions of 1892-1893 would lead to reduced major league crowds. National League salaries plummeted as a result. According to historian Michael Haupert, whereas the top salary in 1889 was $5,000 (Pittsburgh's Fred Dunlap and New York's Buck Ewing), the top salary declined to $2,800 in 1892 (Baltimore's Joe Gunson) and to just $1,800 in 1899 (Boston's Vic Willis).[308]

Given the relatively small number of major league jobs and the National League's salary intransigence, players needed to work harder than ever after 1891 to be successful. Former major leaguers flooded into the minor leagues where they pressed existing minor leaguers for jobs. The result of this compression was some of the best baseball ever played at the top end of the minor and major leagues, and the emergence of an intense aggressive form of competitive play that would become known as "scientific baseball."

In 1892, Baltimore switched from the American Association to the National League, and nineteen-year-old McGraw stuck with them, remaining in the major leagues from then on. He was not yet playing as regularly as he wanted to, but he was at the top. In just over two years, he had gone from being a Butcher Boy who received baseball lessons between trains near the Elmira station, to a semi-pro player in small towns like Olean and Wellsville, to the big leagues in Baltimore. Along the way, he observed, absorbed and deployed the many "scientific baseball" tricks and tactics that would impact the game for generations.

"In 1892, when I found myself on the bench as a result of the twelve team consolidation, I felt as if the bottom had dropped out of the world," McGraw said. "At the same time I felt confident of my own ability to make good eventually."[309]

He would soon become arguably the world's most recognizable athlete.

CHAPTER 9

1892
Binghamton Championship

T he influence of players both from and passing through the Twin Tiers continued to increase throughout the early 1890s. With this influence came an increase in smart, aggressive local baseball that featured skill, speed, precision, and opportunism. Given the failure of the Players' League to give players the economic security they sought as industrialists/magnates in their own right, the players' next best step was to continue to increase their value as craftsmen at the top of the working class ladder while they bided their time prior to reorganizing and challenging the National League's monopoly. This meant building skills and promoting a serious "scientific" approach to the game.

At the minor league level, Bill Heine had an injury-ridden season in 1891 and was now a step behind other major league prospects. His former teammates McGraw, Taylor, Goodall, and Doran had moved on to the major leagues, but Heine still strove to make a name for himself in the Eastern League, sticking with Elmira in 1892.

Heine started the '92 season as a catcher and outfielder and also found himself in the regular line-up. On June 7, he caught for pitcher Oliver Sprogel in a 4-1 loss to Rochester. Former team-mate Herb Goodall pitched for Rochester and held Elmira to just five hits. Joining Heine in the line-up was left fielder Hank Simon, who just five years earlier had refused to pose in the Syracuse team pitcher with Robert Higgins.

Ex-teammate John Doran was also back in the Eastern League. After reaching the major leagues, but failing to hang on in Louisville in 1891, he was desperately working his way back up through the minors. After stints in Troy and New Haven in '91, he was pitching for Albany in '92.

His performance was promising, but inconsistent. Albany management reportedly suspended him briefly in early June,[310] but he was back on the mound on June 11, when he gave up only five hits to Elmira, but lost 8-3 nevertheless. "Doran's wildness in giving six men bases on balls was the principle cause of the defeat," *Sporting Life* reported.[311] The next day, "Doran appeared to be his old form again, and gave the Buffalo batsmen few chances."[312] Within a month, however, Doran "had broken his promise to abstain from the use of intoxicants for the rest of the season on which condition he was reinstated."[313] As a result, Doran's baseball prospects seemed to be in limbo.

The newest emerging star of the Eastern League in 1892 was twenty-year-old Binghamton infielder Willie Keeler. Just 5'4" and 140 pounds, the Brooklyn native was thought by many to be too small for big-time baseball, yet he proved to be a phenomenal hitter for Binghamton, batting near the top of the order and leading the league in hitting. He would eventually join Hanlon and McGraw in Baltimore, but for now was still working his way up.

"He choked up on the bat so far he only used half of it," explained former big leaguer Sam Crawford of Keeler's hitting style, "and then he'd just peck at the ball. Just a little snap swing, and he'd punch the ball over the infield. You couldn't strike him out. He'd always hit the ball somewhere. And could he fly to first! Willie was really fast. A nice little guy too, very friendly, always laughing and kidding."[314]

On June 27, Keeler and Binghamton faced Doran and Albany. Binghamton won the rain-shortened contest 3-2, with Keeler managing just one hit and one run against Doran.[315] The next day, Elmira hosted Syracuse and won 7-0 on the strength of Con Murphy's seven-hit shutout. Heine batted clean-up and played centerfield for Elmira, chipping in two singles and two runs.

On July 4, Elmira and Binghamton hosted each other in a home-and-home doubleheader, with the morning game in Binghamton and the afternoon game in Elmira. John Fitzgerald started the first game in the box for Binghamton, and John Dolan started for Elmira. Fitzgerald gave up two runs in the first, but Binghamton's hitters scored six runs in the second and one more in third to take a commanding 7-2 lead on the way to an 11-3 victory. Fitzgerald's ten strikeouts helped him overcome six walks and five Binghamton errors. Heine started in centerfield and batted clean-up for Elmira, but failed to get a hit. Keeler started at third base for Binghamton, batted leadoff, hit two singles, and scored one run. First baseman Mike Lehane, who had played with Buffalo in '87, led Binghamton's hitting attack with a double and two runs scored. "Elmira put up a very loose game of ball and was defeated," *Sporting Life* reported, no doubt taking note of the seven Elmira errors.[316]

For the afternoon game in Elmira, the scenario was reversed, with Elmira taking an early lead and holding onto it for a 13-10 win. Pitcher Hon Fricken earned the win for Elmira, and two pitchers, Martin Duke and Bert Inks, were ultimately responsible for Binghamton's loss. Heine had a single, two stolen bases, and three runs scored for Elmira; Keeler had three singles, two doubles, and three runs scored for Binghamton. "The Binghamton men played like school boys," *Sporting Life* complained. "The Elmira players played a very good game, but the contest was so very one-sided and the playing so slow and tedious as to make it devoid of much interest."[317]

At the end of the first half of the Eastern League's season, Providence was in first place, Elmira was in fourth, and Binghamton was in sixth.[318] As was common at the time, the League was suffering from financial challenges, and so in July the leaders decided to reduce from eight teams to six, dropping Utica and Elmira, the two least profitable teams. As a result, Heine signed up to join Keeler in Binghamton. Perhaps rubbing elbows with another up-and-coming star like Keeler would give Heine the shot in the arm he needed to get to the majors.

Due to the downsizing, the Eastern League used a split schedule. They counted the first half of the season and then started the second half from scratch. The winner of the first half would then play the winner of the second in a post-season playoff. This gave every team, including Binghamton, a new opportunity to get into the championship chase.

The second half of the '92 season started slow for Binghamton. On August 1 and 2, Binghamton lost two straight games to Troy. Heine and Keeler combined made six of Binghamton's thirteen hits across those two games, but it was not enough. Binghamton's management had been tinkering with putting Heine in the outfield and having Keeler bat lower in the order, but by August 3, Keeler was back in his familiar leadoff spot and Heine was back behind the plate.[319] Perhaps they thought his presence would have a calming impact on the pitching staff.

The changes worked well, and on August 3, Binghamton defeated Providence, 7-3, with a solid pitching performance by Henry Lynch. Heine caught a solid game, despite one passed ball, and chipped in with a triple, while Keeler went hitless. The next day, Binghamton beat Providence again, this time 7-2, with John Fitzgerald pitching. Heine had two passed balls this time, but he also nailed another triple. Keeler made up for his rare off day by stroking two singles and walking twice.

From that point on, with Keeler at third and leading off at bat and Heine behind the plate, Binghamton played very solid baseball. On August 7, they defeated Albany 15-6, with Keeler and Heine collecting two hits apiece, and on August 10, they defeated Rochester 10-2, with Keeler pounding a home run, a triple, and a single, and Heine landing a double.[320]

Despite his prolific hitting, Keeler's fielding at third worried Binghamton management. On August 15, for example, he made two errors–and also happened to go hitless—in a frustrating 3-2 loss to Buffalo. "The game was closely contested on both sides, but Keeler's muff of Fournier's fly in the ninth inning, when two men were out, gave Buffalo the winning run," *Sporting Life* reported. He had two more errors the next day, to go with his two doubles, in a 12-6 loss to Buffalo. At the same time, Heine contributed yet another triple.[321]

Binghamton headed into September in a strong position, even with their losses to Buffalo. In a double-header against Rochester on September 3, Binghamton won both games, 22-2 and 16-7. Keeler feasted on Rochester's pitching to the tune of seven hits in eleven at bats that day, while Heine played center-field and went six for twelve. Keeler also contributed two errors, but they were inconsequential. Jack Barnett, who also contrib-uted a triple and a single, won the second game for Binghamton.[322]

John Francis "Jack" Barnett was born in 1872 in Elmira to Irish immigrant parents Jeremiah and Ellen. Jeremiah was a laborer, and he and Ellen had at least four other children: older siblings Anna and Gerry, and younger sisters Nellie and Mary.

Binghamton headed into the end of September as the winner of the Eastern League's second half of the season, which meant they would be pitted against first-half winner, Providence, in a championship playoff.

The first three championship games were played in Provi-dence, which won two of three. Game four was scheduled for September 23 in Binghamton, and according to *Sporting Life*, "the grounds were in good condition" and 2,500 people showed up to watch the contest.[323]

Providence took an early 3-1 lead in the first inning against starting pitcher Bert Inks, but Binghamton pulled closer in the sixth and then pounced on Providence's starter, Kilroy, scoring six runs in the seventh on their way to a 10-5 win. Keeler went two for four, but second baseman Sam Wise and Lynch were Binghamton's true hitting stars, combining to go six for ten. The two teams were now tied for the championship, 2-2.

In game five, on September 24, more than three thousand people showed up to watch, and Devlin started for Binghamton against Providence's Dolan. The two shut down each other's hitters until Binghamton picked up two runs in the fourth inning and two more in the fifth. Then each team exploded in the sixth, with Providence picking up six runs and Binghamton picking up five, for a 9-7 lead. Barnett came in as a relief pitcher for Binghamton and held Providence scoreless, while Binghamton picked up two insurance runs and won 11-7. Lynch and Wise again swung big sticks for Binghamton, combining to go six for ten, while Keeler picked up one single. Owing to the length of the game, the time of year, and the absence of stadium lights, "darkness ended the game after the eighth inning."

For game six in Binghamton, on September 27, attendance climbed to over five thousand, "and the utmost enthusiasm prevailed throughout the game." Inks started for Binghamton and Sullivan for Providence, and Mike Slattery "won the game for the home team in the first inning. With the bases full he drove the ball to the back fence for three bases, all three men scoring." Keeler had three hits and two stolen bases; Heine, a triple; and Wise and Lynch got five more hits between them to accompany Slattery's big first-inning hit, leading Binghamton to a 7-1 victory and the 1892 Eastern League championship.[324]

"The battle is over, and the Bingos have possession of the flag," *Sporting Life* reported. "One reason for the home team's success this season has been the perfect harmony existing between the players and the management. There was no lushing, and the club was composed of as gentlemanly a set of players as ever represented a city on the diamond."[325]

1892 Binghamton team. Top row (L/R): Slattery, Knight, Wise, Lehane and Cote; Middle row: Heine, Hanrahan, Doescher, Keeler and Lynch; From row: Inks, Barnett and Fitzgerald. Courtesy of the National Baseball Hall of Fame.

Keeler, *Sporting Life* reported, "is a fast runner and has a good, level head," while Barnett "has good curves, plenty of speed," and "the backstop work of Heine this season has been of the gilt-edged order. Besides being a first-class catcher, he was the hardest-hitting back stop in the League."

Keeler appeared to be headed to the majors in 1893, especially given his strong season with Binghamton. Inks was also expected to get an immediate shot in the majors, once Binghamton's season was over. "Bert Inks will finish the season with Washington," *Sporting Life* explained. "Inks has made a record this season that will be equaled by few pitchers in the country. He is without doubt one of the greatest south paw twirlers in the profession."[326] Heine's major league prospects also still appeared to be good, despite being his being overshadowed by the team's other stars.

It was a good season for the champions, but not so much for another south-paw twirler, John Doran, who, after compiling a 14-6 record with a 0.86 earned run average for Albany, found himself playing for a number of semi-pro teams after leaving Albany in July. In early August, Doran pitched for the Oneonta Normals, shutting down the Cooperstown Athletics in two grand contests when the Athletics found his "league" pitching a "puzzle."[327] In other words, the Cooperstown hitters had a tough time figuring out his curve balls. He also reportedly played for a team in Northampton, Massachusetts. "The way of the drinking ballplayer is hard and the end sure," lamented the *Philadelphia Inquirer* in considering Doran's situation.[328] Just a year removed from the major leagues, Doran must have thought a change of scenery would help him get back on track.

CHAPTER 10

Baseball Innovations

P itchers like Doran faced an immense challenge in 1893 when organized baseball moved the pitcher from a pitcher's "box" that was 4' x 5.5' with the center front edge (the release point) fifty feet from home plate, to a two-foot long and six-inch wide pitcher's "plate" that was 60'6" from the rear of home plate, where it has remained ever since. Before this change, a pitcher could start his wind-up anywhere in the box, provided that the release point remained within the pitcher's box. Subsequent to the change, a pitcher's release point could be anywhere, provided that he started his wind-up on the pitcher's plate. Although it may not seem like much of a change, it made a huge difference for some in how and where pitches broke and was especially taxing for pitchers who relied on finesse. It also gave the batter a split-second longer to size up oncoming pitches.

Some critics of the change thought that the magnates were manipulating the rules in an effort to slow down the players' efforts to increase their skill, value and bargaining power, but if that was their intent, it was ultimately unsuccessful.

In fact, as a hitter, Doran's ex-teammate Harry Taylor looked forward to the advantage. He had taken quite an impressive road from quiet Halsey Valley, on to Ithaca, Cornell, Canastota, Waverly, Elmira, and then on to Louisville. He had performed well at each stop and learned a tremendous amount about baseball and leadership.

After winning the pennant in 1890, Taylor stuck with Louisville and Chapman through the dismal, disappointing years of 1891 and 1892. By the end of 1892, Chapman had been replaced as manager in Louisville, and for the 1893 season, he moved back to manage the Buffalo Eastern League team.

Although he planned to finish law school at Cornell in the spring of 1893, Taylor wanted to stay in the major leagues through the 1893 season to earn the money needed to initiate his practice. Unfortunately, his relationship with the new Louisville ownership group was increasingly unpleasant. In the fall of 1891, he and Jennings challenged the reserve rule by negotiating a back-up contract with the New York Giants, while still under contract in Louisville. This back-up contract was in case the Louisville franchise or the American Association as a whole collapsed. This action did not put either player in ownership's good graces, especially after Chapman left. After the 1891 season, when the American Association folded and merged its four financially strongest teams, including Louisville, into the National League, Louisville's management increased the tension on Taylor and Jennings. They moved Taylor to the outfield, for example, from his preferred position at first base. The two played out the 1892 season with each playing only marginally well. Taylor hit .260 in 125 games (his season abbreviated on account of injury)[329] and Jennings just .224 in 152.

Ned Hanlon took over the reigns as Baltimore's manager in 1892, and was in the process of shaking up the team. His memory of Jennings helped him negotiate a deal in June 1893 to acquire Taylor, considered Louisville's star, and Jennings, considered a throw-in, for Tim O'Rourke and cash.[330] The Orioles were just beginning to earn their reputation for aggressive, intelligent, no-holds-barred play, and although Taylor was the senior player in the deal, Jennings was the one Hanlon really wanted.

Hanlon, a Brotherhood leader and captain of the 1887 World

Champion Detroit Wolverines, was a keen judge of talent. As a player, he was "best known for his aggressive base running and his superb defensive abilities,"[331] and he put all of these skills to work in building his Baltimore team.

Taylor and Jennings joined a club that already featured twenty-year-old McGraw, twenty-one-year-old Joe Kelley, and twenty-nine-year-old Wilbert Robinson. Other Baltimore stars included catcher William Jones Clarke, nicknamed "Boileryard" for his loud raspy voice; outfielder Steve Brodie, a career .303 hitter; and pitcher Frederick "Crazy" Schmit.

The trade turned out to be one of the most momentous in baseball history, as it represented one more piece of the puzzle in Hanlon's efforts to build a dynasty. Historian Burt Solomon explains:

> Hanlon had the ball players work the hardest on whatever they were worst at. "Work, work, work, all the time"–that was how Hughey Jennings described Hanlon's method…They perfected the meticulously timed deception of the hit-and-run. He drilled them on placing bunts for hits, not for sacrifices. They practiced fouling off pitch after pitch. The infielders practiced picking off runners and covering first base on groundballs. The batsmen worked on a tactic that would become known as the Baltimore chop. George Van Haltren had first tried it–swinging down on the ball, at an angle, to bounce it so high off a sunbaked infield that the batter could scamper to first base by the time it came down.[332]

The Orioles' aggressive style of play befitted its city:

> Baltimore straddled the boundary not only between Catholic and Protestant but also, more virulently, between North and South. The issue of slavery had left the city fractured in despair. Baltimore had been the

commercial capital of the South until the Civil War and was still a place of southern pace and sentiment. Poor whites kept streaming into the city from Virginia and Appalachia. No city to the north was home to so many black people; none to the south had so many immigrants. More and more, the rising numbers of Germans–nearly a quarter of the populace–and Irish and Russian Jews and such had lent an air of northern diligence.[333]

Taylor immediately fit in at first base, and Jennings went to work at shortstop. Jennings and McGraw would grow very close over the years, with Jennings, at both Taylor's and McGraw's urging, eventually following McGraw to Allegany College to do off-season undergraduate coursework in exchange for coaching the baseball team. McGraw and Jennings did not join the major leagues with the same academic background as Taylor, but they worked hard to catch up.

"Hugh Jennings and I became pals immediately," McGraw later wrote. "Jennings was a red-headed, freckle-faced kid, and fresh, like myself. We took to each other the first time we met, both of us having the same ambitions and aspirations."[334]

They were still learning at this stage how best to compete without running afoul of the umpires, and sometimes their gambits got the best of them. On September 16, 1893, for instance, McGraw, Jennings, and Taylor were all in Baltimore's starting line-up against Cleveland starter Cy Young. Taylor peppered Young with a double, two singles, and one run; while McGraw scored two runs; and Jennings had a single and a run. Baltimore scored eleven runs against Young, but also gave up eleven; at the end of the seventh inning, the score was tied, 11-11.

Cleveland got two base runners in the eighth, and Baltimore started to stall for time, thinking that otherwise there would be time for Cleveland to take the lead, but not enough time for Baltimore to come back. There were no lights, so the ballgame had to be finished before nightfall. The September dusk began to set in, and the umpire told Baltimore to speed things up. Cleveland went on to score four runs in the eighth and take a 15-11 lead, whereupon McGraw and company stalled even more, figuring that if it grew too dark before the complete inning ended, the score would be returned to 11-11. According to *Sporting Life*, the umpire cautioned the Orioles repeatedly, but "the Baltimores fooled with the game. [Catcher Wilbert] Robinson refused to pick up the ball, and, after being asked three times if he would play ball, said that he would not."[335] As a result, the umpire awarded the game to Cleveland by forfeit. Young would go on to win thirty-four and lose sixteen games for the full 1893 season, with an earned run average of 3.36. It was his second consecutive season with over thirty wins.

Taylor's last day as a major league player was in a double-header in St. Louis on September 26, 1893. He batted third in each game, going a total of one for eight on the day with a single, two stolen bases, and one run scored. McGraw was in his customary leadoff spot for both games and went two for eight, with two singles and one run scored. Baltimore won the first game 8-7, but lost the second 3-1 to St. Louis pitcher "Kid" Gleason. Before the decade was over, Gleason would become a star with both the Orioles and the New York Giants. Taylor's old Elmira teammate, Frank Shugart, manned center field in both games for St. Louis.[336]

The Baltimore team was already earning a reputation for perfecting smart, fast, "inside" or "scientific" baseball, but was not yet ready for a championship run, finishing the 1893 season in eighth place with a mediocre 60-70 record. Hanlon would need to make further adjustments. Team captain Taylor[337] had a solid season at first base, and batted .283 with fifty-four runs batted in eighty-eight games. Jennings batted just .255 in sixteen games and would spend time with McGraw during the off-season, working on his batting. At age twenty, McGraw had had a very strong season, batting .321 and leading Baltimore with 123 runs scored, 101 walks, and sixteen hits by pitch, already a noted Oriole tactic.

Whereas Baltimore was fast turning into a crucible for the new aggressive style of "scientific baseball," the old line style was best personified a long train ride away in Chicago, where Cap Anson's "Colts" continued to draw crowds of National League fans. The summer of 1893 was also notable for the World's Columbian Exposition, better known as the Chicago World's Fair, held to celebrate Christopher Columbus's 1492 voyage to the New World. The World's Fair drew over twenty-seven million people from around the world to the six hundred-acre site in Chicago and brought together an unprecedented display of culture and technology. The nearly two hundred white stucco buildings, constructed especially for the event and designed in a neo-classical style, earned the fairgrounds the nickname "The White City."

The Fair helped bring a new baseball stadium to the windy city, as in May a new West Side Park was opened at the southwest corner of Polk and Wood Streets, near where the University of Chicago Schools of Medicine and Pharmacy are located today. The new ballpark boasted capacity of 13,000, and was a welcome new home for Cap Anson's club, especially for Sunday games during the Fair.

Special railroad fares from New York and Pennsylvania towns to the Chicago fairgrounds were common all summer and were prominently advertised in local newspapers. In late August, Nellie Davis Hemingway, the author's great grandmother, left her husband home alone to tend the family farm near Dryden, New York, and traveled to Chicago via train with her brother and other family members to visit the Fair.[338] Like many other visitors, she stayed in the Chicago area with family or friends and brought home many souvenirs, like silver spoons, booklets, puzzles, and toys to commemorate the event, some of which are still in the family's possession.

Cap Anson was the same age as his old teammate John Clapp, but whereas Clapp was already several years removed from his player/manager stint in Waverly, Anson had been player/manager in Chicago since 1879, and was still going strong, batting .314 and knocking in 90 runs in 103 games. In fact, he only began using a glove the previous season, at the age of forty, the last National League first baseman to wear one.[339] He would go on to play four more seasons in his Hall of Fame career.

Anson's club finished the 1893 season in a disappointing ninth place, twenty-nine games behind pennant-winning Boston, and by season's end welcomed 23-year-old Clark Griffith to the roster. Griffith would eventually be one of the key leaders with Taylor, Jennings, Clarke and others in the creation of a new player's union, but in 1893 was still looking to get a major league foothold. By the very next season, he was one of the aces of the pitching staff, winning twenty-one games in the first of six straight twenty-win seasons for Chicago. The staff would include former Louisville ace Scott Stratton, who, at just twenty-five, was seeing his career descend just as Griffith's was ascending. By 1896, Stratton, a thirty-one-game winner in 1890, would be out of major league baseball altogether.

One of Chicago's season highlights was a three-game July visit from the up-and-coming Orioles. McGraw batted lead-off and played shortstop for Baltimore while Taylor batted sixth and played first. Anson batted clean-up and played first for the hometown club. Over the three games, McGraw collected just two singles and Taylor five singles, while Anson rapped seven hits, including three doubles and a triple, in leading to a Chicago sweep with a combined score of 26-6. Although any team featuring the cocky McGraw would not have been daunted long by the defeat, his Orioles were clearly not yet the powerhouse they would become just one season later.[340]

McGraw, Hanlon, Taylor and company were bringing a new style of play to major league baseball in Baltimore, and this led players, managers and owners to initiate similar experiments at all levels of the game, including the minor leagues. In New Orleans, for example, a native of Shenandoah, Pennsylvania's coal country, baseball player and manager Abner Powell, had for years tried one innovation after another to keep the turnstiles moving, not unlike Bill Veeck's efforts in St. Louis, Cleveland and Chicago roughly a half-century later. Since coming to New Orleans in 1887 to manage the city's first Southern League franchise, Powell had made every effort to keep the team and the league from collapsing, which was an eternal challenge, particularly in the South's struggling economy. In order to pump up attendance, Powell is credited, for instance, with creating marketing innovations like Ladies' Days, rain checks, and using a canvas tarpaulin to cover the field during rainstorms. He also frequently gave away free soda and hired local bands to entertain fans between innings.

Abner Powell from Shenandoah, PA

Baseball was still a relatively nascent New Orleans activity in 1893, as Powell struggled to fill out a competitive and entertaining roster. Among those he brought to the city in 1893 was thirty-one-year-old pitcher John Doran, still struggling to return to the major leagues. Doran found himself joining Powell, outfielder "Count" Campau, and former Elmira player Dick Phelan, among others, as Powell hoped to put together a strong Southern League season.

Since first playing together for New Orleans in 1887, Powell and Campau had continued their baseball journeys. Powell remained in New Orleans for four of the six intervening years, while Campau had stints in Kansas City, Detroit, St. Louis, and Troy. In 1890, Campau was the only player to ever lead two leagues in home runs in the same season (the International League and the American Association).

At twenty-nine, Campau was still very much in his prime as a ballplayer. A learned graduate of the University of Notre Dame, he was also very popular with the local media, and during the baseball season, wrote an article in the *Times-Picayune* entitled "Advice to Amateurs" regarding the "science" of baseball: "Many a time I have been asked for my views on the successful way to make a good ball player. From a player's standpoint a ball player is born and not made. But with continued practice and coaching from an older and experienced head the amateur will probably reach the top notch in the profession." Among those whom Campau cited as examples of such "older and experienced" ballplayers were Anson, Ward, Comiskey, O'Rourke and Taylor.[341]

In 1893, New Orleans had a population of almost 250 thousand. Although situated in the deepest part of the Deep South, its Southern League baseball team was primarily comprised of ball players from the North, like Doran and Campau.

Like the rest of the South, New Orleans was coming out of Reconstruction, and Jim Crow laws were beginning to leave their mark, producing an increase in racial disharmony. Traditionally more Spanish and French than English in its demeanor, New Orleans had a long tradition of integrating its layered cultural influences, and this integration was not fully in-tune with the rest of Louisiana and the region as a whole.

"There were wide differences in life styles and attitudes among the 'colored' population of New Orleans," wrote historian William Ivy Hair. "The 'Creoles of color,' mostly descendants of the ten thousand free Negroes of the city's antebellum era, ranked high on the economic ladder; most held skilled jobs or were in business or the professions. A few were quite wealthy. Nearly all the Creoles of color were of visibly mixed ancestry; many spoke French as a first language, and some could pass for white."[342]

The racial tapestry that created the Creole culture relied on a degree of nuance that many whites rejected. A growing number New Orleans whites, backed by rural Louisianans, demanded complete racial segregation. In response, in 1892, a group of African American activists recruited "octoroon" (one-eighth black) Homer Plessy to test the limits of segregation by riding a New Orleans streetcar intended for whites. The activists thought they had put together a good legal case to end segregation in its infancy, but instead, when they lost the case (Plessy versus Ferguson) in 1896, it spawned the "Separate but Equal" construct that lasted until the Brown vs. Board of Education case in 1954.

The racial tension in 1890s rural Louisiana was even evident in the ways that various groups interpreted the word "Creole." In October 1893, for instance, a meeting of Lake Charles citizens issued a resolution stating that "a certain wandering troupe of negro female half breeds, who are advertising themselves as 'The Creole Beauties'" was insulting to "Creole families of Louisiana that have always been the pride of the State." The citizens resolved:

> We urgently request all fair minded citizens who are unwilling thus publicly to pronounce the fair daughters of Louisiana as of mixed blood to resolutely turn their backs on this slanderous show.[343]

The show went on in Lake Charles and appears to have closed soon thereafter. A few days later, an article in the New Orleans Times-Democrat summarized the author's attitude (assumed to be on the newspaper's editorial staff) ominously.

> While we are opposed to negro shows—one and all—we did not approve of the action of the committee [to make a public protest.] A few determined men beats

all the public meetings you can have. Last but not least, meetings held over saloons to defend the names of the fair sex is [sic] entirely out of order.[344]

These sorts of sentiments would continue to lead the Louisiana legislature to enact increasingly restrictive legal rules, Jim Crow laws, on people of "African descent" regardless of education, ethnic background or other considerations.

It was in this atmosphere that Abner Powell's New Orleans baseball team pursued the 1893 season, opening with early exhibition games on March 29 and April 3 against Pittsburgh, which was conducting its spring training in the area. In the first game, Doran "pitched well" against his former teammate Hank Gastright, but lost 9-7. In the second game, Leach started for New Orleans against Terry and lost 4-0. Former Doran teammate Frank Shugart started both games at shortstop and went three for ten for Pittsburgh, while Campau went three for seven for New Orleans. Piggy Ward led off both games for New Orleans and went just one for seven.[345]

Mobile also hosted Pittsburgh early that spring, losing 8-4 on March 30 and 7-1 on March 31. Charlie Hamburg, playing for Mobile, went one for four against former teammate Ehret in the first game and one for three against Baldwin in the second.[346]

Mobile and New Orleans faced one another frequently throughout the season. In April, Doran faced Mobile twice, beating them 6-3 the first time and 18-1 the second.[347] Hamburg was a combined zero for six against Doran in these games. He fared better against Birmingham pitching, lighting up Underwood on April 21 for a single, double, triple, and stolen base and leading a twenty-three-hit attack and a 24-6 Mobile victory.[348] Doran finished the month losing 5-4 to Nashville in the first game of a double-header. Hamburg finished it going zero for four against "Iron Joe" McGinnity in a 4-3 loss to Montgomery.[349]

As the summer progressed, Hamburg was not up to his usual standards in Mobile, batting just .198 in twenty-eight games.

Doran did not do much better, posting a 5-6 record with New Orleans and, later, a 1-3 record with Mobile. Campau, on the other hand, had another strong season, batting .337 in ninety-six games with a team-leading nine home runs.

The '93 season did not end well for the New Orleans team as a whole. Despite Powell's best efforts, the Southern League folded before the full season was out, and New Orleans finished in eighth place. Eventually, Powell would manage to resuscitate the Southern League and his team, and in 1896, New Orleans would win the league championship. Still, the '93 season stung with disappointment.

Doran's lack of success in New Orleans and Hamburg's in Mobile did not bode well for their return to the major leagues, yet each would continue to strive. Each would head north to Pennsylvania in 1894: Doran to mentor younger pitching prospects from his hometown area in Athens before trying out with Scranton, and Hamburg to take a spot with Harrisburg.

CHAPTER 11

Winning Baseball
Baltimore Sets An Example

T hanks to Ned Hanlon's success in building a super-team in Baltimore in 1894, professional teams throughout the country had a model to follow for winning championships. The model was one of speed, skill and smarts, an elevation of the players' role from simple cogs in a larger machine to individual craftsmen.

After finishing dead last in 1892 and in eighth place in 1893, in '94, Baltimore added former Binghamton star Willie Keeler, former Detroit star Dan Brouthers, and pitcher/second baseman William "Kid" Gleason; in doing so, they won the National League championship. All eight of Baltimore's starting fielders hit over .300 (led by Joe Kelley at .393), seven each stole over thirty bases (led by McGraw with seventy-eight), six each scored over one hundred runs (led by Keeler and Kelley with 165), and five each knocked in over one hundred runs (led by Brouthers with 128).

Baltimore was baseball's dominant team during this period. In the six seasons from its first pennant in '94 through the National League's last twelve-team season in '99, Baltimore won three pennants, two Temple Cups (given to the winner of a post-season series between the first and second place teams,) and a League-high 538 games over that span—a record that was totally unprecedented in baseball history at the time.

Moreover, following that first championship '94 season and completely unbeknownst to McGraw and his mates, Baltimore's baseball legacy received a special blessing on February 6, 1895, with the birth of future great George Herman "Babe" Ruth.

Young George was born into a fanatical baseball environment. Baltimore baseball was the talk of the sporting nation during that period. The Orioles ended the '94 season with a 20-9 win in Chicago and an 89-39 record. During their long train trip back to Baltimore, cheering fans greeted them at the stations in Grafton, West Virginia; Cumberland, Maryland; and Washington, DC, before arriving home.

"When the train pulled into the Camden Station [in Baltimore] on October 2, the reception was unlike anything ever before in the history of the national game," Jennings' biographer, Jack Smiles, explained. "There were 50,000 fans crammed in and around the station and the nearby streets. Fireworks exploded as the players disembarked. A fife-and-drum corps escorted the team through the station. A parade ensued to the Fifth Regiment Armory. Two hundred groups had signed to march in the few days since they clinched, some on decorated floats. Half the city, 200,000 people, lined the parade route."[350]

The 1895 Orioles were champions yet again, going 87-43 and finishing three games ahead of Cy Young and Chief Zimmer's Cleveland Spiders. Led by McGraw, the Orioles were earning a reputation as hard-nosed aficionados of the inside game–bunt, steal, hit-by-pitch, hit-and-run, the Baltimore chop–anything that would give them an edge over their competition. "Heck, they knew baseball inside and out," Sam Crawford explained. "You know, ball players were tough in those days, but they were real smart, too. Plenty smart. There's no doubt at all in my mind that the old-time ball player was smarter than the modern player."[351]

Crawford recognized that the Orioles were not easy to play against, either: "After you'd make a trip around the bases against them you knew you'd been somewhere. They'd trip you, give you the hip, and who knows what else. Boy it was rough. There was only one umpire in those days, see, and he couldn't be everywhere at once."[352]

1896 Baltimore Orioles. Front row L-R: Doyle, McGraw, Keeler and Pond. Middle row L-R: Brodie, Hoffer, Kelley, Hanlon, Robinson, Jennings and Reitz. Back row L-R: Quinn, McMahon, Esper, Hemming, Bowerman, Clarke and Donnelly.
From the New York Public Library.

The Orioles were also pros at doctoring or "doping" their home field to suit their team's strengths. "The team was composed of fast men who were brilliant bunters and hard base runners," said Christy Mathewson, who played for McGraw years later in New York. "The soil of the infield was mixed with a form of clay, which, when wet and then rolled, was almost as hard as concrete. The ground outside the first and third base lines was built up slightly to keep well placed bunts from rolling foul, while toward first base there was a distinct down grade to aid the runner in reaching that station with all possible expedition."[353]

The Orioles were a scrappy, talkative team, "as lively as crickets," and each player had his own way of dealing with clutch situations. "Each of them had his own way with the umpires," historian Solomon wrote. "Willie was apologetic. Robbie would smile and kid them. Hughey would try to reason with them. Joe Kelley would scream. John McGraw would tread on toes and use vile language that Harry von der Horst worried ladies might hear, which sometimes they did."[354]

"Our Baltimore club had a reputation as umpire fighters," McGraw wrote. "I guess we did make life pretty miserable for some of them. This was due largely to the never-die spirit that we had built. It was our second nature to fight for the smallest point and, as a consequence, the umpire often had to take the brunt of our wrath."[355]

In response to criticism that arguing rarely led the umpires to change their calls, McGraw insisted that the argument was still necessary, in order "to impress upon the umpire that the players are not going to let anything slip by them."[356]

Since the early twentieth century, Baltimore's success in the 1890s has been attributed to dirty tactics and unfair trickery. Whether this attribution was due to jealousy of the Orioles' success in general, their high-spikes-sliding, belt-loop-grabbing, and ball-hiding reputation was largely undeserved, according to detailed research of contemporaneous news accounts. In his study, "Cap Anson 3," for example, historian Howard Rosenberg found very little corroboration for accusation of outright rule-breaking. In fact, Baltimore's reputation at the time appears to have had more to do with cussing, arguing with umpires, and aggressive opportunism than with outright cheating.

Hanlon may have been the architect of the team, but the young eager players gradually took it upon themselves to be a creative force for the team's drive to success.

"Nerve was what the Orioles had–and smarts," explained

Solomon. "They were too young and too full of themselves to know they could not invent whatever they wished. Night after night, in the vicious heat of the Baltimore summer, McGraw and Keeler and Kelley and Jennings sat up and puzzled out schemes to win ballgames. Who needed Hanlon? For hours they calibrated the chances of a runner's scoring from third base on a sacrifice bunt if he dashed for the plate at the pitcher's first motion. On the diamond they discovered that, on a bunt anywhere inside the foul lines, the runner could not be thrown out if he left instantly."[357]

For veteran players—like Kid Gleason, for example—whose stints with the Orioles were brief, playing for Baltimore elevated their individual performances. Gleason had one of the best years of his twenty-two-year major league career, while playing with the Orioles in '95, batting .309 and scoring ninety runs. His career average was just .261. No doubt he thrived on his teammates' energy and intensity.

The Orioles worked hard, played hard, and identified closely with the Baltimore community. McGraw and Robinson purchased houses next door to each other on St. Paul Street, not far from where the team played at Union Park, and opened a popular billiard and bowling emporium called The Diamond at 519 North Howard Street, across from the Academy of Music. The emporium was reminiscent of Clapp's and Pearce's spots in New York. According to local Baltimore sources, the sport of duckpins was first invented at The Diamond.

Throughout their dynasty, the Orioles epitomized and perfected the type of "intelligent," "fast," "inside," and "scientific" baseball that was effective and popular at the time–a game that thrived on speed and surprise. John McGraw, the old Truxton butcher boy, was the ambassador for this style of baseball in the 1890s and would continue to be so when he moved to New York. His was the name most associated with this style of play until Babe Ruth, Baltimore's free-swinging son, came of age and joined McGraw in New York twenty years later.

Buffalo and the Eastern League

For ex-Oriole and ex-Waverly star Harry Taylor, the 1894 season opened with him fully retired from the game, passing the New York state bar examination and establishing himself in Buffalo–back near his good friend, Jack Chapman. Business was slow due to the national economic depression though, so Taylor organized amateur games in the Buffalo area, calling his team the "Pastimes" and scheduling games with Cornell, St. Bonaventure, and others.[358] He also spent time tutoring players on the Cornell baseball team during the spring. Among the players on his "Pastimes" team in Buffalo was Al Lawson, who at the time was still dabbling in professional baseball and not yet fully engaged in the aircraft manufacturing work that would eventually be his greatest claim to fame.[359]

According to *Sporting Life*, Taylor's first legal case was not a success: "Harry Taylor has already risen in his profession; he is now managing clerk for Attorney Eugene Falk. Harry tried his first case a few days ago; a little girl was run over by a milk wagon, and the parents of the child sued the owner of the wagon for damages. Taylor represented the child in a very able manner. He tried hard to 'water the old man's milk' as he put it in his droll way, but the merits of the case and the jury were against him."[360]

Taylor was beginning his legal career in the midst of an economic recession that had more immediate impact on more people than prior recessions. This was because there were increasingly fewer independent farm workers relative to wage workers in the U.S. economy. Wall Street panic related to surprise insolvencies in the spring of 1893 led to the failure of roughly fifteen thousand companies and 491 banks, and to "unparalleled economic suffering," as indicated by an unemployment rate that went from three percent in 1892 to over eighteen percent in 1894. Such unemployment was a new experience for much of the population, since by 1900, one in three U.S. families was dependent on a regular paycheck from a company, whereas forty years earlier, only one in five was.[361] Such was one of the brutal by-products of industrialization.

The depression created renewed impetus for greater regulation of Wall Street, trusts and industrial "robber barons," as well as calls for repeal of the Gold Standard that was perceived by many rural citizens, particularly outside of the Northeast, to be a boon for the rich at the expense of the poor. Caught up in this movement was a young former baseball player from Illinois, William Jennings Bryan, who moved to Nebraska in the 1880s, won election to Congress, and in 1896 would ride a populist wave to the Democratic Presidential nomination.

As mentioned, for the 1894 baseball season, Taylor's former teammates Hamburg and Doran each headed to Pennsylvania. Hamburg joined the Harrisburg team, while Doran pitched in Scranton for a little over a month[362] before settling in Buffalo with Chapman. This would be a key season for both Hamburg and Doran.

Bill Heine, still working hard in the minors, joined Chapman and Doran in Buffalo late in 1894, after stints with Troy and Binghamton. He may have also pitched a game in Harrisburg.[363] Between Buffalo, Binghamton, and Troy, Heine batted a solid .296 for the season.

The 1894 Buffalo team also featured thirty-five-year-old Sandy Griffin from the '87 Buffalo team and future Hall-of-Famers Jimmy Collins and Pud Galvin. The twenty-three-year-old Collins had batted just .286 in 1893, but would improve to .352 in '94. Thirty-seven-year-old Galvin, who had been Chapman's St. Louis teammate in '75 and Clapp's Buffalo battery mate in '79, only played in three games in '94, batting .125.

Jimmy Collins was not yet the star third baseman he would become, instead still rotating among infield and outfield positions, as Chapman instructed. Collins had been born in the village of Suspension Bridge near Niagara Falls, the second of four children of Irish immigrants Anthony and Alice Collins. In 1872, while Collins was still a toddler, the family moved to Buffalo, where

Anthony worked as a policeman and eventually rose to the rank of captain. The family initially lived in Irish immigrant neighborhoods in the city's southern section, but by the time son Jimmy Collins graduated from St. Joseph's College downtown, they had moved to Niagara Street on the predominantly native-born west side. Jimmy Collins worked as a railroad clerk while playing for an amateur Irish team, the Socials, in the late 1880s, and by 1892, was playing third base for a team in the northern manufacturing section of town. In was there that, in May of '93, Buffalo manager Chapman recognized his talent and offered him a contract.

Also breaking into the Eastern League in 1894, with Springfield, was French Canadian Phil Nadeau. Nadeau was born in 1872 in Montreal, Canada, and, although stocky at 5'8" and 175 pounds, was surprisingly nimble and quick. He played an outstanding outfield and was also able to play a capable infield when needed.

Nadeau's rookie season started extremely well, with some hot hitting–particularly in May, before his hay fever kicked in and limited his effectiveness. On May 10, for example, he had three singles and scored two runs to lead Springfield to a 20-5 victory over Syracuse. The next day, he hit two home runs, a triple, and a double; scored three runs; and made five "difficult" catches in left field in a close 10-9 loss to Troy.

A common feature of the Eastern League in 1894 was continuous performance problems with its top pitching prospects. Binghamton's Jack Barnett, for instance, was characterized as the best pitcher in the league, "when in trim."

"Whether his poor work heretofore has been owing to sulking, to poor condition or to anything else is best known to him," *Sporting Life* reported of Barnett. "To the spectators at the games, it looked like a genuine case of the sulks, while on the other hand, to the players, it looked like an off day, as they term it."[364]

This criticism followed a week in which Barnett had actually not performed all that poorly, giving up just five runs in a 24-5 victory over Buffalo. Collins ripped a triple and Griffin had a double and two runs scored off Barnett, but it was still an easy victory for Binghamton. Barnett had even helped out, hitting a double and two singles and scoring three runs.

As a pitcher who had enjoyed more than his share of media glory and criticism, Doran could have used more rehabilitation time before the season began, but perhaps this was indicative of less than stellar work habits. He started the year going 1-5 with twenty-six strikeouts in just over forty-eight innings with Scranton. Twenty-one-year-old pitching prospect Edward "Davy" Dunkle was also on the Scranton team, and he posted a 3-10 record for the season, but he seemed earmarked for bigger and better things.

It is unclear what prompted Doran's move to Buffalo in July. Upon his arrival, the media reported him to be "in first class shape…like a race horse. Doran in the past has been his own worst enemy, but under the contract which he signed with the local club he will not find it profitable to tread any but the straight and narrow way."[365] Unfortunately, he did not stick with Buffalo long, as on August 17, the *Sayre* (PA) *Evening Times* reported that Doran had pitched for his hometown Athens team against a YMCA squad from Towanda in a "largely attended" contest, earned a 9-9 tie after eleven innings.[366]

Cooperstown and Amateur New York Baseball

Contests between local amateur teams sponsored by YMCAs or other organizations were common in the mid-1890s, and teams were often put together for brief stretches simply to play in multiple series with nearby teams.

For example, years before it was lauded as the birthplace of baseball and decades before it became the home of the National Baseball Hall of Fame, Cooperstown had a competitive town team, nicknamed the "Athletics." Doran had pitched against the Athletics club in '92 as part of an amateur team from Oneonta.

In '94, the Athletics played several times a week from mid-July through September, amassing an impressive winning percentage as they did so. Their most common opponent was a team from Poughkeepsie, but they also played numerous games against the Cuban Giants and at least one, on August 1, against the team from Middletown Asylum.

Cooperstown began as a frontier settlement on Otsego Lake in 1786, and was originally incorporated as the village of Otsego in 1807. It was renamed Cooperstown in 1812 after its founder William Cooper, whose son, James Fenimore Cooper, would become arguably the most prolific American writer of the early nineteenth century, penning *The Last of the Mohicans*, *The Pioneers*, and numerous other works of both fiction and nonfiction. James, who grew up in the village, was among the very first American novelists to include African, African-American, and Native American characters in his stories. By 1894, Cooperstown was still largely a rural, agriculture-oriented town.

Cooperstown's '94 baseball club was captained by J. Hollister. A youngster named Fred Talada, a protege of John Doran's from Athens, Pennsylvania, was also reported to have played for the team.[367]

The Cuban Giants of 1894 featured the same Frank Grant and Clarence Williams who played for Harrisburg prior to its climb to the Atlantic Association in 1890. Both were still very potent. At twenty-eight, Grant was in his prime, and he helped lead the Giants to a 27-11 victory over the Athletics on July 26. The next day, the Athletics returned the favor with a 9-7 victory. Grant and Williams both had "excellent" performances, according to the local Cooperstown newspaper.[368]

The Athletics had previously faced the Giants in '93, with the *Otsego Farmer* describing Grant as the team's star: "He is quick, alert, a swift runner and a splendid thrower and so good humored that he takes at once with the crowd," the paper said. "He covers an immense amount of ground. In the eighth he made the most wonderful running catch that has ever been seen here."[369]

According to Grant's childhood friend, Bliss Perry, those who witnessed his exciting hitting style saw "the ball shoot in over the plate and the statue-like batsman swing forward quick as lightning, with a stroke like an axeman's, clean and hard. The dry sharp ring of the ash was swallowed up by the roar of voices, as half the spectators sprang to their feet to watch the ball on its long, low flight down the field. The grand stand was full of clapping hands and stamping feet and cheers."[370]

The week after the July 26 and 27 split against the Giants, the Athletics had a big game against Middletown Asylum. As its name indicates, the Asylum team was comprised of employees of the Middletown State Homeopathic Hospital in Middletown, New York.

Despite the fact that running a baseball team was relatively expensive, the hospital managers intentionally sponsored and promoted a baseball team for its patients to watch and follow among its on-going activities and argued for continuing to do so in light of its positive influence on patients:

> While our patients have been obliged to forego, during the year from which we have just emerged, some of the attractions which pertain to health and home, we may state with considerable satisfaction that the amusement known as "baseball" has continued without interruption at this institution. Like the mellifluous flow of Tennyson's book, the ecstatic inspiration of baseball "goes on forever."[371]
>
> This game will draw more patients out of the slough of despond, and set their feet upon the heights of hilarious jollification than any other means known in medicine or hygiene. There is nothing else to be found in the history of games that can so effectually turn back the hand upon the dial plate of time, and make old men renew their youth, as the American game of baseball.[372]"

A game of baseball usually occupies about two hours

of actual time, but the excitement preceding and following a game is sometimes continued for days and weeks in succession. In the mind of the lover of the sport there is a long continued bright anticipation before the game, and an equally long continued cheerful contemplation of the incidents pertaining to the contest itself.[373]

Among those recruited to work for the hospital and play for the team was a twenty-year old right-hander from North Adams, Massachusetts, named John D. "Jack" Chesbro. According to his SABR biography, Chesbro earned his nickname, "Happy Jack," while working for the hospital, "after a patient noted his cheery disposition and friendly grin." He was the fourth of five children of Chad Chesbro, a shoemaker, and Martha Jane Fratenburgh Chesbro.[374]

At the August 1 contest against the Cooperstown Athletics, Chesbro and his mates fell 10-7.[375] Still, the Asylum club enjoyed a 21-7 record in 1894, including a 3-2 record against Frank Grant and the Cuban Giants.

"Happy Jack's" success at the Asylum led to professional stints in 1895 with Johnstown and Albany in the New York State League and with Springfield in the Eastern League, along with his fellow Asylum teammates Art Madison and Pat McGreevy. Within a few years, Chesbro would become one of the major leagues' most effective spitball pitchers.

Unlike some of the rivalries described earlier between upstate New York towns, the Athletics' rivalries were not typically reported as being overtly aggressive. However, on August 27, the Athletics defeated a team from Richfield 5-0, and the Richfield fans were reportedly very disturbed by the treatment accorded them by the Cooperstown fans. The next day, the teams met again, and Richfield allegedly bribed the umpire, Mitchell. The ensuing calls from said umpire so enraged the Athletics that Mitchell got into an altercation and later had to settle with the local judge for damages. The Cooperstown club paid the fine on the umpire's behalf.[376]

CHESBRO, N. Y. AMER.

Jack Chesbro. From the Library of Congress.

Harrisburg and the
Pennsylvania State League

Their respective performances in the '94 season set Hamburg and Doran on divergent paths in 1895, with Hamburg moving up from Harrisburg to Rochester, and Doran moving down from Buffalo to Harrisburg. Fortunately for the dogged hunter Hamburg, his move from Harrisburg did not come too early to prevent him from duck hunting on the Susquehanna River in late March.[377]

"Charley Hamburg is too well known in base ball circles to need an introduction from your correspondent," reported *Sporting Life*. "Suffice it to say that he played with Mobile last season [1893], and for some time was a member of the Louisville and Buffalo teams." [378] In Harrisburg, in 1894, Hamburg returned to being the steady, competent player he had been when he played for Chapman in Buffalo and Louisville, batting .310 with eighty-four runs scored in ninety-six games.

In an effort to start out on a good foot with his new team in 1895, Doran recommended that Harrisburg management also sign a pitching prospect from his Athens hometown, twenty-one-year-old Fred Fremont Talada.

"Harrisburg expects to open the season with a strong team," reported *Sporting Life* on February 16, 1895. Among the first signings announced were "Catcher Andy Roth, formerly of Royersford and the Philadelphia State League team; pitchers Jack Doran, formerly of Scranton, and Fred Talada, a youngster who played his first professional season in the New York State League last year, whom Doran recommended."

Talada, born on March 26, 1874, in or near Athens, was the son of Guy and Mary Talladay. In the 1880 census, the Talladays were living in Barclay, Pennsylvania in a decisively working class neighborhood. Guy was listed as a thirty-four-year-old "Brakesman" born in Pennsylvania, and the family's neighbors included laborers born in Ireland on one side and Guy's father,

Solomon, an "Engineer Locomotive," on the other. The broader neighborhood included numerous coal miners born in Ireland or Pennsylvania, at least two of whom could neither read nor write.

According to local news reports associated with his arrival in Harrisburg at the start of the 1895 season, Fred Talada pitched the 1894 season in the New York State League, and was extremely successful. Unfortunately, no evidence has yet been uncovered to support this record. His alleged team in Cooperstown, was semi-pro and not in the New York State League. Moreover, his alleged 24-5 pitching record more closely approximated the record of George "Deke" White, who was a dominant pitcher for Cooperstown in 1894, and would eventually pitch in the major leagues and become one of the founding fathers of the National Baseball Hall of Fame.

In recommending Talada, it's possible that Doran—or even Talada himself—exaggerated the youngster's credentials for the media. There is one game account, from July of 1894, stating that Talada was pitching for the well-known Williamsport Demorests during the season, which was also not part of the New York State League.[379] It's possible that Talada played on a per-game basis for numerous area teams, including Cooperstown, similar to how Doran likely played prior to his '87 Elmira season. He also could have played using an alias.

Harrisburg gave Talada at least two pitching opportunities early in the 1895 season. On April 6, he was one of three pitchers who faced the Carlisle Indian School in an 11-8 loss. Carlisle scored five runs in the eighth inning to secure the win. Talada is the last pitcher listed in the batting order, so it is probable that he was at least partially responsible for those final five runs.[380]

On April 13, the *Harrisburg Telegraph* reported that Talada was among the Harrisburg pitchers defeated by Philadelphia 25-7 or "slaughtered by 'Yanigans,'" a reference to Philadelphia's second team, since in exhibition season major league teams frequently used split squads to maximize playing time, as they continue to do today. "[Ed] Ames and Talada were simply peaches and cream for these same 'Yanigans,' while Willy McGill [an experienced major league pitcher] wasn't handled with kid gloves either."[381]

On April 16, the *Harrisburg Telegraph*, in an article entitled "Another Exploded 'Phenom;" reported that the team had released Talada. "Fred Talada, the New York State League 'phenom,' signed on the recommendation of Pitcher Jack Doran, himself on the 'sick'-list at his home, has gone the way of all exploded 'phenoms,' and is now hunting a job."[382] Ironically, unlike Doran, Talada barely had any time in the "phenom" spotlight.

Talada's rough treatment may have been part of the local backlash against Doran. Just weeks earlier, on March 26, 1895, the *Harrisburg Telegraph* had reported what many by then suspected–that there was more to Doran's uneven performance than an injury or sore arm: "There is no better pitcher in the business to-day than Jack Doran if he abstains from the drink habit. He holds some great pitching records, shutting the Worcester team, of the Atlantic Association, out without a hit and striking out twenty men May 5th, 1890, while in New Haven. On Decoration Day he shut Washington out 8-0 without a hit, and on the afternoon of that day gave Baltimore but two hits in fourteen innings, the score being a tie."[383]

Given that both Doran and Talada appeared to be washouts, Harrisburg had to look to other prospects for pitching help, most notably Vic Willis, a nineteen-year-old future major leaguer from Newark, Delaware, who would go 4-4 for Harrisburg in '95 before the team folded in June.

For the remainder of the 1895 season, Talada went back to the Athens area and played baseball wherever he could find the opportunity. In mid-August, according to the *Towanda* (PA) *Bradford Star*, Talada and his battery mate Ayers played for Towanda in a town team match-up against Troy (PA), which was led by Lock Haven star Davy Dunkle, who had played with Doran at Scranton the previous year. Talada and Towanda defeated Dunkle and Troy 11-0, with Talada striking out twelve batters to Dunkle's ten.

WILLIS, PITTSBURG

Vic Willis. From the Library of Congress.

Later in 1895, while pitching against Williamsport, Dunkle allegedly perfected the "potato trick" originally concocted by "Wild Bill" Setley. With a one-run lead in the ninth inning, two outs, and a runner on first, he threw a potato he had hidden in his pocket over the first baseman's head, leading the runner to believe he could safely advance to second. As soon as Dunkle saw the runner head to second, he fired the actual baseball to second ahead of the runner, who was tagged, thus securing the last out of the game.[384] George Stovey was reportedly the umpire for the game, and called the runner out after "considerable wrangling." Stovey later won a $25 bet when National League President Nick Young agreed that "it was up to the base runner to keep his eyes open and not be caught."[385]

Talada pitched in numerous contests for Towanda that season, including a game in which Talada and Ayers teamed up to lead the "cigarmakers" to victory over the "printers" 6-2. These were likely amateur teams comprised of a combination of workers from those industries and associates. Talada and Ayers also teamed up to earn a ten-inning 9-8 victory over Troy. Playing second base for Troy in that game was Bill Heine, who got three hits off Talada, including a game-tying shot in the ninth.[386]

For his part, Doran held on with Harrisburg as long as he could. On May 25, *Sporting Life* lamented that the "famous southpaw" had not yet regained his pitching prowess, but also remained optimistic.[387] On June 1, the paper's Harrisburg correspondent reported: "Doran, the once famous twirler, is slow in regaining his skill. He was a complete failure in the first game he essayed to play, and this is the only opportunity he has had to show what he can do. He has been practicing to get himself in shape, but whether he will ever again fill the bill as a pitcher cannot now be stated."[388]

The 1895 season wound up being a very challenging one for Harrisburg. Following the big busts of Talada and Doran, the team went 19-16 in the first half of the Pennsylvania League season before folding. Revenue was not sufficient to meet expenses. The team's best players, including twenty-one-year-old catcher Roth and pitcher Willis, finished the season with other teams.

The Harrisburg team's loss of revenue was reflective of baseball's broader economy. It was not easy to lure spectators to games day after day. There were built-in advantages for town teams to join leagues, particularly in terms of stability and prestige, but there were also disadvantages, such as the expected number of games, the requisite expenses, and the dependence on a set number of opponents who might not be interesting to locals. Meanwhile, unaffiliated town teams had more flexibility to lure good players and opponents with promises of higher—though less stable and reliable—returns.

PART THREE

The Hoodlum Element

Baseball in the Late 1890s

"Popular culture—entertainment high and low—rises from the bottom if it is to gather the strength needed to endure. It does not start at the top of the social ladder and then descend."[389]

– JOHN THORN, BASEBALL IN THE GARDEN OF EDEN.

CHAPTER 12

Waverly, 1896

F rom the earliest days of organized baseball in the 1860s, it was a challenge to corral both enough good, regular players and "cranks," or spectators, to make it a viable business. From the view of "proper" society, baseball continued to waiver between catering to the "respectable class" versus catering to the "hoodlum element." For many the game was not taken seriously; in fact, to many, it was dangerously rowdy, or, at best, a waste of time. As part of catering to the respectable, team officials often sought to lure ladies and children to games by offering them discounted, or, in many cases, free admission. However, if there were gamblers, hustlers or other questionable characters about, the games themselves were not always "civilized" entertainment.

Local teams sometimes formed into leagues to better organize themselves, set rules, and leverage advertising. The leagues also attempted to control players to benefit their own interests, but the existence of so many leagues meant the best players still had options. Unfortunately, the game's underlying financial foundation was unstable, and leagues were unreliable. Change seemed to be the only constant.

Since the American Association folded after the 1891 season, baseball had just one major league–the National League—with twelve teams in the cities of Baltimore, Brooklyn, Cleveland,

Cincinnati, Boston, Chicago, Pittsburgh, New York, Philadelphia, Washington, St. Louis, and Louisville. In 1896, there were three minor leagues one level below this: the Atlantic, Eastern, and Western leagues. The Atlantic was comprised of teams from Newark, Hartford, Paterson, Wilmington, New York, Lancaster, Philadelphia, and New Haven. The Eastern was made up of teams from Buffalo, Providence, Rochester, Scranton, Springfield, Syracuse, Toronto/Albany, and Wilkes-Barre. The Western League, under the control of Ban Johnson, was comprised of Columbus, Detroit, Grand Rapids, Indianapolis, Kansas City, Milwaukee, Minneapolis and St. Paul. These were all mid-sized-to-large cities with, for the most part, consistent paying attendance.

The next level of minor league baseball below that was comprised of five leagues, including the Pennsylvania State League, which operated in seven cities: Carbondale, Easton, Hazleton, Lancaster, Philadelphia, Pottsville, Shamokin/Reading, and York. For the most part, these were slightly smaller cities. The other four leagues at this level were the New England League, Southern Association, Virginia League and Western Association.

There were three more leagues a rung below this and many more that were considered "independent" leagues. In total, according to SABR, there were forty-one active leagues in the U.S. and Canada in 1896. In Pennsylvania alone, there were, in addition to the aforementioned leagues, the Cumberland Valley League (with teams in Carlisle, Chambersburg, Hagerstown, and Hanover) and the Central Pennsylvania League (with teams in Shamokin, Sunbury, Williamsport, Milton, and Mount Carmel). Both of these leagues were made up of teams from much smaller towns with less reliable attendance.

According to the *Philadelphia Inquirer*, some of the "independent" town teams were considered "amateur" rather than professional or semi-professional. Among the Pennsylvania coal country towns with amateur teams the *Inquirer* covered in '96 were Freeland, Mauch Chunk, Hazleton, Wyoming, and Lattimer.[390]

In 1895, the New York State League included the towns of Albany, Amsterdam, Binghamton, Elmira, Gloversville, Johnstown, Schenectady, and Troy, and it was dominated by teams from the Capital district and the Mohawk River valley. Unfortunately, the league failed to launch a season in 1896.

This created a unique opportunity for semi-professional teams in the area to pick up regional support.

By 1896, Waverly and its neighboring Penn-York Valley towns of South Waverly, Sayre, and Athens were aspiring to be considered at the same level as towns that had professional minor league teams. The combined population of the four towns had grown significantly since Waverly's 1887 professional season, now approaching 15,000. Although this was still short of Elmira and Binghamton, it put the valley community in the same size category as the aforementioned Pennsylvania towns. It fact, it was now larger than New York towns like Cortland, Ithaca, Canandaigua, and Corning, which, like Waverly, were vying for both economic and sporting success. In terms of competing with existing New York State League towns, the community was larger than Johnstown and just a shade smaller than Gloversville and Amsterdam. Most importantly, its growth trajectory over the prior two decades was much higher than all of these towns.

Waverly's '87 semi-pro baseball success still echoed into the mid-1890s. By 1891, local enthusiasts were pursuing another crack at organized baseball in Waverly, often citing its central location. "Why could not a six-club league, comprised of Susquehanna, Binghamton, Athens, Owego, Waverly, and Elmira, be formed for the season of 1891?" wrote "A Sport" to *Sporting Life* on April 15 of that year. "The circuit would be a compact one and could be conducted on a paying financial basis. All the towns are good ones, and the matter should be talked over. Waverly would do her share to carry off the bunting at the close of the season."

Waverly, NY, at the corner of Broad and Fulton Streets.

At least one member of the 1887 team, Percy Lang, was still a prominent member of the Waverly community and directly involved in managing the local baseball effort as President of the Waverly Athletic Club (WAC), out of which the Baseball Committee that would run the team was established. Local media was very supportive of Waverly's bid to have a semi-pro team in 1896. Having a competitive local team would put Waverly on par with Elmira and perhaps even lead to an increase in business ventures.

In early May, according to the *Waverly Advocate*, Lang and others on the WAC were seriously at work building a baseball diamond at the Howard Street Grounds, and recruiting local players. Local merchants A.N. Ford and P.W. Towner were named the manager and secretary/treasurer of the new baseball team, respectively. Among the possible players mentioned was Fred Talada, if he could be persuaded to move from the Cleveland area where he was then currently pitching.[391] As Lang recalled, Waverly's success in '87 hinged on containing expenses, which meant having strong local players, especially pitchers.

The types of entertainment that baseball would be competing against in Waverly continued to be varied. There were other
sports like boxing and pedestrianism, musical acts like minstrel
shows, vaudeville and band concerts, and of course there were
traveling circuses and western shows. Such so-called exotic performances also included gypsy bands like "Roving Ned's" that
spent a week in Waverly in March as part of its regional tour,
performing "wonderful feats in fortune telling, mind reading,
etc.", complete with "a reproduction gypsy camp with dogs, camp
fires, etc."[392]

The *Free Press*'s May 16th edition, in the midst of news about
farmers; the comings and goings of ordinary citizens; Erie, Lehigh
Valley, and Lackawanna train schedules; and advertisements for
such products as corsets, Wright's Pills, flower seeds, and Battle
Ax plug tobacco, featured a story about baseball, reporting that
local ball players on the "Regulars" and "Colts" had recently competed at the Howard Street Grounds. The game proved, the *Free
Press* asserted, that "we have plenty of good material in Waverly
from which to form a strong team, and that such a team will be
organized there is no doubt."[393]

Among the local players who played in the game and were
being considered for the team were nineteen-year-old shortstop
Owen Dunham, a sign painter who was said to be "quick and sure
on ground hits and a strong, accurate thrower," twenty-one-year-
old third baseman John "Bud" Waller, a local African-American
laborer, who was "all right on third base," and twenty-one-year-
old catcher Ervin A. Mix, a blacksmith who was "a good batter
and an excellent catcher." Others evaluated were Quick, who
"with proper coaching will make a good pitcher," and center fielder
H. M. Leonard, "who is a sure fielder and a heavy batter."[394] The
other players in the "Regulars'" line-up for the game were twenty-
five-year-old Irving Washington Brewster, Jr., a bartender and
the son of a Civil War veteran and mason, seventeen-year-old
Theodore "Tosh" Gillan, whose father was a blacksmith at the
Lehigh Valley shops, Herrick, A. N. Ford, and Harris.

The team's management selected Dr. Carmody of Sayre to help train and coach the team, since Carmody reportedly had "many years" of college baseball experience.[395]

Management's first mission was to build a team that would be competitive with other local teams. Fortunately, Waverly's financial backers were willing to field out-of-town talent to defeat the neighboring town teams, but wanted to highlight Waverly's home players and contain expenses if possible. "The outlook for a good team and a successful season is very bright," the *Free Press* reported. "The committee are [sic] very much encouraged at the prospects. All desiring positions on the team will be given an opportunity to demonstrate their ability. The best players will be selected and no favoritism will be shown."[396]

The following week, the *Free Press* reported that "the athletic grounds are being enlarged by the extending of the fences" and that "the diamond is also being newly graded."[397] This Howard Street Grounds location, was south of the local cemetery, on the south side of Providence Street, east of Spaulding, west of Cayuta, and north of Broad, on the site of the old circus grounds.

In other news of the day, a big point of pride for the local railroad yards and its hundreds of employees, the *Free Press* on May 23 excitedly reported that the "Lehigh's new fast train, 'Black Diamond Express,' made her initial trip over the road" the previous Friday, complete with the most modern and luxurious Pullman coaches. There would now be two daily trains through Sayre, one leaving New York and the other, Buffalo. "They are the handsomest and fastest trains in the world," the *Free Press* claimed, a statement that very much aligned with the community's eagerness to show off its cutting edge.[398]

In terms of recruiting for this new team, the talent emphasis was on speed and agility, per the Baltimore Orioles example, as rapid excitement was what people would pay to see. "Baseball was a more exciting game in those days," said ex-major leaguer Tommy Leach, who played for Auburn in the New York State League in 1898. "It was more rugged, first of all. Take the equipment. We had little gloves that would just fit over your hand. Now they have those big nets, and they catch the ball in the webbing. But we had to catch the ball with our hands."[399]

As the major league champions, the Orioles, had demonstrated, speed was indispensable in modern, "scientific" baseball–and contributed significantly to the game's entertainment value.

Riding on a wave of local excitement, the newly uniformed Waverly team was unveiled in the afternoon of May 30 at the Howard Street Grounds. Admission to the game was twenty-five cents per ticket, and, given that the seating accommodations were still incomplete, the attendance was very respectable at seven hundred. The starting batting order for Waverly was Dunham leading off at shortstop, twenty-two-year-old Harvey "Doc" Pearce at third, Mix at catcher, Garrison in right, Leonard in center, Waller at second, Brewster in left, Gillan at first and Quick on the mound. They faced a tough Corning squad, arriving just before game time on Erie train number eight, led by its pesky lead-off-hitting leftfielder Willie Reilly and its talented left-handed pitcher Parker.

The teams warmed up eagerly before the crowd, as the Corning players took in the Howard Street Grounds for the first time.

When the game commenced at four o'clock, the Corning bats lit up Quick right away, as Reilly led off the game by smacking a double and racing around the bases on a subsequent single to take a 1-0 lead. Parker meanwhile held the Waverly bats quiet and Corning took a 7-0 by the seventh inning, thanks not only to clutch Corning hitting, but sloppy Waverly fielding.

The sloppy fielding was due in part to the field conditions, and Waverly used this to their advantage in their half of the seventh, as Leonard hit the ball to Corning's shortstop and raced to first. The shortstop botched the play, and Leonard was safe at first.

This brought up Waller, Waverly's best hitter.

Bud Waller in football gear. From the Waverly Historical Society.

Waller had reached base earlier in the game when one of Parker's pitches hit him. After trotting to first, he immediately stole second in an effort to get into scoring position, and to prove he was not intimidated. Unfortunately his teammates were unable to get him home, and he was stranded at second.

Now he eagerly dug in against the scrappy southpaw. The crowd, perked up by Corning's error and wondering perhaps if Parker might hit Waller for a second time, cheered loudly as Parker wound up and sent a pitch right down Waller's alley.

Waller took a big swing and met the ball squarely, cracking it over the left field fence for the first home run of the game, the first of the season, and the first ever at the Howard Street Grounds. Corning's lead suddenly shrank to 7-2.

Waverly scored two more runs in the eighth on a double by Mix and singles by Leonard and Brewster, but Corning scored twice more to take a 9-4 lead into the ninth inning. Quick then almost single-handedly attempted a comeback against the tiring Parker, as he belted a single, stole second, stole third, as then scored on an error, making the score 9-5. Unfortunately, Waverly could manage just one more run, losing by a final sore of 9-6.

Overall, the Waverly team and fans took the loss in stride. "The work done by all the men was excellent, considering everything," reported the *Advocate*, "and the game they put up against the Corning aggregation, which is acknowledgedly a strong one, won them many praises from the baseball cranks who witnessed the contest."[400]

Buoyed by the strong start, Waverly continued to place its hopes in the hometown players, and prepared for its next opponent. On June 6, Towanda rolled into town, and Waverly had a much easier time against them than it had against Corning. Ford replaced Brewster in the line-up and moved to right field with Garrison moving to left, but otherwise Waverly fielded the same line-up as a week earlier. This time, though, Waverly was the one to take an early lead and never let go, burying the "gentlemanly" Towanda visitors 15-5 before a "good crowd" in an "interesting contest despite the one-sided score." Waller, the team's "slugger," again had a big game, with another home run to go with two doubles, a single, and four runs scored. Towanda meanwhile was "unable to connect with Quick's pitching, scarcely getting the ball out of the diamond." Gillan's first-base work was also a "feature" of the game.[401]

Two games into the season and Waverly felt very optimistic. The following week, on June 13, Waverly played its first away game, at arch rival Sayre's home opener. It was a highly anticipated contest for both teams.

Waverly thus far prided itself on having a team made up almost entirely of Waverly residents. The one exception, Pearce, was a machinist at the Lehigh Valley Shops and a Sayre native. His father, Richard, was born in England and had worked as an engineer on the railroad as well as a foreman at the stocking mill.

Immediately prior to the Sayre opener, Pearce defected from the Waverly team and joined Sayre. In response, Lang and the other WAC officials asked the Sayre police chief to prevent Pearce from playing for Sayre, but this effort was unsuccessful. Pearce started at shortstop for Sayre and batted second.

The loss of Pearce meant Waverly had to retool its line-up with no opportunity to practice, thus moving twenty-four-year-old outfielder Frank Kennedy to shortstop and Waller to third.

The twenty-two-year-old Herrick pitched for Waverly, while Pierson, a ringer from Ithaca, pitched for Sayre. Sayre's catcher, Shannon, was from Athens. "Sayre's battery was an imported one while not a man played on the Waverly team that is not directly identified with the town," the *Advocate* lamented.[402]

As the eager Sayre crowd looked on, each team scored a run in the first inning, Waverly went up 2-1 in the third, and then Sayre tied the game in the fifth. Things stayed quiet until the seventh, when Sayre scored four two-out unearned runs on a single, an infield error, a wild pitch and three more singles. Then they scored five more runs on sloppy play in the eighth to go up 11-2 on their way to an 11-3 victory. Waller was held hitless, and the Waverly line-up wound up with more errors (seven) than hits (six). To make things worse for Waverly, their former teammate Pearce led the Sayre hitting attack, with a double, a single and four runs scored.

"Herrick's work throughout was good and if he had been properly supported in the field and Waverly had hit Pierson a little bit the result would have been different," the *Advocate* reported.[403]

"Herrick pitched a fine ball for Waverly," the *Free Press* echoed, "and had he received perfect support in the fifth, seventh and eighth innings, the score would have told a different tale."[404]

A week later, on June 20, Waverly faced the Binghamton YMCA at home and lost 13-11. The team now had a record of one win and three losses. Waverly had much larger baseball ambitions, so losing to Sayre and the Binghamton YMCA was totally unacceptable. Local crowds would not support a sloppy losing team, and without strong local support, becoming a regional powerhouse was impossible. Perhaps it would be necessary to secure better out-of-town talent.

Management began to scour the region from city to farm, and team manager Giles Viele thought he found the answer seventy miles away in a very young, husky right-hander from Factoryville named Christy Mathewson.

Mathewson was just fifteen years old and was already earning rave reviews for his amateur pitching feats in the Factoryville area. Having heard of the exploits, Viele received the WAC's permission to secure young Mathewson, and traveled to Factoryville to scout the youngster. Liking what he saw, he approached the pitcher and his family and believed he earned Mathewson's commitment to join the team.

Upon returning to Waverly, Viele was confident the team's fortunes would soon change, but Mathewson never showed up in a Waverly uniform.

According to an account from Mathewson's mother, Christy pitched a game for Factoryville at Honesdale, and "a man who saw that game at Honesdale made Christy an offer to pitch on a professional team." He talked it over with her and his father, noting that he could "make ten times as much money playing ball as he could at farming."

According to Mathewson himself, perhaps apocryphally:

> But one fine day the captain of a team belonging to a town about five miles away came to me and asked if I would pitch for his nine.
>
> "We'll give you a dollar a game!" he said in conclusion.
>
> "What! How much?" I asked, in amazement, because it was such fun for me to play ball, then, that the idea of being paid for it struck me as "finding money."
>
> "A dollar a game," he repeated; "but you'll have to walk over, or catch a ride on some wagon."
>
> There was no trolley route connecting the two villages then. I told him he needn't mind how I got there, but that I would certainly come.
>
> So, for a time, I went regularly over to the other town–Factoryville's old rival–and pitched every Saturday; and often I had to walk both ways. But they always

gave me my dollar, which was a satisfactory consolation and a good antidote for foot-weariness.[405]

Viele insisted that he "booked" Mathewson for Waverly, but another team moved in and the future superstar backed out of their agreement.[406] Whether Viele was the man Mathewson's mother recalled and whether the scenario is similar to what Mathewson himself described, the future Hall-of-Famer did not make the seventy-mile trek to Waverly, but instead played for semi-pro teams closer to home before enrolling at Bucknell University.

Having lost Mathewson, the team looked elsewhere for pitching talent. On June 23, John Doran's protégé, right-handed twenty-two-year-old Fred F. Talada, the "fine ball player" and "crack pitcher" from nearby Athens who, although having failed at Harrisburg the previous year, had been "pitching for the 'West End' athletic team in Cleveland, Ohio;[407] arrived in Waverly to join the team.

Fred Talada from Athens, PA.

Talada was no Mathewson, but he was an excellent addition, and Waverly now searched for others who might be able to join him and strengthen the team. Whereas management had primarily looked in the Southern Tier of New York for talent, similar to John Clapp's 1887 team, the recruitment drive for Mathewson led them to other talent in the Northern Tier of Pennsylvania. If pure talent was limited, maybe entertaining talent would be available. Not far from Waverly, for example, the 1896 Pennsylvania State League's Easton team featured journeyman "Wild Bill" Setley, whom the *Philadelphia Ledger* said "furnished much amusement to the spectators." Setley, who was primarily a pitcher, used "peculiar" arm motions, according to the *Ledger*. "His first was to swing his arm around windmill fashion, then he would have a sort of pendulum swing, and again he would tie himself up until one wondered how he got straightened out again. These gyrations were at times even too much for the Athletic batsmen, who could scarcely bat for laughing."

Setley, born in 1859 in Camden, New Jersey, had a long career in minor league baseball–first as a player and then as an umpire–playing with leagues all across the country, and told tremendous stories, both real and imagined. That he moved so frequently from team to team throughout his career was a testament to both his skill and his bent for comedy and distraction.[408] Among the highly skilled players who joined him in Easton at the beginning of 1896 were journeyman Bill Heine and manager Hank Ramsey.

Unfortunately, entertainment value alone did not guarantee financial success. By the end of May 1896, the Easton team was having financial problems, as were other teams in the Pennsylvania State League. Particularly problematic was the fact that the players were not being regularly paid. Setley, who had just become a father for the first time and needed a regular paycheck, attempted to jump to a semipro team in Bangor, Pennsylvania, but Easton would not release him. He pitched his last game for Easton on June 3, finished with a loss, earned his release, and took his 5-4 record to Newark in the Eastern League. The Easton team folded soon afterward, and Heine also jumped to Newark, bringing with him his .321 batting average.

As other Pennsylvania teams suffered from financial problems in early June, Waverly was one of many towns vying for the services of the orphaned players. "Numerous applications from outside men are being received almost daily now," the *Advocate* reported, "but we believe that outside of pitchers we have enough first-class talent right here." [409]Waverly did not attract Setley or Heine at that point, but it did attract their teammate George Koehl, who had been in the minors for two years.

The Waverly baseball committee continued to make every reasonable effort to build an exciting and winning team. They even arranged for a grandstand to be added to the ball grounds, which the *Free Press* declared "a great improvement."[410] Unfortunately, the team lost again to Sayre 9-3 on June 26. The *Free Press* tried to coax more attendance for the next day's game against Troy, saying, "Troy is a strong team–were only beaten twice last season–and a lively contest can be looked for. Waverly expects to win this game. Come and see this game as Waverly will have a reorganized team in the field."[411]

Baseball was not the only activity competing for citizens' attention in the peak of the summer. In the same issue, the *Free Press* also announced that the Erie Railroad was offering special excursion tickets to the Democratic National Convention in Chicago: "good going July 3, 4, 5 and 6, good returning July 12, inclusive, at round trip rate of one first-class limited fare one way."[412] The Erie was also running special "cheap" rates for a weekend trip to the New York City area June 27-28. "The famous Wyoming Valley Nyack band will accompany the excursion in both directions and will give a concert at Coney Island Sunday afternoon."[413]

So it was with anxious anticipation that Waverly met the Troy visitors that Saturday afternoon. It was Talada's first start as pitcher, and "he had Troy guessing from start to finish. He pitched very effectively, being credited with seven strikeouts." His pitching "caught on with the crowds," the *Free Press* reported. "He was warmly applauded when he first stepped up to the plate."[414] In fact, Waverly's entire line-up showed the impact of the new players, including outfielders Koehl and Ayers, shortstop Carnochan, catcher McKee, and pitcher Talada.[415] The team was gradually transforming itself from a hometown amateur squad to a team of hired professionals.

Waverly scored three runs in the second inning and never trailed, tallying three more in the sixth and holding off a late Troy rally to win 8-6. Easton veteran Koehl paced the Waverly hitting attack with two doubles, a triple, a single, and three runs, while Waller and Leonard each chipped in a double and a run. Perhaps more importantly, Waverly only committed three errors,[416] a significant improvement overall.

For those players whose talent allowed them to escape mine work, even the hard labor of semi-professional baseball was preferable to the toil and danger of mining. A perfect illustration of this occurred the morning following the Troy game, when, just over eighty miles south of Waverly, in Pittston, Pennsylvania, the roof caved in on two hundred acres of the Red Ash Vein in the Newton Coal Company's Twin Shaft Mine, entombing as many as eighty miners. According to the *Scranton Tribune*, heroic rescue efforts immediately ensued, drawing experts from throughout the region.

Among the survivors was a nineteen-year-old "driver boy" named John Ricker, who was working the periphery of the mine prior to the collapse and witnessed a "Polander" whose:

> …clothes and hair were singed showing that he had touched off the gas, but he was unable to talk much English and we could not ascertain just where he met the gas. After we got down in the mine we heard the coal cracking and flying as it had been during the day and we went to work though some of the men were very timid.

We were traveling toward the foot of the shaft and passed Frank Keough and Thomas Wall, also drivers going in with loaded cars. Before we had gone more than one hundred feet from the point where we left Langan there was a rush of air and Adams said, 'Look out Jack for the gas.' I pulled off my cap and blew out my light to prevent an explosion and then the wind came tearing along at a frightful rate and we could hear the coal crackling and tearing and striking against the back of the last car. Then I got a ride I shall never forget. Down along the gangway the cars were driven at a frightful rate of speed by the wind. The dust was choking and the darkness terrible. How far I went on that car I don't know, but I have a recollection of being thrown off and of fortunately catching a prop. I hung onto it until the wind ceased and then got to my feet and call for Adams. He said he was not injured much and we started to feel our way toward the foot. In an instant came the second fall and again the frightful rushing of the air which carried me I know not how far but certainly a considerable distance. I had only struggled along a short distance when the third fall occurred. The air had little effect on me this time for I found myself at the foot of the shaft and had just strength enough to pull the bell as a signal to the engineer to hoist and then fell over on the cage exhausted. Adams had gone up before me. On the way up I revived and felt better when I reached the top. I was almost choked with dust and my head still feels as if it was full of it.[417]

A subsequent investigation found that there had been an audible "squeezing" of the pillars holding up the roof about two weeks prior to the collapse and that extra pillars had been added as support, which indicated the pillars were straining under the weight. Some miners, including a man named Edward Hughes, left their shifts early the night of the collapse when "the crackling grew worse," but most kept at work.

Ultimately, forty-nine of the eighty men and boys who had been trapped died in the collapse. The dead were primarily Irish and Lithuanian immigrants.

Back in the Southern Tier, on Tuesday, June 30, Waverly traveled to Binghamton to play that city's semi-pro Athletic Club team, which had also recently been reinforced with new players. Binghamton defeated Waverly 15-4, who "seemed to play indifferently and without their usual ginger," the *Free Press* explained. "Had the Waverly team played the game of which they were capable the result would have been different." Koehl made his first start for Waverly, absorbing the loss.[418]

The next day, July 1, the Binghamton team traveled to the Howard Street Grounds and Talada started for Waverly. Waverly took an early 6-1 lead in the second inning, led 9-3 going into the eighth, and held off yet a late rally to earn the 9-6 victory.[419] Ayers batted leadoff and provided Waverly's hitting with the necessary spark–scoring three runs in the game–while Mix contributed two singles and two runs, and McKee added a triple, single, and one run. Talada hit a double and a run, Carnochan hit a double and a single, and Waller contributed with a single and a run. "The game was a well-played and interesting contest from a Waverly standpoint. Talada pitched ball and particularly so when men were on bases. The home club had no less than four double plays to their credit, and played a fast game from start to finish."[420]

Leading the four double plays that day was sparkplug second baseman Bud Waller, still Waverly's only African-American player and likely one of the very few whom Waverly's opponents encountered during the season, outside of barnstorming teams.

It was an especially touchy time for race relations in the country at large, as it had been just a little over a month since the U.S. Supreme Court decided the New Orleans Plessy versus Ferguson case. In the nine years since the International League had attempted to fully integrate baseball, the sport's color line had hardened, and this hardening was a reflection of society as a whole. Parallel economies grew up on opposite sides of the color line; only in smaller towns like Waverly, where the overall labor pool was not large enough for the two economies to be fully separate, was there still enough mixing that the races could play competitive baseball together.

The fact that the Waverly team was only semi-pro and not officially part of a formal league lessened the significance of Waller's participation for the time being, but if Waverly intended to take the field in exhibition games against league teams, it would need to reconsider him, despite his strong performance. Moreover, even in semi-pro contests, Waller likely had to be careful, as the old concerns about white players taking liberties with their slides and spikes still existed.

On July 4, Waverly defeated Corning in both games of a double header, 9-2 and 14-6. Waverly's winning streak was getting on the neighboring towns' nerves, with Sayre and Athens complaining that Waverly was using out-of-town players.[421] *The Waverly Free Press*, flipping on its previous position, called such talk "boy's prattle," noting that "no town or city has a nine entirely of its own residents. Waverly hires a part of her players and pays for them."[422]

While the official team was traveling, Waverly organized an amateur fundraising game on the home diamond, featuring businessmen from the "Northside" against those from the "Southside." The Northsiders won, thanks in part to the exploits of banker and second baseman Percy Lang, the shortstop from the '87 team. "Lang dislocated his liver-pad in that second two-base hit," joked the *Free Press*.[423]

The businessmen must have attracted a tonier crowd than usual, as the game's spectators complained about seating conditions, and such complaints had not been previously published. "If smoking in the grand stand were prohibited the association would be a gainer," wrote the *Free Press*. "Many ladies will not take seats there because of the nuisance."[424]

Just two days later, Waverly hosted Bainbridge in "the best game ever played on the Southside grounds," though it unfortunately resulted in another loss for the home team, this time 6-3. "The visitors are an exceptionally strong team. They played thirty-five games last season and lost but nine, and have been defeated but once or twice this season," the *Free Press* explained.[425]

Perhaps due in part to the team's inconsistent performance, the *Free Press* made an extra effort to urge patrons to attend the next game with Bainbridge: "Waverly will play the Bainbridge team again next Monday. The home team will be strengthened and a desperate effort will be made to win. Every lover of the national game should go over and see this great game. Game called at 3 o'clock. Admission 25 cents; ladies free. Show that you appreciate the effort that the management is making to give Waverly good ball by patronizing this game."[426]

Unfortunately, Waverly's rematch with Bainbridge was cancelled when the visitors received a telegram calling them home for a game. Evidently, Bainbridge was likely to make more money from the home game, so opted accordingly. Such interruptions were relatively rare, but not unheard of, as independent teams generally stood to make more money against a strong opponent at home than on the road, unless the road trip was to a large urban area, whereby the expected revenue had to be netted against the travel cost. Waverly went on to defeat the Binghamton YMCA 17-3 on Thursday, July 16, with Talada "doing great work for the home team, striking out eleven men."[427]

In their attempt to build up the team, Waverly also picked up several veteran players from other Pennsylvania teams over the coming weeks, including Joe McKee from York, W.J. Graffins from Sunbury, twenty-year-old Charles Kutzner from Shamokin, and twenty-five-year-old Clinton "Goldie" Seavers from Pottstown.

As Waverly's season headed into mid-July, the base ball committee began to run into financial difficulties. "All persons in arrears for dues to the baseball association should settle at once," the *Free Press* reported. "The association now have [sic] a strong base ball nine in the field and they are playing winning ball, but it requires money to keep them there. All dues to July 1 were remitted by the association, and need not be paid but a prompt payment of the dues for this quarter is urged. The money may be left with P. W. Towner, the collector, or with F. C. Simmons."[428]

On July 23, Waverly lost 5-4 to Sidney. Following this loss, Waverly patrons were again urged by the Free Press to support the home team at its upcoming games. "The management must be financially sustained if they are to give Waverly good ball. The admission will be 35 cts, boys 10 cts, ladies free."[429] Unfortunately, the urgings and discounts appeared to have little impact.

On August 1, the long-awaited rematch with Bainbridge occurred, but the home team was soundly defeated, 12-1. "It was not our day anyhow, but we played 'just for fun,'" the *Free Press* apologized. "Next time we get a crack at those fellows, we shall simply annihilate them and leave their bones on the bleaching boards, grim monuments of our victory."[430] The team's unofficial record now stood at a mediocre nine wins and nine losses.

Taking a page from the playbooks of other teams that attempted to re-invent themselves in the middle of a season, the *Free Press* reported that management had "disbanded" the team after the Bainbridge rematch and signed a "new team": "An effort is being made to raise funds to support a nine whose time shall belong to the association and who will not be playing in some other town when we want them. To this end a subscription paper is being circulated and about $200 has been already subscribed."[431]

It was challenging enough to sustain an independent team with good talented players, and even more so when management wanted to win right away and lacked the patience to build up a winning team slowly. Semi-professional players generally did not get paid unless they played, so they could not be blamed for bidding themselves out to surrounding teams, especially if their primary team was only playing one game a week. Even Waverly's

DONOVAN, DETROIT

Bill Donovan. From the Library of Congress.

best players, like Waller and Talada, found themselves playing with rivals on off days. This loose affiliation made it even more challenging to lure paying fans to the games.

On August 13, Waverly's "new team" played Athens. Although some of the players had been carried over from the first half of the season, there were also several newly signed additions, including the first officially recorded appearance in Waverly of nineteen-year old right-hander Bill Donovan.

The son of an Irish-born carpenter, Donovan was born in Lawrence, Massachussets, and moved with his family as a child to Philadelphia, where he had been playing amateur ball before signing with Waverly. In addition to Donovan, the new Waverly players included J.A. Singer at shortstop, Eddie Lee at second base, W.M. Dodge at first base, Ernest Dorsett in left field, Dennis Ryan at third base and F.W. Skelton in center field. Among those missing from the first half of the season were Ayers, Mix, Carnochan, McKee, Gillan, and Waller.[432]

In an effort to help the baseball team increase respectable attendance, the Hall & Lyon furniture works, the town's largest employer, shut down for the afternoon to allow its employees to attend the August 13th game.[433]

Donovan was not yet being called by his major league nick-name, "Wild Bill," but the hard-throwing right-hander gave up three walks, one wild pitch, and one error to counter his six strikeouts in his first outing with the new club. His catchers were credited with four passed balls, and his fielders with six errors, including two by Dodge. Although losing 15-6, Donovan was tagged with only six earned runs. He also helped out at bat with two singles and two runs scored.[434]

Donovan had another shot at a local rival on Wednesday, August 19th, when Waverly hosted Sayre. Waverly got out an early 3-0 lead in the third inning and piled on seven runs in the 8th to eventually win, 15-3. Donovan gave up just seven hits and one walk and had five strikeouts and surprisingly no wild pitches. He also helped his case with a double and a run scored. The real hitting star for Waverly, however, was George "Red" Ross, the new second baseman, making his first appearance in a Waverly uniform with two home runs and a double.[435] The *Free Press* reported that Ross "certainly is a fine player and is a tower of strength to the local team."[436]

The next afternoon, August 20, "the largest crowd of the season witnessed the Corning-Waverly game." Koehl started as Waverly's pitcher, but fell behind 6-3 after three innings. Unfortunately, errors again confronted the home team, and they fell further behind to 9-3 in the fourth and 12-3 in the fifth, committing a total of eight errors in the game. In right field, Skelton alone had three errors, and Talada in left field added two more. The final score was a 16-5 Corning victory, a major disappointment to the large crowd. "The local outfield played a very weak game, allowing the visitors to score nine or ten runs of their total of sixteen from their misplays," the *Free Press* sadly noted.[437]

As the team's inconsistent play indicated that business might be coming unglued on the field, so did the activities off the field. The Sayre and Athens teams continued to scold Waverly for pulling in players from outside the area. Soon, local newspapers began to get into the act, attacking Waverly for all sorts of offenses on behalf of their respective teams. *The Sayre News*, for instance, complained about how some of the Waverly fans behaved during the August 19 game: "The management of the Waverly ball club will have to do something to stop the low, insulting language used by a low class of supposed-to-be ladies of that place who take seats in the grand stand while games are played there. During the game Wednesday a number of respectable Waverly people were driven from the stand by the low and disgusting talk of others. In one case, a young girl was calling other ladies vile names because they cheered the Sayre players."[438] Rumors also circulated that gambling and drinking associated with the Waverly team were getting out of hand.

On August 21, Waverly traveled to Towanda and defeated the home team 7-3. Talada earned the victory for Waverly, while Ryan and Singer each contributed home runs.

The very next day, Towanda traveled to Waverly for a rematch. Donovan pitched for the home team and held them close, 2-2, through the fifth inning. In the sixth, however, the error bug began to return, and Waverly gave up four runs to fall behind, 6-2. They rallied in their half of the seventh to pull ahead again to 7-6, but eventually succumbed in ten innings, 9-7. Waverly wound up with five errors, and Donovan had one wild pitch and four walks against eight strikeouts. Ayres and Carnohan were being kept busy by Waverly's opponents, as both were in Towanda's line-up for the two games.

Based on this aggressive schedule, management was clearly doing its best to keep the players busy and paid. Even when not pitching, Talada and Donovan were both asked to play other positions, hopefully to prevent them from taking their pitching arms elsewhere.

On August 28th, Waverly traveled back into Pennsylvania, this time to play Towanda. Talada pitched, and Donovan was back in the line-up, playing center field. Towanda jumped out to a quick 3-0 lead, but Waverly tied the game in the sixth, and scored five runs in the eighth to secure an 8-3 win. Singer led the hitters with a home run and two runs scored.

On August 31, Waverly traveled to Towanda to play in front of one of the largest crowds of the season. It was a close game up to the eighth inning, when Towanda scored four runs; they ultimately won 7-3. It was a rough game as well, as Dorsett "had one of his fingers badly split"[439] and a pitched ball fractured Talada's left forearm. The loss brought Waverly's unofficial season record to sixteen wins and thirteen losses.

"Somewhere bands are playing. Somewhere hearts are light," chided the Elmira *Daily Gazette and Free Press*, "but Waverly is not the place. Yesterday the crack base ball team went to Towanda accompanied by a delegation of Waverly cranks and met defeat by a score of 7 to 3. It is said that a large amount of 'long green' changed hands."[440]

This was the first media confirmation that gambling was becoming more common at the games, which was not necessarily bad for team managers hoping to stoke attendance, but it definitely tended to attract the hoodlum element at the expense of women and families. Balancing the two would be critical to the team's ultimate success. This was an expected outcome of the growth of the team's popularity, since, according to historian John Thorn, the three "essential ingredients facilitate[ing] the growth of any localized game to national sport" are gambling, statistics, and publicity.[441] Local newspapers were increasingly publishing box scores and other game details, which encouraged gambling.

On September 5, Waverly faced off against Sayre once more, and lost 16-4. Koehl and the newly acquired "potato trick" practitioner, Edward "Davy" Dunkle, lured from Lock Haven to take the injured Talada's place in the rotation, took the loss for Waverly.

Edward "Davey" Dunkle from Philipsburg, PA.

The *Free Press* was more literary than usual in describing the bitter loss: "Waverly ball tossers went out on the green award last Saturday forenoon, stepping as high as an Athens girl, and in a few short hours we brought them home on a stretcher, figuratively speaking, Sayre furnishing the red fire, slow music, and other accessories, and incidentally gathering in the game, together with a grist of good hard dollars that our local sports are said to have let drop with a dull, sickening thud. It was sad, but we'll see to it that they don't do it again."[442] The "good hard dollars" comment almost certainly referred to yet more gambling at the game.

Waverly went on to win three easy games in row versus Corning, Towanda and Troy (PA) by a combined score of 43-14, before hosting "the champions" of Hornell on the Howard Street Grounds on September 10. Talada was healthy again, and the team seemed to be operating on all cylinders. The large home crowd anticipated a big win.

Unfortunately, Hornell took an early lead and was leading 10-7 in the seventh inning. Waverly loaded the bases and the crowd expectantly watched as Ryan came to bat.

Ryan had already had a strong game, but he surprised his teammates, the crowd and perhaps even himself as he belted a mammoth grand slam home run to put Waverly ahead, 11-10. Bedlam ensued, as the *Free Press* noted:

Then a mighty cheer went up, the "rooters" hoisted "Denny" on their shoulders, carried him to a seat, and a shower of silver coin poured into his lap. It was the second home run he had made, and next time he went to bat he up and did it again. From that on Waverly continued to roll up the score, and at the close it stood 17 to 10 in our favor. Talada pitched a magnificent game and was well supported at every point.[443]

In addition to these game details, the *Free Press* confirmed again that "considerable money changed hands" on the game.[444] The win brought Waverly's unofficial season record to twenty-two wins and fourteen losses.

Immediately following these four consecutive victories, on September 11, Waverly lost a double-header to Towanda 18-7 and 13-0. The *Free Press* was beside itself:

> Waverly's base ball aggregation has been playing all sorts of ball of late, a genuine succotash in variety, not always a thing of beauty, and far from a joy forever.
>
> While we were preparing to paint the nine and the diamond a rich rosy red and dreaming of the long golden autumnal days that were to be filled with victories and gladness, we just sent the nine down to Towanda Friday morning to keep them in practice, you know, and what did that measly Towanda nine do but pick them up bodily and bang them all over the grounds.[445]

To make matters worse, the next afternoon, Waverly went to Sayre and lost 8-1.[446] The team recovered somewhat on September 14 by defeating visiting Towanda 8-6, but the inconsistency was surprising and suspicious, leading many to believe some players were intentionally throwing games. Talada earned the Towanda victory, and, with Donovan, Dunkle and a couple others, seemed to be among the very few Waverly players above reproach. "Talada's pitching was the feature of the game," the *Free Press* noted. The very next day, Waverly made a return visit to Towanda and won again 15-7. As though to prove it still could not sustain a streak for long, however, Waverly hosted Sayre on September 16 and lost 9-5.[447]

At this stage of the season, the Cuban Giants were making their summer pilgrimage through the region. Emblematic of the segregated legal framework that was driving race relations in general at the time, by 1896 the best African-American players had joined independent "colored" barnstorming baseball teams, and these teams were becoming increasingly popular. Teams like the Cuban Giants traveled across the country every summer to entertain and compete with local teams, and they frequently used local African-American players to augment their line-ups.

For example, on September 15, the day before they defeated Waverly, Sayre hosted the traveling Cuban Giants–described as "a colored nine"–and won 15-14. Playing shortstop for the Giants was Waverly's Bud Waller, who "played it well." According to the *Free Press*, Waller "will play with the Cubans next year."[448] This may have been wishful thinking on Waller's part, since there is no evidence that he played any additional games with the Cubans beyond that one. That this would have been his ambition, rather than to move further into white baseball, however, was a sign of baseball's limited reality for African-Americans.

An even more prominent sign of this limited reality was that Waller's probable infield mate at second base for the Cuban Giants in that game was a player who had already proven his ability to compete against the best white players–the "incomparable" former Buffalo and Harrisburg star Frank Grant.

At age thirty, Grant was still a solid and exciting player, having been with the Cuban Giants since '91. "Some folks claim that the Cubans are not as strong as last season," reported "G. Whiz" for *Sporting Life*. "[This writer doesn't] see it that way. They are stronger. Manager Bright knows the game, and gets the players. He is the same clever gentleman that he always was, and is bound to succeed. Frank Grant is with him, and as good a player as ever."[449]

Frank Grant. From the New York Public Library.

By the time the Cuban Giants were traveling through the region in mid-September of 1896, Waverly added new players to its roster to replace several, such as Lee, Clark, and Ryan–the very same Denny Ryan who had been so prominently lauded just a week earlier on September 10– whom the *Free Press* accused of "playing very loosely, making many costly errors, in fact it was so rotten an exhibition of how not to do it that the management dismissed Clark and sent him back home to Corning."

It appears that there were serious concerns that the players were more likely playing for wagers than for wages–or were perhaps drinking or cavorting themselves to inconsistency: "The managers showed their disapproval of the yellow playing by their prompt assurance that proof of crooked work on the part of any player will be followed by prompt dismissal. Now if anyone knows of 'funny work' let them report it or forever hold their peace."[450] As a part of this disciplinary purge, Koehl was reported to have been "dismissed" on the 14, because "he tarried too long with the flowing bowl."

On September 18, Waverly played host to the Cuban Giants, the same team that had lost to Sayre the week before, and lost 7-1. Here, "Waverly played a very rocky game," the *Free Press* reported.[451] Neither the *Free Press* nor the *Advocate* published a box score for the game, but in other contests that featured the Giants that summer, the lineup included Grant, infielder Sol White, first baseman Jack Fry, and outfielder Shepard Trusty.[452] Dunkle pitched for Waverly and took the loss. Without a box score we are unable to confirm if Waller played for either the Giants or Waverly in the game, but it is certainly possible.

Sol White. From the New York Public Library.

"The fact is the baseball loving people of the place have become thoroughly dissatisfied with the turn baseball matters have taken in Waverly," the *Advocate* reported. "While the dusky colored players were prepared to put up a good article of ball the home team was listless and did not put any snap into its playing whatever."[453]

Possibly in its effort to draw as spectators both the "reputable class" and the "hoodlum element," Waverly was drawing too much of the latter to also draw the former.

On September 23, Waverly traveled to Towanda and lost 15-7, with Talada and Seavers pitching for the visitors. The townsfolk of Waverly were clearly growing tired of their club's losses: "One thing is certain–about half of the members of the Waverly base ball aggregation are not playing ball, and do not intend to, and they should be summarily bounced. Waverly will patronize a good game but is tired of being buncoed."[454]

The next day, Towanda returned the favor by visiting Waverly and losing 8-6 in "a very good game" before a "very small" crowd.[455] Despite the win, Waverly's unofficial season record was still decidedly unimpressive at 23-21. No further comment from the *Free Press* could be found. According to the *Advocate,* Waverly played two more games against Sayre, winning the first 8-6 with 25-year-old future major leaguer Frank Gatins at third base cracking a single, and losing the second 12-4. The split brought Waverly's final season record, according to available records, to 24-22.

Frank Gatins from Johnstown, PA.

The *Advocate* confirmed in its season summary that gambling rumors haunted the team's final weeks and likely suppressed attendance. "The fact is the suspicion gained ground that the games were 'fixed,' the *Advocate* reported. "This is not known to be a fact and we are not inclined to believe it. But there is no doubt the rumor had much to do with the falling off in the attendance at the games."

The *Advocate* also speculated that another temptation of the "hoodlum element," excessive late-night carousing, was also to blame. "A man can't 'bum it' all night and play ball the next day. Baseball is a noble game and requires level headed men to play it. The whole nine must work together like a machine, every part performing its function. If there is a weak place in the team the opposing side quickly discovers it and the result is that the game is lost on account of the defect."[456]

The *Advocate* reported that the team finished the season just over $600 in arrears to players ($268) and local businesses that supplied services to the team ($339).[457]

"The betting and gambling indulged in openly at the games was revolting and distasteful to many who would otherwise have been glad to attend the games," the *Advocate* wrote. "If the sport cannot be enjoyed without such wicked and foolish proceedings as wagering large sums of money on every strike and run let us forego the pleasure."[458]

From all indications, it appeared to be the end of semi-pro baseball for the Waverly team. Within a week, the *Free Press* was eagerly covering football, noting on the front page that Waverly's high school team defeated Athens 16-0 and that the upcoming "Cornell-Harvard game at Ithaca will be one of the great games of the year. Local enthusiasts are arranging for an excursion over the Lehigh and doubtless many from this place will see the game." Percy Lang was the Waverly High School football coach and was also a local college referee occasionally officiating Cornell games.[459] Despite all the excitement and opportunities for baseball, perhaps Waverly was a football town after all.

On October 17, *Sporting Life* included a very short blurb that most readers probably missed, but which dramatically hit home an example of how far the mighty can fall, even in the relatively sedate media climate of the 1890s: "Ex-pitcher Doran is living in Athens, Pa., a physical wreck from dissipation."[460]

This had been the first season since 1888 that Doran was not recorded as pitching for any teams, and it was also the first in which his protégé, Talada, had a good deal of measurable success. Where this success would take Talada and Waverly in the coming seasons following the largely unsuccessful 1896 season, however, was anyone's guess.

Waverly's pro baseball experience in 1896 was a microcosm of the national experience. The town sought to attract a good mixed-race crowd with good talent, but could not afford to overpay for the talent. Moreover, publicity was vital, but too much reliance on promoting individual star players drove up the stars' value and price. So, the team struggled to find the right balance, often shifting lineups, with inconsistent play, a large gambling influence, potentially thrown games, and small crowd sizes the result.

It would be several seasons before Talada and his fellow Waverly baseball enthusiasts would try to convince the public to again launch professional baseball at the Howard Street Grounds. In the meantime, the Grounds hosted football.

CHAPTER 13

Labor Strife

William McKinley defeated the populist William Jennings Bryan in the Presidential election of 1896, so pro-industrialist Republicans continued to lead national affairs in Washington. This boded well for the monopolist titans of industry, such as Carnegie, Rockefeller, and Mellon, but not so well for labor activists. John Ward and other professional ballplayer union organizers—still licking their wounds after the failure of the Players' League in 1890—had yet to put together a fully effective labor organization.

The National League remained the only major league, and its twelve teams' rosters were overtly manipulated by team owners for financial advantage, with little regard for whether the teams were winning or losing. Fans grew increasingly frustrated with the owners and attendance fell. As a result, players at all levels–from major league to semi-pro—struggled to find the best fit for their time-limited talent more than ever before. Declining attendance in the major leagues also had players worried about the game's future. As major league options dried up, would the minor leagues, with all of their requisite financial uncertainty, be the only professional option? Would they dry up as well?

Similar to other workers throughout the nation near the end of the economically challenged 1890s, baseball labor was antsy but disorganized. John Ward's first baseball players union, the Brotherhood of Professional Baseball Players, had been wiped out following the unsuccessful Players' League season of 1890. The potential for serious labor strife was ever present.

For his part as an enterprising young semi-professional player now residing full-time in Waverly, Talada attempted to resuscitate the '96 Waverly team for the '97 season, but was unable to secure an affordable lease for the Howard Street grounds. As a result, the remaining Waverly players scattered throughout the area. Waverly's best prospects (Gatins, Dunkle and Donovan) each moved into the formal minor leagues. Gatins went to Lock Haven and Dunkle to Sunbury in the Central Pennsylvania League, and Donovan went to Waterbury in the Connecticut State League.

Lacking his own team, Talada pitched for semi-pro teams around the Athens-Waverly area. On June 4, for example, he was the starting pitcher for Athens against Sayre. "Talada, last year's Waverly pitcher, was in the box for Athens, and except that he was a little wild, pitched a splendid game, but his support at times was very ragged," reported the *Elmira Daily Gazette*.[461]

The game's umpire, Bud Waller from the '96 Waverly team, upset the Sayre team with his calls. According to the *Daily Gazette*, "The players took exceptions to the umpire's decision calling a man safe at first, and left the field,"[462] resulting in their losing the game by forfeit.

Dunkle's new home, the Central Pennsylvania League, was, in 1897, comprised of the towns of Bloomsburg, Lock Haven, Shamokin, Milton, Pottsville, Sunbury, and Williamsport. Several less prominent former Waverly players also joined this league: Ryan joined Dunkle in Sunbury, Clark and Dunn went to Shamokin, Singer went to Milton, and Seavers went to Bloomsburg and Pottsville.

Charles Kutzner, who had played for Shamokin and Reading in addition to Waverly in '96, ended his organized baseball career in favor of a position as a "chainman" (surveyor) with the Mineral Railroad and Mining company, the predecessor of the

Susquehanna Collieries Company, a company that would later control approximately 5,823 acres of coal lands on both sides of the Susquehanna River at Nanticoke Dam.[463] Such were the decisions facing young men at the time, even celebrated local ball players like Kutzner. Many such men had to ask themselves if their baseball abilities were more valuable economically than the other abilities they had. How long should they continue to work in semi-pro or minor league ball in the hope of making the big leagues, as opposed to taking another good professional opportunity when it arises?

Among the veteran professionals in the Central Pennsylvania League in 1897 was 31-year-old George Stovey, arguably the greatest African-American pitcher of the century. He was the same pitcher who, a decade earlier, was removed from the Newark line-up at Cap Anson's request due to his skin color, precipitating the hard "color line" in organized baseball.

Stovey started 1897 with the Cuban X Giants, a traveling barnstorming African-American team like the Cuban Giants, where among his early season appearances were a 14-10 win over Elizabeth on April 17 and a 13-7 loss to Trenton on May 6. On May 28, in a game where Stovey played leftfield, the X Giants defeated North Adams 5-4. The *North Adams Transcript* headline describing the game read "The Darkies Won." The account of the game was rife with such racist commentary as, "North Adams went at the game with a rush and made two runs in both the first and second innings. Then they stopped their sprinting for the 'coons' got the dust out of their eyes."[464]

Stovey reportedly pitched for part of the 1897 season with his hometown Williamsport Demorest team and was therefore the last of the 1887 International Association "colored" pioneers to hang on in organized professional baseball. By mid-season, he had moved to umpiring the Demorest contests, earning kudos from the national baseball media. "He is certainly a great improvement," *Sporting Life* reported in August regarding Stovey's performance relative to other umpires. "We are sure he will be a success, as he is an old player and understands the game."[465]

The kudos were not unanimous, however, as, according to the *Philadelphia Times* on August 26, "a forty minute wrangle" held up the Williamsport-Bloomsburg contest when Bloomsburg reportedly refused to play with Stovey as umpire. Stovey declared that Bloomsburg had forfeited the game, but Williamsport stockholders called off the forfeit, and the game proceeded with a "Martin" as the umpire. Whether the "wrangle" was over Stovey's perceived partiality to the home team, his skin color or something else was not explained.

Of all the region's professional leagues in 1897, two with the most interesting balances of future and former major league all-stars were the Atlantic and the New England. The Atlantic League started the season with teams in eight cities–Philadelphia, Hartford, Lancaster, Newark, Norfolk, Paterson, Richmond, and Reading—while the New England League was comprised of six cities–Newport, Brockton, Pawtucket, Fall River, Taunton, and New Bedford.

Charlie Hamburg began the season with the Atlantic League's Philadelphia Athletic club, after having played in Lancaster in 1896. At thirty, Hamburg was one of the seasoned veterans on the team. He still played excellent outfield and looked to continue his solid hitting, having been one of the leaders in Lancaster, along with future major league home run leader Socks Seybold, with a .304 average.

Twenty-nine year-old Bill Heine, still just a step away from the majors, also began the season in the Atlantic League, starting out with Hartford after having finished the 1896 season with Newark. Heine batted .295 in 1896 and was among the league's top fielders.

"The signing of Bill Heine, the crack short stop of the Newark club of last season, gives Hartford a man without equal in his position in the Atlantic League," *Sporting Life* reported on February 27. This was high praise, especially since among the League's other promising stars were pitcher Jack Chesbro in Richmond, outfielder Socks Seybold, catcher Andy Roth in Lancaster, and a twenty-three-year-old, 5'11" 200-pound phenomenon from Chartiers, Pennsylvania, in Paterson, named Honus Wagner.

At the time, Paterson, New Jersey, had a population of just over 105,000–a 34 percent increase over its 1890 population of 78,347 and more than double its 1880 population of 51,031. Paterson was founded in 1792 by the Society for Establishing Useful Manufactures. It was a company founded by, among others, Alexander Hamilton, seeking to channel the power of the seventy-seven-foot-high Great Falls on the Passaic River for manufacturing. They hoped to establish the United States' manufacturing capabilities, allowing the young nation to become even more independent of Great Britain. Mills and other industrial buildings—particularly those related to textiles—sprung up throughout the area, earning Paterson the nickname, "Silk City."

Paterson's baseball club was managed by a tough young executive named Ed Barrow. Born in 1868 in Springfield, Illinois, as a teenager, Barrow worked at a local newspaper in Des Moines, Iowa, climbing his way up from mailing clerk to head of circulation, all while pitching for a local town team. Enterprising and hot-tempered, he purchased the Inter-State League's Wheeling franchise in 1895, and in 1896, he bought into the Paterson club and signed Wagner.

Wagner was not yet the Paterson club's regular shortstop, but he batted .348—seventh-best in the league—in 1896, and in 1897 continued to play wherever he was needed. Heine was not playing shortstop, either, frequently finding himself in the outfield instead. In a May 31, 1897, contest with Heine's Hartford club, for example, Wagner played third base and batted clean-up with one single in a 5-3 loss. Heine, meanwhile, played left field for the victors and batted fifth with a single and a run scored. "Bill Heine is playing a strong game in left field, although the outfield is entirely out of his latitude," *Sporting Life* reported.[466]

Honus Wagner. From the Library of Congress.

Wagner's prowess–both in the field and at bat—was noticeable. His former teammate, Tommy Leach, said of him:

> Up until 1903 he played almost every position on
> the team. One day at short, the next day in the outfield,
> the day after at first base. He didn't look like a shortstop,
> you know. He had those huge shoulders and those bowed
> legs, and he didn't seem to field balls the way we did. He
> just ate the ball up with his big hands, like a scoop shovel,
> and when he threw it to first base you'd see pebbles and
> dirt and everything else flying over there along with the
> ball. It was quite a sight! The greatest shortstop ever. The
> greatest *everything* ever.[467]

Sam Crawford similarly recalled: "In my opinion, *the* greatest
player who ever lived was Honus Wagner. He could do everything. In fact, when I first played against him he was an outfielder,
and then he became a third baseman, and later the greatest shortstop of them all. Honus could play any position except pitcher
and be easily the best in the league at it."[468]

Despite Wagner's prowess, Heine had every reason to feel
that he was able to compete capably with the phenom. This was
borne out on June 1, 1897, as Hartford and Paterson played a double-header. In both games, Wagner batted clean-up and played
right field while Heine batted sixth for Hartford and played left
field. Hartford won the first game 8-4, despite Wagner's three
singles. Heine hit a double and a single for the victors.[469] In the
second game, Hartford won again, this time 12-3. Wagner had
just one single and a stolen base, while Heine had three singles
and one run scored. Pitcher Lee Viau, the same pitcher who, in
1891, gave up multiple hits to a young McGraw, took the loss
for Paterson.[470]

Like Heine, Hamburg also competed well against Wagner
early in the season. Two days later, on June 3, for instance,
Paterson was playing at home against Philadelphia, and this

time, it was the Philadelphia club that dealt Paterson a loss, 10-4. Wagner batted clean-up again, this time starting at third base. He also picked up two doubles and a single. Hamburg started in right field, batted clean-up for Philadelphia, and had a double and a single.[471]

Wagner was not only a top major league prospect, but he was known to be mild-mannered, having had but few disagreements with teammates. One notable exception occurred in 1896, when pitcher Lee Viau, who was known to be a heavy drinker, had an altercation with Wagner. Viau had pitched in the major leagues for Cincinnati, Cleveland, Louisville, and Boston, but he had drifted around the minors since 1892, landing in Paterson in 1896. Manager Ed Barrow had strict rules regarding gambling and drinking, but some players failed to comply. One day, when he was scheduled to pitch, Viau arrived at the park intoxicated. Several players, including Wagner, took issue with his state. In response, Viau "grabbed a water bucket and emptied it over Wagner's head. An unamused Wagner wrapped his large hands around the pitcher's throat, lifting him off the floor. After a few seconds, Wagner regained his composure and dropped the shaken man. It was a seldom-seen side of the mild-mannered Wagner."[472]

By the first week of June, Paterson had a 20-21 record and sat in sixth place within the Atlantic League, but was still within firing distance of the leader, Newark, who stood at 20-15.

Just days after Hartford's three-game sweep against Paterson, Heine was "loaned" to Newark, and on June 7, Newark traveled to Paterson to face Wagner and Viau. This time Heine failed to come through, as he started at second base for Newark and had no hits in Viau's 8-0 four-hit shut-out. Wagner started in left field for the victors and had three singles, two runs scored, and a stolen base.[473]

The two teams faced each other again on June 12, this time in Newark. Heine started at shortstop for Newark and smacked two doubles, but it was not enough to earn the victory. Wagner started again in leftfield and clouted a home run and a single, as well as scoring two runs to pace Paterson's 10-4 victory.[474] Paterson cranks, likely sensing that Wagner was not long for the minor leagues, designated June 20 as "Wagner Day" in "testimonial for his earnest work."

A few miles south in Richmond, Charlie Hamburg had a far more frustrating day, as Richmond's starting pitcher, Jack Chesbro, bested Hamburg and the Philadelphia Athletics, 12-2. The game was very close right up until the eighth inning, when leftfielder Eisley led Richmond's hitters to four runs in the eighth and seven more in the ninth. Hamburg went 0 for 4 in the loss.[475]

As June wrapped up, Wagner continued to compile big numbers. On "Wagner Day," he started at third base against Philadelphia and laced a single to help pace a 4-1 victory. By July 17, he was headed to the National League's Louisville Colonels, where he would begin his twenty-one-year Hall-of-Fame major league career.

At about the same time, Louisville-native Hamburg was traded to Paterson. Former Waverly player Clinton Seavers, who had been a regular with the Bloomsburg club in the Central Pennsylvania League, replaced him on the Philadelphia team.

Heine made one more move before the 1897 season was over; having received a release from Newark, he headed to last-place New Bedford in the New England League for the month of August. On August 2, he started at shortstop against Newport, batted fifth, and hit a single.[476]

The New England League had a reputation for turning out top ballplayers. It was particularly effective in the mid-to-late 1890s, just as the National League was increasingly flexing its muscle in claiming top players for less than their value. One reason for this was that in 1892, the league's owners elected former John Clapp teammate and current Boston baseball reporter Tim Murnane as its president. "Murnane brought two critical elements to the New England League presidency. As a newspaperman, he could deliver publicity for the league. More importantly, his connec-

LAJOIE, CLEVELAND

Napoleon Lajoie. From the Library of Congress.

tions with the major-league owners meant that he could secure better financial compensation from them on behalf of the New England League owners for mid-season player sales. He could also marshal the latter's concerns about their relationship with the major league."[477]

Among the top New England League players during this period was future Hall-of-Famer Napoleon Lajoie. In 1896, the twenty-one-year-old Lajoie hit .429 for Fall River before being called up to Philadelphia. In Fall River, Lajoie had played centerfield and led the team to the league's hitting record. The great Cy Young remembered, "Lajoie was one of the most rugged hitters I ever faced. He'd take your leg off with a line drive, turn the third baseman around like a swinging door, and powder the hand of the left fielder."[478]

Lajoie did particularly well against both Brockton—who had their own promising outfielder, Phil Nadeau—and Portland. In a two-game series against Brockton on July 28 and 29, 1896, Lajoie went six for ten with a home run, a stolen base, and three runs scored, while Nadeau went two for eight with just one run scored.[479] Meanwhile, Fall River went 9-3 in the season series against Portland, featuring one four-game stretch in mid-July where Lajoie went nine for seventeen with a home run, two doubles, a stolen base, and eight runs scored. Demonstrating complete confidence against pitchers with recent big-league experience, Lajoie faced Portland's crafty John "Sandy" McDougal on July 14 and smacked two singles and a double. [480]

John Auchanbolt "Sandy" McDougal was born in 1874 in Buffalo. His father, John, was born in Scotland, and his mother, Jane Brown, in England. Neither was pleased with Sandy's decision to play baseball professionally.[481] He stood 5'10" and possessed reddish hair, prompting his nickname. Sandy played in one game with Brooklyn in 1895, pitching three innings on June 12 and giving up four runs on three hits and five walks. It was hardly a record he wanted to be known for; fortunately, he still had time to get back to the majors and improve it.

John "Sandy" McDougal from Buffalo, NY.

Among the other promising stars in the New England League was Fall River's Joe Delahanty, one of six baseball-playing brothers from Cleveland, five of whom would eventually make the major leagues. The eldest of the brothers, Ed, had been playing in the major leagues since 1888 and would eventually be elected to the Hall of Fame.

Phil Nadeau and Sandy McDougal remained top league prospects in '97. Nadeau batted .330 in 1896 and stuck with Brockton, while McDougal moved in 1897 from Portland to Taunton.

At the time, Taunton, Massachusetts, had a population of about 31,000–a 22 percent increase over its 1890 population of 25,448. Taunton had been incorporated as a town in 1639, and by 1656, it contained the first successful ironworks in Plymouth Colony, which eventually led to a local manufacturing industry that produced a variety of important iron-based products, such as stoves, tacks, and machinery. Textiles, brick-making, and other industries also congregated in the area, benefitting from an ideal location for transportation via river or railroad. The proliferation of silversmith operations in the nineteenth century earned Taunton the nickname "Silver City."

Nadeau, who typically batted leadoff for Brockton, faced

McDougal several times during the season. McDougal was a sneaky right-hander who would later be described as having an unorthodox delivery, in which he faced away from the batter just prior to releasing the ball,[482] a move that surely annoyed right-handed hitters like Nadeau.

Early in the season, McDougal started against Brockton twice. The first game, on May 19, was a nail-biter up to the very end, with McDougal holding Brockton to just three runs and Taunton scoring the tie-breaking run in the ninth inning with two outs, winning 4-3. Nadeau had only one single in the contest. The second game, on May 22, was not as close, with Nadeau and the other Brockton hitters getting four runs in the third inning to take a 5-3 lead. Two more in the fifth and another in the sixth clinched their 8-5 victory. This time, Nadeau had three singles, two runs scored, and a stolen base against to pace the victors. Brockton finished that week in second place at 11-6, while Taunton was in last place at 5-13.

The New England League finished its season in early September with Brockton and Newport tied for first place. Nadeau finished the season with a .293 batting average and 96 runs scored in 106 games, while McDougal pitched one last game for Taunton on September 8—an 8-3 loss to Newport—and then packed his bags for Toronto and the Eastern League. This was a great opportunity for him to pitch closer to home, as well as take another step to a return to the major leagues.

Just two days after pitching in Newport, McDougal was on the mound again, this time in Toronto against Wilkes-Barre, the team representing the second-largest city in Pennsylvania anthracite coal country—and the one the closest to major labor unrest.

At the time, Wilkes-Barre had a population of nearly 52,000—more than double its 1880 population of 23,339. Nestled in the Wyoming Valley near the Susquehanna River, the area's original European settlers had lived in the midst of often-hostile native tribes. During the Revolutionary War, joint British and Iroquois forces attacked Forty Fort, located in present-day Wilkes-Barre, and drove most of the settlers out in what is commonly called the Wyoming Massacre. This attack—and others like it along the frontier—prompted Washington to launch the Sullivan-Clinton campaign that would wipe out most of the remaining Native Americans in the region.

Wilkes-Barre's population was still less than 5,000 as late as 1860, but, like the rest of the region, it skyrocketed as demand for anthracite coal rose and as thousands of recent European immigrants sought jobs in local mines, collieries, and associated industries. The importance of the hard, shiny anthracite coal to Wilkes-Barre earned the town its nickname: The Diamond City. It was a collection-point for many disparate cultural groups, and the tension of labor disagreements and poverty often boiled over into ethnic violence.

As both a distraction and a means of assimilation, baseball was popular throughout the coal region, from the larger Eastern League cities, to the towns of the Central Pennsylvania League, to the amateur small town teams in the Anthracite League, and to less-formal pick-up contests everywhere. Regardless of the level, in 1897, the game was played during a summer of labor tension, much of it exacerbated by labor activism that favored English-speaking "natives" at the expense of more recent immigrants from Eastern Europe.

"People were flocking to the cities, into their sweatshops and slums, and began to embrace baseball for its touch of green," wrote historian Burt Solomon. "A Gilded age was giving way to something grimier. Economic warfare had its battles in the Haymarket riot in Chicago in 'eighty-six and the deadly Homestead strike on the outskirts of Pittsburgh in 'ninety-two. Nothing honorable was at stake–only survival and greed."[483]

Memories of ethnic-oriented violence, personified by the Irish secret society, the "Molly McGuires," were still fresh in many local people's minds. The Mollies were agrarian anti-English-occupation resistance fighters in Ireland, some of whom had U.S. connections. Many anthracite mine owners and/or managers were of English or Welsh descent, and they ascribed much of the violent crime committed by Irish labor interests in Pennsylvania's anthracite coalfields during the early 1870s to a Molly conspiracy, thus promoting fear and obedience among the general populace. Eastern European immigrants did not have the same associations with edgy violence, but many locals now felt they were just as secretive and threatening as the Irish had been twenty years earlier. As is true in most such scenarios, especially in times of scarcity, people tend to be afraid of and biased against those who are different.

Unfortunately, labor tension in the anthracite region was unavoidable in 1897. Despite the strike of 1887-1888, and the on-going efforts of organized labor to improve working conditions, the coal economy continued to suffer from years of short-term monopolistic manipulation of coal supply, which threatened long-term profits and put heightened pressure on expenses, the largest of which was labor. Coal mine owners placed limitations on labor by cutting hours, cutting pay, increasing fees, tying wages to coal prices, and even charging job-seekers a fee for obtaining a job, all of which resulted in multiple waves of strikes and violence. Mine owners and superintendents squeezed costs as much as they could while attempting to avoid costly shutdowns; the poorest workers, the recent immigrants from eastern Europe, felt this squeezing most acutely. Compounding this squeeze was a three-cents- per-day wage tax on un-naturalized alien workers imposed by the Pennsylvania legislature. The still-nascent United Mine Workers (UMW) union supported this tax, with UMW organizer John Fahey going so far as to note that the tax does the foreign workers "a power of good by keeping them out of the coal mines where all is cruel poverty and misery,"[484] an odd statement only understandable in the context that at the time the UMW primarily represented the top levels of the labor pool, not the least-skilled, non-English-speaking laborers and their families.

In the midst of this labor tension even coal towns without league teams aspired to put competitive semi-pro and amateur baseball teams on the field. For example, around midsummer, young men in Mount Carmel were rumored to be organizing a baseball team "as good as any of our neighboring towns" that would compete for the independent "Championship of the Coal Region." These town teams tended to schedule games independently against one another, and attract as many families to the games as possible.

Among the families touched by baseball in coal country was the Picus family who had emigrated from Slovakia in 1884, then part of the Austro-Hungarian Empire. Michael, born in 1854, was a miner in Pottsville in the late 1890s,[485] and his son John, born in 1883, was, by age thirteen, a miner further west in Johnstown.[486] John Picus would eventually pitch semi-pro baseball in the Pottsville area before becoming Jack Quinn and joining Jack Chesbro in New York as two of the game's greatest spitball pitchers. As a young teenager, John reportedly worked an early shift at the mine so he could play sandlot baseball in the afternoon. "I always had a good arm, developed in stone fights we used to have as kids," he recalled later. "Those fights probably helped me to gain control as well as develop the strength I needed to break in as a big league pitcher."[487]

537   THE BREAKERS, HAZLETON, PA.   ILLUSTRATED POST CARD CO., N. Y.

Hazleton, PA, coal breaker.

Another such family was the Brodericks of Freeland. Ireland-born miner James Broderick of Lattimer and Milnesville had been a Knights of Labor activist during the 1887-1888 strike and remained an activist in the summer of 1897. A possible close relative, Martin, immigrated to Pennsylvania from Ireland some time prior to 1850, and by 1850, was a laborer in Blythe. By 1880, Martin's son John was a miner in Lattimer with four sons under the age of thirteen. One of those boys, Matthew, was one of the area's outstanding ball players by the mid-90s. John worked his way up to Outside Boss at the mines near Freeland and Lattimer, while Matthew played for teams in Freeland and Mauch Chunk. Meanwhile, his younger brother, Charles, worked at the mines as a mule driver, and his younger sisters worked at the local silk mill and the overalls factory.[488] Matthew and another Freeland boy, Bernard "Barnie" McFadden, were considered the "best ball players in the Lehigh region." Following the summer of 1897, they both earned spots with Villanova College.[489]

Coal towns of all sizes worked as tirelessly as ever to promote their games and bring cranks to the stands. Boxer John L. Sullivan umpired the game at Shamokin on August 11 as part of a promotion to get more fans to put their tensions aside and attend the game. His going fee for such appearances was reportedly a full half of the gate receipts.[490]

The Anthracite Baseball League was an excellent example of towns coming together in 1897 to use baseball as a means to promote healthy competition and relieve labor tension. It was comprised of amateur teams from the four neighboring towns of Freeland, Lattimer, Drifton and Hazelton, right in the middle of coal country amidst active mining operations. The teams played approximately 15 games apiece against one another from May through early September, and tensions remained relatively contained in the area during this period, despite active strikes. Drifton won the League championship with a record of 12-4.[491]

The summer of 1897 was sprinkled with labor violence, and much of the most serious such violence stemmed from relatively small actions. On August 12, for example, Gomer Jones, Superintendent of the Lehigh and Wilkes-Barre mines, placed restrictions on where mule drivers could leave their animals at the Honey Brook mine.

Many laborers already had long-standing complaints about Jones. "Mr. Jones has made his record by cutting down wages and brutally tyrannizing over the men under his charge," a *Freeland Tribune* correspondent reported. "His name was used by the industrious mothers at Upper Lehigh many years ago as a bugaboo to frighten refractory children. The exclamation, 'Go to sleep, Jackey, and your own mamma won't let the nasty Gomer Jones carry away her own dumpling darling little Jackey,' had a very salutary effect on washday—such being the man's record in the community."⁴⁹²

As a result of Jones's new order, mule drivers, who, like seventeen-year-old Charles Broderick, tended to be young and paid already low wages, now had to take longer to get to and from the mines without a requisite increase in pay. Thirty-five of these drivers—many of whom were from southern or eastern Europe—went on strike immediately. Within four days, 350 mule drivers went on strike and were supported by over 3,000 miners. At the time, the UMW was not actively managing the strike, its membership being relatively small. The UMW to date had made only token efforts to organize immigrant labor, not only due to their support of the immigrant wage tax, but because many of the immigrant laborers were too meagerly paid to afford the dues.

Throughout the remainder of August and into early September, miners and mule drivers throughout the region around Wilkes-Barre were on strike, marching for greater rights; some local newspapers termed it "idling." The number of strikers was soon too large for the mine owners to break with private coal and iron police, so they appealed to Luzerne County Sheriff James F. Martin to stop the marches and enable the mines to re-open. Martin formed a posse of over one hundred English-speaking citizens (which he considered his "deputies") to satisfy the mine owners' request. In the first week of September, Martin issued a proclamation, reading in part that "notice is hereby given to all good citizens to refrain from tumultuous and unlawful assembly and from all acts of disorder or violence, and from all acts interfering with the liberty of other citizens, or tending to a breach of the peace. Notice is further given that all such acts of disorder and lawlessness will be summarily repressed in accordance with the laws of the land."[493]

On September 8, roughly one thousand strikers, most of whom were of Polish, Slovakian or Lithuanian descent, marched from Michalchik's Hall in McAdoo to the Hazleton area, where Martin and his deputies greeted them. Martin read from his proclamation and asked the strikers not to enter Hazelton, but few of those who were able to hear him could understand English, and, confused, some disbursed and others continued marching toward Cranberry. Martin and his men proceeded behind the men and violent confrontation was avoided. A larger group of strikers had reportedly congregated in Pottsville, and violence was avoided there as well. In addition, the mine company announced it was willing to make a wage concession, bringing the most recent offer to one dollar and ten cents per day. Not everyone was pleased with this lack of confrontation, even though it seemed like Martin's approach was thus far reasonable.

"The situation is a grave one and clashes between the strikers and the operators' armed men have been narrowly averted several times this week," reported the *Freeland Tribune*.[494]

The good news of the wage concession prompted the strikers to call off marches scheduled for Thursday, but on Friday, September 10, when a group of nearly five hundred strikers marched to an operating coal mine in the town of Lattimer, the pressure was on Martin. The likelihood of a confrontation was very high.

According to local news accounts at the time, many of the deputies in Martin's posse were eager for a confrontation, bragging to one another about how many marchers they would kill, essentially de-humanizing the "foreigners." The idea of participating in live gun battles was not far from the public consciousness, as battles against Native Americans had last occurred only a few years prior. In fact, that very summer, a "large wagon" made its way around the region, selling access—for a nickel—to a man in a cowboy hat who claimed to have killed Sitting Bull. *The Elmira Daily Gazette* reported on June 30 that the wagon was at the corner of Broad and Waverly Streets in Waverly, and that "a large crowd dropped their nickel to see the wonderful curiosity."

Lattimer's baseball team was not scheduled to play that afternoon, but the Wilkes-Barre team was in Toronto, and it was in this climate that McDougal took the mound for Toronto against Wilkes-Barre on September 10. It was not supposed to be a close contest. At that point, Syracuse led the league with a record of 79-46, Toronto was second at 70-47, and Wilkes-Barre was dead last at 29-80.

McDougal did not do well in this outing, however, as Wilkes-Barre jumped out to a 7-0 lead in the first inning, with first baseman Fatty Diggins, right fielder Patrick Meaney, and left fielder Billy Bottenus leading the attack. Fortunately for McDougal, Wilkes-Barre pitcher Fritz Odwell did not do much better, giving up four runs in the first inning and then six more in the third. Welcome Gaston and Bill Dinneen soon relieved McDougal on the mound. Catcher Doc Casey and left fielder Billy Lush led Toronto's hitting attack, and they wound up winning 11-10. The victory brought Toronto closer to first place and dealt Wilkes-Barre yet another unwelcome loss.[495]

As the game was proceeding in Toronto, five hundred unarmed miners marched behind an American flag to Lattimer. Sheriff Martin and his armed police force ordered the crowd to disperse, but the marchers continued on; many of them did not understand English. When someone from the armed posse reached for the flag, skirmishes and confusion ensued. Amidst the confusion, Martin's deputies fired into the crowd.

The *Philadelphia Times* reported on the incident:

Accounts of the strikers and deputies here differ as to who was most at fault, but in a trice the guns of the deputies belched forth a tongue of fire. The report seemed to shake the very hillsides and a cry of dismay went up from the strikers. They scattered those of them who could move, and another volley was fired into the now retreating and disorganized strikers. Others fell dead or wounded, and the scene which followed beggars description. The excitement was simply indescribable. The moans and screams of the wounded and dying filled the air. The deputies, seeing the strikers fleeing in terror and leaving their dead and wounded on the field, went to the aid of the unfortunate men.[496]

When the shooting stopped, nineteen men were dead and between seventeen and forty-nine others were wounded (reports differed wildly). It was one of the deadliest labor confrontations in U.S. history. Medical evidence showed that nearly all of the strikers had been shot in the back.

"Strikers Shot Down," declared the next day's *Scranton Tribune* headline; the paper characterized the marching strikers as a "mob." *The Scranton Republican* called the marchers "Infuriated Foreigners," as the dead and injured were overwhelmingly Polish, Slovakian, or Lithuanian. [497]

The Freeland Tribune, edited and published by Thomas A. Buckley, the Freeland Justice of the Peace and himself an immigrant from Wales, was much more sympathetic to the strikers, noting that "a score of men were deliberately murdered on the public highway near Lattimer on Friday afternoon by one of the bands of armed thugs which have been parading the region for a week past."

The *Tribune* further noted that the "massacre was the result of a deliberate laid plot, hatched early last week in the private offices of the coal offices of this region, to aggravate the striking miners" and give the "militia" a "pretext" so that "the coal corporations could reassert their long undisputed title of supreme master of every living thing in their territory."[498]

Depiction of the Lattimer, PA, massacre on September 10, 1897. From The Philadelphia Inquirer.

In the wake of the massacre, local English-speaking families were concerned that thousands of "foreigners" would raid their villages and homes in retaliation. Sheriff Martin and his deputized posse, which was comprised of members of relatively well-to-do local families, were subsequently cleared of any potential murder charges, which only heightened fears of retaliation in the region. James Broderick and other labor leaders organized "indignation meetings" in an effort to unify workers' concerns and activities. In response to the violence and potential for "mob rule," Governor Hastings called in troops.

As the feared "retaliation" did not transpire, people soon came to understand that the incident was less about "foreigners" and more about labor rights, regardless of the workers' national origins. Moreover, while thousands of workers went on strike immediately following the incident, nearly all of the collieries resumed operations within two weeks, which helped diffuse the tension.[499]

Lattimer Mine owner Calvin Pardee, the son of former mine owner Ario Pardee, was a Union Civil War officer who had served in the battle of Antietam, and was in Germantown at the time of the massacre. He had opposed raising miners' wages prior to the incident and was eager to re-open the mines afterwards. The incident had little impact on him, and he was still anti-union three years later when yet another strike loomed. "Under no circumstances will the operators yield to the United Mine Workers," he said of this later strike in 1900. "It will be a fight to the finish and the operators will win." He went on to explain that workers at the Harwood and Lattimer collieries earned a monthly average wage of $40 and $38, respectively–arguing that this proved that "the miners are better paid than the average workingman."[500]

Socialists and labor activists insisted that the Lattimer incident revealed something sinister not only about labor relations, but about the nation's political system as a whole. The Socialist Labor Party's newspaper noted:

> The Hazleton Sheriff's posse was made up, not as formerly, from the toughian class, but from their own, the capitalist class. The Hazleton capitalists, rather than stand the expense of hiring assassins, and the trouble thereof, now did the work themselves–they saved just so much money.
>
> Thus the Tom Platt Republican machine and the Tammany Hall Democratic machine answered, in politics, to the work of the roughs in the Sheriff's posses. The parallel is exact. Just as the roughs knew their value to their real employers and made these pay for them, the Tom Platt Republican and the Tammany Hall Democratic politicians found THEIR value to the criminal capitalist class and made this class pay through the nose for their services they rendered to them. If the

capitalist needed legislation, it had to be bought from the machines; and, worse yet, the machines would initiate the extortion of money from the capitalists by introducing unfavorable legislation, that had to be bought off, or threatening prosecutions that had to be hushed up with good round sums.[501]

Russian native and popular social reformer Emma Goldman—whom J. Edgar Hoover would eventually label "one of the most dangerous women in America" and whose roommate was serving a prison sentence during the summer of '97 for the attempted murder of Henry Clay Frick over labor unrest at the Homestead steel mill in '92—drew similar connections between the Lattimer miners and broader political issues in a speech to a Boston crowd shortly after the incident:

> When I think of this latest legalized murder, it seems like a mockery to the dead miners today to talk and talk, when it is necessary to act. The workingmen were fired upon because they were human beings who wanted bread for their children and homes for their families. They have been kept starving by the authorities and then fired upon because they peaceably asked for bread. You do not need to be an anarchist. If you want bread you are an enemy to society and must be put down. The order to kill the workingmen was given because they asked peaceably for the necessaries of life. If such a thing is a crime against society then society should be attacked and put down.[502]

Due to the violence at Lattimer and the unrest that followed in its wake—including the general public's indignation—John Fahey's UMW union membership grew considerably. "By the opening of the ninth annual national convention of the UMW at Columbus, Ohio, on January 11, 1898, the 15,000 members

John Fahey had enrolled in the Hazleton district made his region the second largest in the country," wrote Michael Novak in his excellent book about the Lattimer incident.[503]

Still, labor unrest at the mines continued. Not only was mine ownership disdainful of labor's on-going demands for better wages and improved safety, but they also systematically retaliated against witnesses who testified at Martin's trial. For example, Joseph Meki, who was wounded during the incident, was fired the day after his trial testimony. "Meki showed the jury the scars in his left arm where the bullet had gone in at the back and come out in front," explained the *New York World*. "He still wears his old coat with a bullet hole at the back and one at the front. He is a poor man. He has worn the coat all winter."[504]

Labor tensions remained in coal country, but the most urgent fears in the immediate Lattimer area following the massacre dissipated enough by the end of September to allow for the Cuban X Giants to visit, defeating Mauch Chunk 8-7 on September 18, and the Freeland Tigers, led by Barnie McFadden, 7-4 on September 19.[505] Sol White led the Giants attack, just as he had the previous season against Waverly.

Up to this point, immigrants from Eastern Europe had not been prominent in professional baseball, just as they were still working their way up the working class ladder. It typically took more than one generation for immigrants to integrate into American life, and baseball was no exception. The Irish who arrived in the U.S. in the 1840s through 1860s best exemplified this progression, for although baseball was a heavily working-class sport, it was dominated by Irish and other white English speakers at the turn of the century. "Well into the 1890s," wrote Frank Deford, "probably up to 40 percent of major leaguers were of Irish descent."[506]

Reacting to the notion that there was a noticeable lack of non-English speakers in baseball, *Sporting Life* ran a letter from Wilkes-Barre in its October 2 issue that made a case for a good team of top national players of German extraction: "The assertion has been made that the German could not think quickly enough to be a base ball player. The following team would make any Irish team hustle: First base. Heckley; second base. Reitz; short stop. Long; third base. Dahlen; left field. Stenzel; center field. Lange; right field. Stahl; sub infielder. Shoch; sub outfielder. Selbach; Pitchers: Hoffer, Klobedanz, Breitenstein and Cuppy; catchers, Peitz and Zimmer. I think would win a majority of games in a contest."[507] Based on their performances in 1897, the writer could also have included Hamburg, Wagner, and Heine.

CHAPTER 14

Baseball in Wartime

As the 1898 season started, the last thing organized baseball needed was something to take the public's mind off entertainment. The sport had suffered a great deal during the economic downturn of 1893 and the labor strife of 1897. Moreover, organized baseball was benefiting from the U.S.'s good relations with Cuba, as evidenced by frequent touring trips there. In fact, for Cubans, according to historian Riess, "baseball symbolized liberty, progress, modernization and opposition to the Spanish colonial regime."[508]

Unfortunately for baseball, from the time President McKinley assumed office in 1897, the public's calls for war with Spain over its imperial activities in Cuba and the Philippines continued to grow. By 1898, the voices calling for war had grown to a roar.

On February 15, the clamor rose to a fever pitch when the battleship USS Maine exploded in Havana Harbor and sank, killing 266 out of the 355 sailors on board. It either exploded from an internal accident, such as a combustion fire in the coal bunker, or from an external cause, like a mine. On March 28th, the U.S. Naval Court of Inquiry ruled that the cause was a submerged mine.[509] The national media turned up the volume of its indignation, stoking the public's anger and desire for vengeance and painting Spain as the culprit. McKinley urged patience but ultimately decided to take action; on April 20, he demanded that Spain withdraw from Cuba. The U.S. blockaded the island on April 21, Spain declared war on April 23, and the U.S. declared war on April 25–all right at the beginning of the baseball season.

As a result, the 1898 season started with low attendance numbers, and it never really picked up throughout the summer. With much of its paying public either gone to war or actively following the war, baseball struggled to maintain its financial stability. Local teams tried to find local explanations for the low attendance and to stay optimistic, but the larger issues were difficult to ignore.

On May 7, *Sporting Life* reported:

> Although the attendance at the two games thus far played in Cleveland has been below expectations, President Robison believes there are plenty of explanations therefore, and declares firmly that his horoscope shows a most successful season ahead.[510]
>
> "The opening games at Cleveland," said Mr. Robison to-day, "came just at a time when the people were in a flutter of excitement over the departure of the soldiers. Moreover the weather was cold and threatening, and it was like beckoning pneumonia to come and abide with you to go out and sit in the stands Friday and Saturday."[511]

Sporting Life also made some general comments on May 7 regarding the war's impact on the game:

> Well, the war is on and still the League is doing business at the same old stand, despite the gloomy view of some pessimists. Squadrons may blockade Cuba and naval battles may be fought, but base ball goes on forever. It is a significant fact that the principal pastime among Uncle Sam's soldiers in the different encampments is a game of base ball. Soon some of the boys in blue will be making home runs while holding some fort in the

"pearl of the Antilles." As soon the white-livered Spanish butchers have quit, as is their style, the jolly tars will be only too glad to handle the bat and ball when they get shore leave. In the meantime business keeps right on and lovers of base ball will continue to urge on their respective teams. After a while the scareheads on the war subject will become so wearisome to the public that they will turn to the sporting page for relief. No such little thing as a war with the pesky Spaniards can put a damper on the great race for the League championship.[512]

The clubs and the national sports media were clearly anxious for baseball to continue to be successful, and, as the season progressed, many teams encouraged ties to patriotism by inviting military bands to games, recommending teams march to games in military uniforms, and giving free tickets to soldiers and sailors in uniform. Management was desperate to equate an afternoon at the ballpark with patriotism and the American flag.

The war also affected Americans' perceptions of race and ethnicity, which affected all aspects of society, including baseball. An incident in May of that year involved Cleveland Native American outfielder Louis Sockalexis and a case of mistaken ethnicity. According to *Sporting Life* and the *St. Louis Republic*, Sockalexis and the other Cleveland players were heading to Cincinnati by train when Sockalexis entered a smoking car and encountered a group of Army recruits who mistook him for a Spaniard. Heated words ensued, which led to a fight.

"When he started to leave one of the blood thirsty recruits tried to upper-cut the big Indian," wrote the *Republic*. "There was a mix-up and for about five minutes Uncle Sam's new candidates for military honors found in Socks the toughest proposition they ever tackled outside of a Missouri mule. He was simply chock full of fight and when the Rubes gave him the opening he was quick to take advantage of it."[513]

In the New York State League, Charlie Hamburg started the

season with the Canandaigua club, managed by Hank Ramsey. Ramsey promised to put together an inexpensive but capable club led by Hamburg; second baseman James McQuaid, who had played with Hamburg at Lancaster the previous year; pitcher Fred McFall, who had pitched with Jack Chesbro in Roanoke in '96; pitcher George Allen, who started his professional career in '95 in Austin, Texas; and catcher Jack O'Neill from Ireland.

The other 1898 New York State League towns were Auburn, Cortland, Johnstown/Palmyra, Lyons, Oswego, Rome, and Utica. At the beginning of the season, the teams all had solid prospects: Auburn was led by outfielder Tommy Leach, infielder Tim Shinnick, and pitcher Mal Eason; Cortland featured pitcher Mickey Mullin and outfielder Fred Ketchum; Johnstown/Palmyra starred outfielder Carlton Molesworth and shortstop Jim McGuire; Lyons was expecting big things from outfielder Bill Gannon and infielder Billy Gilbert; Oswego was looking to outfielder Jimmy Barrett and utility man She Donahue; Rome was led by infielder Pete O'Brien and pitcher Bill Cristall; and Utica featured catcher Jerry Hurley and infielder John Nugent.

Cranks of the New England League were also eager for the start of the new season. McDougal was back in Taunton after his Toronto stint, Nadeau was back in Brockton, and Seavers was signed up with Fall River.

The Atlantic League was also primed for a big season, war or no war. It was now comprised of the cities of Allentown, Hartford, Lancaster, Newark, Norfolk, Paterson, Reading, and Richmond. Each team had at least one veteran star. Richmond still boasted Happy Jack Chesbro as pitcher, while Lee Viau pitched for Paterson, Scott Stratton pitched for Reading, Billy Bottenus played outfield for Hartford, and Andy Roth caught for Lancaster.

Batting leadoff and playing outfield for Newark in '98 was former University of Pennsylvania star Zane Grey, just twenty-six years old and not yet embarked on his famous literary career. Grey's younger brother, Reddy, would go on play one National League game for Pittsburgh, and Grey was a decent player himself. In the early part of the season, on May 25, Grey faced Richmond in a double-header and picked up a double in the first game, but still faced a 3-2 loss.[514] In the second game, Grey led off against Chesbro and picked up a single and a run scored in four trips to the plate. Richmond won the game as well, 5-3.[515]

A few days later, on June 5, Grey picked up a single in an 8-1 victory over first-place Lancaster, while Roth, batting clean-up for Lancaster, went hitless.[516] The next day, Grey faced Hartford and outfielder Billy Bottenus. Both Grey and Bottenus smacked doubles and scored runs, but Harford prevailed 2-1 in ten innings.[517]

Although he was still an umpire for the Central Pennsylvania League—comprised of teams from Lock Haven, Milton, Sunbury, and Williamsport—George Stovey's temper revealed itself early in the spring, when he was injured in what sounded like a bar fight. "George Stovey, formerly pitcher for the Cuban Giants," reported the *Philadelphia Times* on April 1, "was badly used up in a fight with 'Son' Williams, a well-known colored character, last night. Stovey received several bad wounds, and he alleges that Williams cut him with a razor. It is thought that Stovey will recover."

The cities of Binghamton and Elmira–two mainstays of organized baseball since 1885–were both without organized franchises for the third straight season. For the Southern Tier of New York, not having organized baseball in its largest towns was a blow to both the local economy and to the sport. Even games in the Iron and Oil League or the Central Pennsylvania League were too far away for the casual fan in Waverly, Elmira or Binghamton. Those in the area interested in watching the national pastime would have to travel to Cortland or Canandaigua, or settle for semi-pro, barnstorming, and amateur contests and following the organized leagues, which contained many familiar players, via newspapers.

The New York State League promised to be highly competitive that season. Canandaigua and Cortland met to start the season with a double-header, which resulted in Canandaigua sweeping Cortland 11-5 and 17-3. Canandaigua quickly went on to win six of its first seven games, taking an early lead over Oswego, who won five of its first six.

Cortland started the season 2-4, doing well after their first two loses to Canandaigua. On May 20, Mickey Mullin shut down Tommy Leach and Tim Shinnick's Auburn squad to earn the win, 7-0. "In each of five out of the nine innings, but three visitors were allowed to step up to the rubber, so effective was the work of Mullin, and so perfect was his support," the *Cortland Standard* reported.

Twenty-two-year-old Michael J. "Mickey" Mullin[518] was born in Pennsylvania and had pitched in the New England League for Salem in '95 and '96 and Pawtucket in '97. Despite his potential, Mullin's '97 season was inauspicious, and by the end of May he was released. He then headed to Hornellsville and also spent time pitching during the season for Canandaigua.

That same day, May 20th, Canandaigua lost to Oswego 8-4. "Threatening weather and a cool wind kept the crowd down to about 500," the *Standard* said, "but the enthusiasm was unbounded."

On June 7, Cortland traveled to Canandaigua for a rematch, with its star pitcher, Mullin, opposing McQuaid, Hamburg, and the other big Canandaigua hitters. Mullin held them to just two runs in a 4-2 victory. Hamburg had two singles and a stolen base; McQuade, a double and a run scored; and Jack Lawlor, a double and two singles, but it was not enough. Mullin helped out with a double and a run scored. Ketchum, Cortland's big hitter, played centerfield and batted third, but went zero for five in the winning effort.[519]

As the games continued, so did the war, and patriotic fervor was evident in small towns throughout the country. Among the tunes selected by the Waverly City Band for its first outdoor concert of the summer in early June was John Phillip Sousa's new march, "Stars and Stripes Forever"[520]–a march just published and performed for the first time the previous summer at Willow

Grove Park in Philadelphia. Many Waverly citizens undoubtedly heard the march for the first time that evening.

Many of the players' peers were also directly engaged in the war. At least sixty-six young men from the Elmira area signed up for military service, and most of those signed up within the first two weeks of May.[521]

A number of ball players left baseball to go into active military service, including John Titus of St. Clair, Pennsylvania, in the middle of coal country. Titus, who had worked in the local coalmines throughout the previous year's labor trouble, was still playing amateur ball and had not yet begun his professional baseball career. He enlisted with Company K of the 8th Regiment of the Pennsylvania Infantry. His unit trained in Georgia and Virginia and was deactivated before they could be deployed to combat. He would eventually play the 1901 season in Pottsville of the Pennsylvania State League before embarking on an eleven-year major league career.

Also enlisting from the middle of coal country was Jacob Coveleski, the eldest of the five baseball-playing Coveleski brothers from Shamokin. He served with Company E of the 21st U.S. Army Infantry Regiment in the Philippines and unfortunately died of chronic dysentery at Corregidor Hospital during the U.S. occupation in 1899.[522] His youngest brother, Stan, would eventually be elected to the Baseball Hall of Fame. Jacob never played beyond the amateur ranks prior to his untimely death, but, according to Stan, he "could throw a ball as fast as you could hit one."[523]

Warren Wallace Beckwith, a twenty-three-year-old Iowan whose father was born a short train ride from Canandaigua, played in the Texas League in '97, and had the double distinction of enlisting in '98 as a private with Company F of the 50th Iowa Infantry and of eloping with Abraham Lincoln's granddaughter, Jessie Harlan Lincoln. He sired two children with her before divorcing in 1907. Jessie's father, Robert Todd Lincoln, was dissatisfied with the marriage and reportedly referred to Beckwith as a "baseball buffoon."[524]

Some of the sports reporters who covered baseball also served in the war. James Nolan of the *Louisville Dispatch* suffered a leg wound that left him "crippled for life" when a shell burst near him at Coamo in Puerto Rico. As a result of the ordeal, Nolan was said to have dropped from 250 to 150 pounds. "In common with most of the volunteers," *Sporting Life* reported, "he speaks harshly of the official neglect that soldiers were subjected to and declares that he has had enough of war."[525]

On June 14, the *Waverly Advocate* ran a letter from volunteer soldier Eugene Whitley, who was stationed at Camp Cuba Libre near Jacksonville, Florida, with the Second Regiment of New Jersey Volunteer Infantry. Whitley complained about the sand being impossible to clean and noted that within the army:

> …the rebel feeling is still very strong among the Southern troops. They object to our playing "Yankee Doodle" and "Hang Jeff Davis on a Sour Apple Tree," etc. I am afraid if they get too fresh there will be trouble between the Northern and Southern troops. They insist on playing "Dixie" and we insist on sticking up for the Yankees.
>
> We are on the St. John's River, two miles from Jacksonville, a city about as big as Elmira or a little smaller. The white people here are very kind to the New Jersey boys, as a majority of the business men are from New York or New Jersey and we have the run of the town.

In Washington, the war with Spain prompted Assistant Navy Secretary Theodore Roosevelt, nearly a decade after he welcomed baseball's world tour home at the big Delmonico's dinner, to resign his post and serve as a colonel with the 1st United States Calvary, better known as the "Rough Riders." Following weeks of training, the Riders arrived in Cuba at the end of June, ready to fight.

On July 1, as Roosevelt led his troops in a dramatic assault up San Juan Hill, first-place Canandaigua hosted struggling Palmyra, which was just four games ahead of last-place Utica. Bill Heine had joined Palmyra from Dayton on June 21, and for this game, he started at shortstop and batted sixth. Meanwhile, Hamburg started at first base and batted second, Lawlor started in center field and batted third, and McQuaid started at second base and batted clean-up for Canandaigua.

Canandaigua took an early lead and never relinquished it as starting pitcher George Allen held Palmyra scoreless until the seventh inning, eventually winning 6-2. McQuaid and Allen lead Canandaigua with two doubles each. Both Hamburg and Heine went hitless.

Just four days later, Palmyra battled fourth-place Cortland and lost 10-5. Mullin started in the box and got the win. Deisel, who got three singles; Ketchum, who landed a double and two singles; and Jones, who hit two doubles and a single, led the winners' sixteen-hit attack. Shortstop Heine and centerfielder Colton Molesworth paced the losers–Heine with two singles, a stolen base, and one run scored and Molesworth with a triple and two runs scored. Only 425 fans attended the game in Cortland; they may have been worn out by the Fourth of July holiday double-header the day before against Rome.[526]

Starting as catcher for Cortland on July 4 was eighteen-year-old Frank LaPorte from Uhrichsville, Ohio.[527] LaPorte, the son of a furniture dealer, had spent the first part of the season far from home in Birmingham, Alabama, in the Southern League, where he hit .380 in twenty-eight games. He was now going to see if he could handle New York State League pitching.

Roughly equidistant between Pittsburgh and Columbus, Uhrichsville had a thriving business community that benefited from the canal and railroad routes and was situated in an area so rich in clay that it was nicknamed the Clay Capital of the World. Uhrichsville had a population of roughly 4,600 and was frequently paired with its neighbor Dennison, known together as the "Twin Cities." For its part, Dennison was the home of forty acres of railroad yards and shops, including roundhouses, turntables, and foundries that, at their peak, employed 3,000 people.

Uhrichsville was the home of numerous Union veterans of the Civil War who were active members of the Grand Army of the Republic, the foremost fraternal organization dedicated to Union veterans, so LaPorte was no doubt familiar with the kind of fervor Cortland displayed for holiday celebrations. The Civil War's impact could still be felt within many families in both Uhrichsville and Cortland. Twenty-four-year-old Wallace Moore, for instance, a cornet player in the Uhrichsville Band and a day laborer at the clay works, had a special connection to patriotic parades and concerts, as his father, James, had served as a private in the 97th Ohio Infantry. Similarly, in Groton, just outside Cortland, a thirty-three-year-old farmer and machinist named Orlando Hemingway had a special connection to the firework displays on the Fourth of July, as his uncle and namesake, Sergeant Orlando Hemingway, had died during the war of typhoid fever in Alexandria, Virginia, while serving with the 143rd New York Infantry. Wallace and Orlando would eventually become in-laws when their children, Margaret Moore and William Riley Hemingway, the author's maternal grandparents, married in 1925.

On July 5, the *Cortland Evening Standard* noted that day's baseball victory over Palmyra on page seven, but paid much more attention to news of the war, with page one headlines such as: "Glorious Victories," "Spain's Fleet Destroyed," and "Our Troops Reach Cavite."[528]

After listing multiple victories, the *Evening Standard* noted that the day was a "thrilling record of such a Fourth of July as has not been known since the bell of Independence Hall rang out the tidings of American freedom. It was a day when one momentous event followed another in constant and rapid succession, each hour bringing forth some new feature more starling than what had gone before."[529]

On July 6, LaPorte caught again for Cortland against Utica. LaPorte was familiar with the opposing pitcher, "Wild Bill" Setley, having played against him while in the Southern League. LaPorte cracked a double and scored a run against Setley in four trips to the plate, but Utica won 10-4.[530]

LaPorte had only two more recorded games for Cortland before his season ended early, going one for three in a 3-2 loss to Lyons on July 8 and going zero for three in an 8-1 loss to Setley and Utica on July 10.[531] Cortland was no longer keeping pace with the league leaders, and LaPorte, despite having shown potential, was released, most likely due to the team's finances. According to BaseballResearch.com, LaPorte did not play organized professional baseball again until 1903, and in 1905 joined the New York Highlanders (eventually the Yankees) and embarked on an eleven-year major league career with New York, Boston, Washington, St. Louis and Indianapolis. He then settled in the Uhrichsville area as a farmer and a foreman for a tool manufacturer.

The war continued to take a toll on baseball attendance as the season progressed, and team owners hoped for a quick victory over Spain. Many teams and leagues teetered on the brink of solvency. By the end of July, Palmyra was out of the New York State League due to financial trouble. The directors were reportedly "caught up" on expenses, but "not desirous of putting up any more money for the team." [532]

Canandaigua continued in first place, "a position which they have maintained throughout the season." Manager Hank Ramsey was touted as "a man well qualified to manage a team in a higher league." Many of his players no doubt harbored similar ambitions. Jimmy McQuaid "is playing a remarkably fast game at second," wrote *Sporting Life*. "He is taking great care of himself, and will surely be in faster company next season." The publication also noted "Hamburg at first is gamboling around that territory like a colt, and with his big stick is proving a terror to pitchers."[533]

Despite the grand victories of early July, hostilities and war news lasted through midsummer and only ended on August 12

LA PORTE, N. Y. AMER.

Frank LaPorte. From the Library of Congress.

with a Protocol of Peace between Spain and the U.S. Many of the soldiers and sailors already deployed for combat would remain deployed for months, especially those involved in the occupation of the Philippines and other territories. For their sakes, teams continued to offer discounts and other patriotic promotions. *Sporting Life* reported:

A dispatch from Cleveland on Wednesday stated that President Frank De H. Robison has telegraphed to President Young the suggestion that all soldiers and sailors in full uniform who took part in the Spanish war be admitted to all League games free.[534]

In days when the welfare of professional base ball is threatened by men who should be its staunchest supporters, it is pleasant to note that the national game is the most popular outdoor sport of the national defenders, the rank and file of the regular army. Before the war there were so few troops stationed in the East that very little was heard of them or their doings, but since the establishment of the camp at Montauk interest in anything pertaining to the regulars had increased a hundred fold. Speaking of base ball in the army, a non-commissioned officer of the Twelfth Regiment, U.S.A., said recently:

"Yes, the game is a great one among the boys, even in the far West. While I was a bit too old to play, I saw plenty of base ball there before coming East to Chickamauga and Tampa at the beginning of the war. Our regiment, the Twelfth Infantry, is the acknowledged champion of the army. I don't believe the Twelfth's team has ever been beaten, and it has met some strong opponents, too, among the Southern League clubs. When they are practicable trips to other posts are frequently made and in an out of the way garrison a rattling good base ball game is no ordinary event. Everybody turns out to see the play."[535]

Not to be outdone, Civil War veterans recalled their days of base ball and battle. "When President Young was a soldier during the Civil War he organized baseball teams among his fellow soldiers, and many hot games were played in between marches and battles," *Sporting Life* reported.[536]

By early September, many local New York and Pennsylvania veterans, like Eugene Whitley of Waverly, began to make their way back home safe and sound, while their communities embraced the sick and wounded, and held somber ceremonies in honor of those who died in the war.

Fred Talada, who had been a leader of the '96 Waverly team and hoped to bring baseball back to the village, spent the summer of '98 neither serving in the armed forces nor playing ball, but rather quarantined at the home of prominent Waverly physician and coroner, Doctor John T. Tucker. According to the *Waverly Advocate*, Talada had a "very mild attack" of smallpox. "Mr. Talada will be out as soon as he regains his strength," the *Advocate* reported on August 18. "The village is to be congratulated in that the prompt handling of the case by the authorities prevented a spread of the dread disease."

Dr. Tucker was born in Ithaca in 1859, attended Cornell, read medicine with Dr. George Cady in Nichols, New York, and practiced in Long Island and Brooklyn before relocating in Waverly in 1894.

Talada and Tucker took advantage of the quarantine to further build upon a partnership that would have an important impact on baseball in the village. The two had traveled to New York City together in mid-1897, and sometime in 1897 or '98, they purchased a Waverly cigar factory and store on Broad Street, naming it "Talada and Tucker." From this venture, Talada could build financial stability and encircle himself with a strong regional network of sporting and business contacts–the sort of foundation upon which a successful professional team could be launched.

The New York State League ended September with a competitive finish, as Canandaigua held its lead not only on the strength of first baseman Hamburg and the other hitters, but also on the acquisition of a key pitcher: "Wild Bill" Setley. Manager Ramsey was used to Setley's idiosyncratic behavior, having managed him two years earlier in Easton, and so he was also familiar with Setley's expertise on the pitcher's mound. Canandaigua was Setley's fourth league team in just six weeks, following drop-in appearances with Utica, Johnstown, and Auburn.

On September 7, Canandaigua played second-place Oswego. Setley only struck out two batters, but he held the opponent to just five hits, winning 7-2. Hamburg led Canandaigua with three hits and a run.[537] The next day, Setley pitched again and was losing 5-0 until the ninth inning, when Canandaigua tied the score. Hamburg and Lawler each smacked a double to lead the hitters, and Setley himself chipped in with a single, a stolen base, and one run scored. Oswego's players refused to continue the game when Canandaigua's spectators allegedly began throwing "gravel stones" at them, and the umpire awarded a 9-0 win to Canandaigua, clinching the championship.[538]

Setley's brief time with Canandaigua was highly successful, as he won four games in a four-day stretch, improved his season record to 14-4, and led the team to a 55-42 record and the league championship.

Canandaigua's franchise would unfortunately not survive beyond the season, as the team folded just a week after winning the pennant, having lost over $1,100. "No sane businessman would think of running his business this way," one team director commented.[539] In addition to suffering from relatively low attendance and interest due to the war, each New York State League team was required to pay a War Tax of ten dollars. Players were asked to take a 10-to-20 percent reduction in pay to keep the league afloat.

There was no indication at the time that professional baseball would return to Waverly in 1899, and on September 20, the *Waverly Advocate* noted that football season was just around the corner. "The Waverly Foot Ball Club held a special meeting at the

YMCA last night," the *Advocate* noted. "Fred Talada was elected manager and Theodore Snook captain. A list of about twenty players has been made, all of whom will engage in practice at the Lincoln Street grounds every afternoon at four o'clock."

At the end of the year, the *Advocate* reported that Talada made a trip to Buffalo and that two of his employees, Grant Lindsey and Charles Walters, took a pleasure trip to Michigan. More baseball planning was underway, but the conditions had to be just right for it to be successful. As Canandaigua's season proved, success on the field did not necessarily mean success at the box office.

This was true at the major league level as well, as 1898 attendance remained low all season and people wondered if it would ever recover. Cleveland's attendance, for example, averaged just 1,237 per game, down thirty percent from the previous season, and even in league champion Boston, the average was just 2,902, down a shocking forty-two percent.

Although the war and economy had huge impacts on attendance, it was clear that changes were needed to improve professional baseball's viability and stability.

"Baseball must again be regarded as a true sport more than is the case at present before it will enjoy its old popularity," wrote Brooklyn's *Sporting Life* correspondent, noting that "too much of the business end of the game is held up before the public," alienating patrons.[540]

The tendency of the owners was to think in terms of reducing liabilities, such as the number of teams and player salaries. The tendency of the players, on the other hand, was to think in terms of creating new opportunities for more players, and encouraging the game to flourish.

The next three seasons, coinciding with the turn to a new century, would determine which approach would prevail. The results are summarized in the second book of this story, to be published in 2020.

Summary of Waverly's Professional Seasons

1887 Independent

Documented Record: 6 wins 5 losses

1896 Independent

Documented Record: 24 wins 22 losses

WAVERLY'S PROFESSIONAL
BASEBALL PLAYERS (1887 & 1896)

* Indicates Major League Experience

LAST	FIRST	'87	'96	POSITION(S)	BORN	DIED
Ayers			X	C, OF		
Beam	*Isaac*		X	P	7/1875	
Brewster	Irving Washington, Jr.		X	OF	11/1870	5/21/1910
Bryan			X	3B		
Carnochan	*John M*		X	SS 1B	2/1873	12/12/1928
*Clapp	John Edgar	X		C	7/15/1851	12/18/1904
Chamberlain			X	C		
Clark	George F.		X		4/1875	
Cole	Archie Burton	X		3B	12/1863	7/5/1948
Corbett	James J.		X	1B	9/1/1866	2/18/1933
Daniels	John "Bucky"	X		OF		
Dodge	W.M.		X	1B		
*Donovan	William "Wild Bill"		X	P, OF	10/13/1876	12/9/1923
Dorsett	Ernest		X	OF	3/9/1874	6/4/1944
Dunham	Owen S.		X	SS, OF	6/12/1876	4/15/1916
*Dunkle	Edward "Davey"		X	P, OF	8/30/1872	11/19/1941
Dunn	Mike		X			
Ferris			X	C		
Flynn			X	OF		
Ford	A.N.		X	OF		
Garrison	W		X	OF		
*Gatins	Frank		X	3B	3/6/1871	11/1/1911
Gillan	Theodore "Tosh"		X	1B	1/7/1879	11/11/1956
Graffius	William J.		X		1/1874	7/31/1930

LAST	FIRST	'87	'96	POSITION(S)	BORN	DIED
Hall	Charles L. Harry	X		2B	1866	
Harris			X			
Herrick			X	P		
Hill	Eddie		X	OF		
Kackle			X	P		
Kennedy	Edward A. "Kick"	X		OF	1860	
Kennedy	Frank P.		X	C	3/1872	
Koehl	George		X	OF, P		
Kutzner	Charles		X		12/15/1875	11/22/1924
Lang	Percy L.	X		SS	6/8/1861	4/8/1926
Lee	Eddie		X	C, 2B		
Leonard	H. M.		X	OF		
Lowman	Nathan Bristol	X		P	2/11/1864	8/29/1936
McKee	Joe		X	C, OF		
Mix	Ervin A.		X	C/3B	1/9/1875	6/1923
Moore	Thomas J.	X		1B		
Murtaugh	John F.		X		1875	
Normile	*Frank L.*		X	P	1876	3/28/1953
Pearce	Harvey D. "Doc"		X	3B	12/5/1873	6/19/1936
Quick			X	P		
Ross	George "Red"		X	2B		
Ryan	Dennis		X	3B	10/1872	
Seavers	Clinton "Goldie"		X	P, OF	11/1871	4/25/1951
Sheahan	Patrick J.	X		1B	5/1860	
Siegmund			X	P		
Singer	J.A.		X	SS		
Skelton	F.W.		X	OF		
Smith	Clarence		X	P, OF		
Smith	Johnny	X		OF	1/1866	

LAST	FIRST	'87	'96	POSITION(S)	BORN	DIED
Talada	Fred Fremont		X	P, C, OF	3/26/1874	5/23/1943
*Taylor	Harry Leonard	X		2B	4/4/1866	7/12/1955
Touhey			X			
Vaughn			X	C		
Waller	John "Bud"		X	2B	1/1875	

Names compiled from game accounts, roster references and box scores. First names, birth dates and/or death dates in italics mean the identity is based on limited or contradictory evidence. Sources for birth and death dates: Baseball-Reference.com, U.S. and State Census Records & Obituaries

PROMINENT WAVERLY
OPPONENTS (1887 & 1896)

Indicates Major League Experience

LAST	FIRST	'87	'96	POSITION(S)	BORN	DIED
*Doran	John F.	X		P	8/1861	
Grant	Frank		X	2B	8/1/1865	5/27/1937
Heine	William C. "Bill"	X		2B	1/1868	1929
Watkins	John M. "Pop"		X	1B	5/18/1857	2/22/1924
White	King Solomon "Sol"		X		6/12/1868	8/26/1955

WAVERLY'S PROFESSIONAL
BASEBALL GAMES (1887 & 1896)

YEAR	DATE	DAY	OPPONENT	LOCATION	W/L	SCORE
1887	5/24	Tue	Sayre		PPD	
1887	5/28	Sat	Elmira	Waverly		
1887	5/30	Mon	Painted Post	Waverly	W	25-5
1887	6/3	Fri	Elmira	Elmira	L	8-4
1887	6/4	Sat	Elmira	Waverly	W	6-5
1887	6/10	Fri	Elmira	Elmira	L	8-4
1887	6/11	Sat	Bradford	Waverly	L	13-4
1887	6/15	Wed	Owego	Waverly	W	23-7
1887	6/18	Sat	Susquehanna	Waverly	W	34-7
1887	6/21	Tue	Owego	Owego	L	10-8
1887	6/30	Thu	*Lockports*	Waverly	W	11-10
1887	7/4	Mon	Elmira	Elmira		
1887	7/9	Sat	Watkins Glen	Watkins Glen	PPD	
1887	7/12	Tue	Elmira	Elmira	L	11-5
1887	7/13	Wed	Elmira	Waverly	W	3-2
1896	5/30	Sat	Corning	Waverly	L	9-6
1896	6/6	Sat	Towanda	Waverly	W	16-5
1896	6/13	Sat	Sayre	Sayre	L	11-3
1896	6/20	Sat	Binghamton YMCA	Waverly	L	13-11
1896	6/26	Fri	Sayre	Waverly	L	9-3
1896	6/27	Sat	Troy, PA	Waverly	W	8-6
1896	6/30	Tue	Binghamton AA	Binghamton	L	15-4
1896	7/1	Wed	Binghamton	Waverly	W	9-6
1896	7/4	Sat 1	Corning	Waverly	W	9-2
1896	7/4	Sat 2	Corning	Waverly	W	14-6
1896	7/7	Tue	Troy, PA	Troy, PA	L	16-9
1896	7/9	Thu	Bainbridge	Waverly	L	6-3

YEAR	DATE	DAY	OPPONENT	LOCATION	W/L	SCORE
1896	7/16	Thu	Binghamton AA	Waverly	W	17-3
1896	7/18	Sat	Troy, PA	Troy	W	7-5
1896	7/23	Thu	Binghamton AA	Binghamton	W	19-15
1896	7/25	Sat	Bainbridge			
1896	7/27	Mon	Oxford			
1896	7/28	Tue	Binghamton YMCA	Binghamton	W	17-3
1896	7/30	Thu	Sidney	Waverly	L	5-4
1896	8/1	Sat	Bainbridge	Waverly	L	12-1
1896	8/13	Thu	Athens	Athens	L	15-6
1896	8/15	Sat	Sayre	Sayre	W	11-1
1896	8/19	Wed	Sayre	Waverly	W	15-3
1896	8/20	Thu	Corning	Waverly	L	16-5
1896	8/21	Fri	Towanda	Towanda	W	8-3
1896	8/22	Sat	Towanda	Waverly	L	9-7
1896	8/24	Mon	Troy	Troy	W	13-12
1896	8/27	Thu	Troy, PA	Waverly	W	19-11
1896	8/28	Fri	Towanda	Towanda	W	7-3
1896	8/29	Sat	Sayre	Sayre	W	17-11
1896	8/31	Mon	Towanda	Towanda	L	7-3
1896	9/5	Sat	Sayre	Sayre	L	16-4
1896	9/7	Mon	Corning	Waverly	W	8-4
1896	9/8	Tue	Towanda	Waverly	W	19-2
1896	9/9	Wed	Troy, PA	Troy, PA	W	16-8
1896	9/10	Thu	Hornell	Waverly	W	17-10
1896	9/11	Fri 1	Towanda	Towanda	L	18-10
1896	9/11	Fri 2	Towanda	Towanda	L	13-0
1896	9/12	Sat	Sayre	Sayre	L	8-1
1896	9/14	Mon	Towanda	Waverly	W	8-6
1896	9/15	Tue	Towanda	Towanda	W	15-7
1896	9/16	Wed	Sayre	Sayre	L	9-5

YEAR	DATE	DAY	OPPONENT	LOCATION	W/L	SCORE
1896	9/17	Thu	Wilkes-Barre	Wilkes-Barre	L	13-6
1896	9/18	Fri	Cuban Giants	Waverly	L	7-1
1896	9/23	Wed	Towanda	Towanda	L	15-7
1896	9/24	Thu	Towanda	Waverly	W	8-6
1896	9/26	Sat	Sayre	Sayre	W	8-6
1896	10/1	Thu	Sayre		L	12-4

Acknowledgements

I am grateful for the help of many in the research and writing of this book, especially my parents who from the very beginning nurtured my curiosity. I also thank my many teachers and coaches who built on this foundation, especially Robert Fox, Gene Higgins, Betty Simcoe, Dan Safford, Frank Cichocki, Allan Fisk, James Parente, Robert Sickler, Duane Klinko, G. Lewis Terwilliger, Thomas Abeling, Alan Geppert, and Andy Codispoti from Waverly; Otto Chaney from Berlin; and Warren Roberts, Josef Zacek, Donald Birn and Henry Krosby from Albany.

I am indebted to the staff of the National Baseball Hall of Fame and Library in Cooperstown, most notably Chris Docter, who tirelessly and without complaint fulfilled multiple information requests during my initial visit, and photograph guru John Horne. I also thank the staffs and volunteers of the Waverly Free Library, the Sayre Public Library, the Spaulding Memorial Library, the Susquehanna River Archaeological Center, the Sayre Historical Society, the Chemung County Historical Society, the Tioga County Historical Society and the Waverly Historical Society. Many at each of these institutions were helpful and encouraging, but especially Chris Brewster, Deb Twigg, Rachel Dworkin, Barb Koehn and Don Merrill.

A special thanks is due to the player and townspeople descendants and relatives with whom I was able to communicate by phone and email, especially William O'Shaughnessy, grandson of Fred Tucker (Talada), Jerome Coffey, grandnephew of Bill Ging, and Maureen Kravec, grandniece of Katie Tobin. I hope my work does justice to them and to the characters and times they described to me. I look forward in the future to meeting family and friends of even more players.

Thanks also to my fellow Society of American Baseball Research members, whose work continues to shine light on baseball's past, and without whom much of the context of this book, made possible via Baseball-Reference.com, would have been impossible to discover. In particular, thanks to baseball historian Tony Kissel, who provided insights and answered many of my questions about the nineteenth century game.

Thanks to my editor Elisabeth Chretien for her excellent work and feedback. Any errors remaining following her work are mine alone. Thanks also to Jeremy Jones and my fellow Iowa Writers Workshop Festival participants for their impressions and suggestions.

Significant thanks to Patricia, Kim, Melissa, Nina and the rest of the staff at Luminare Press for their time and expertise in pulling this final product together.

Finally, thanks to my wife, Maria, for her proof-reading, advice, encouragement and patience, and to friends and family members who read (or listened to) portions of the manuscript, whether they wanted to or not, and provided constructive feedback, especially my children, Angie, Sam and Abby, my brothers, Chris and Nate, my son-in-law, Ryan, my soon-to-be daughter-in-law, Allie, and my father, Howard.

Notes

1   Bill Pennington, *Billy Martin: Flawed Genius*, (New York: Houghton, Mifflin, Harcourt, 2015), 326.

2   Joe Reichler, "Martin Claims He Never Started a Fight," Elmira Star-Gazette, July 30, 1953, 30.

3   Billy Martin and Peter Golenbock, *Number 1*, (New York: Dell, 1980), 64.

4   Melvyn Dubofsky, *Industrialism and the American Worker*, (Arlington Heights, Illinois: Harland Davidson, Inc., 1975), 13.

5   Also known to locals as "Shepard's Creek."

6   Elsie Murray, *Teaoga – Annals of a Valley*. (Athens, Pennsylvania: Tioga Point Museum, 1939) 5-6.

7   Lewis Henry Morgan, *League of Ho-de-no-sau-nee, or Iroquois*. (Two Volumes in One.) (New York: Dodd, Mead and Company, 1922), volume II, 133.

8   Morgan, volume II, 102-103.

9   Murray, 6.

10   Morgan, volume II, 134.

11   John Steele Gordon, *An Empire of Wealth*, (New York: Harper Collins, 2004), 8.

12   Richard Palmer, *The Coming of the Railroad to Sayre*, (Sayre, Pennsylvania: Sayre Historical Society, 2017), 3.

13   Population figures from US Census records.

14   Steven A. Riess, *Sport in Industrial America*, (Wheeling,

Illinois: Harlan Davidson, Inc.), 70.

15 "A Miner's Story," from The Independent, 1902. Online miner recollection located at the Ohio State University eHistory archives. http://ehistory.osu.edu/osu/mmh/gildedage/content/minersstory.cfm.

16 North Pennsylvania Railroad Company. "The North Pennsylvania Rail Road and its Connections, October 1853." Map in the Library of Congress.

17 Palmer, 15.

18 Palmer, 17.

19 Harold Seymour, Baseball: The Early Years, (New York: Oxford University Press, 1960), 347.

20 Population figures from US Census records.

21 With respect to the centuries-long English tradition of urban and rural fairs, "the greatest festival of all was Bartholomew Fair, with its menageries, pickpockets, pantomimes of Harlequin and Faustus, card sharpers, plays, exhibitions of wild men and of horsemanship." E.P. Thompson, The Making of the English Working Class, (New York: Vintage, 1966), 405.

22 Riess, p 17.

23 Frank Deford, The Old Ball Game, (New York: Atlantic Monthly Press, 2005), 13.

24 Riess, 26.

25 Seymour, 347.

26 Dubofsky, 53.

27 Lawrence S. Ritter, The Glory of Their Times, (New York: Macmillan and Company, 1966), 333.

28 Ritter, 123.

29 James M. McPherson, Drawn With the Sword – Reflections

on the American Civil War, (New York: Oxford University Press, 1996), 74.

30   Ibid.

31   Duane Schultz, *Quantrill's War: The Life and Times of William Clarke Quantrill,* (New York: St. Martins Press, 1996), 54-55.

32   Thomas Goodrich,. *Bloody Dawn: The Story of the Lawrence Massacre,* (Kent, Ohio: Kent State University Press, 1991), 72.

33   Schultz, 81-82.

34   Goodrich, 77.

35   Schultz, 144.

36   Schultz, 167.

37   Goodrich, 98.

38   Seymour Lowman, *The Lowmans in Chemung County* (Elmira: The Commercial Press, 1938), 96; and "Mrs. Harriet C. Lowman," Waverly Free Press, July 3, 1914.

39   Lawrence State Journal, August 6, 1863.

40   Goodrich, 95.

41   McPherson, 74.

42   Schultz, 232.

43   Goodrich, 118.

44   Schultz, 231

45   Leavenworth Daily Times, August 30, 1863

46   "A New York Ex-State Senator Burned in Effigy," Paterson NJ Daily Guardian, September 10, 1861, US Census Records and "Death of Nathan Bristol," Port Jervis Evening Gazette, March 3, 1874

47   Lowman, 96; and US Census Records

48   Lowman, 97.

49   US Census Records

50   Riess, 68-69.

51   Both Owen and Albert have family backgrounds in Bradford County, Pennsylvania, just over the border from Waverly. Owen's father John settled in the Athens area before 1796 and died there in 1852, and Albert's father James was born in Towanda in 1813, and later moved to Byron, Illinois, where he died in 1859 (and where Albert grew up). According to an analysis of their respective genealogies, both Owen and Albert are descendants of Edward Spaulding who emigrated from Great Britain to Massachusetts between 1630 and 1633. Edward is Owen's fourth great grandfather and Albert's seventh great grandfather. Owen and Albert are fifth cousins three times removed.

52   "Signed and Money Up," Owego Daily Blade, October 5, 1886, and various game accounts

53   Lewis Sheldon Welch and Walter Camp, Yale, Her Class-Rooms, and Athletics, (Boston: L.C. Page and Company, 1899), 574.

54   Waverly Free Press, April 10, 1886 and April 24, 1886, and "Signed and Money Up," Owego Daily Blade, October 5, 1886.

55   US Census Records

56   US Census Records

57   Ritter, 34.

58   Ritter, 121.

59   Robert B. Ross, The Great Baseball Revolt, (Lincoln, Nebraska: University of Nebraska Press, 2016), xvii.

60   Ross, 27.

61	W.B. Gay, *Historical Gazetteer and Directory of Tioga County, New York, 1785-1888.* (Interlaken, NY: Heart of the Lakes Publishing, 1985), 484.

62	Charlie Bevis, SABR Biography of Harry Taylor

63	Thomas Pellechia, *Over a Barrel – The Rise and Fall of New York's Taylor Wine Company,* (Albany, NY: State University of New York Press, 2015), 12; and U.S. Census Records.

64	George H. Geer ,"On the Memorable Canastota-Oneida Bloodless Battle of 1886," The [Syracuse] Evening Telegram, February 16, 1900.

65	Syracuse Standard, July 18, 1886, 4.

66	The Little Falls Evening Times, July 23, 1886

67	Syracuse Daily Standard, August 11, 1886

68	Syracuse Daily Standard, August 18, 1886

69	Both the Waverly Free Press and the Waverly Advocate made frequent references to the "Elm Street" grounds and the "Elm Street" diamond in 1886 and 1887, but it is not clear from local records where this was. According to an 1888 Sanborn Insurance Map of Waverly, Elm Street was not yet laid out, and even as late as 1898 it only reached part of the way from Spaulding Street east to Cayuta Avenue. It's possible that the grounds were located where the Elm Street School and football stadium were later built, north of the cemetery. It's also possible, despite the name, that they were located in the same then-vacant area as the Howard Street grounds, between Providence and Howard Streets, south of the cemetery.

70	"Shut Out," Owego Daily Blade, September 7, 1886.

71	"Signed and the Money Up," Owego Daily Blade, October 5, 1886.

72	"Owego vs Waverly," Waverly Free Press, October 9, 1886.

73   "Seven to Three," Owego Daily Blade, October 8, 1886.

74   "The Spaldings Victorious," Waverly Advocate, October 8, 1886.

75   Letter from Harry Platt published in the Owego Daily Blade, August 22, 1888.

76   Clapp's career statistical profile in organized baseball, including the teams he played for, is readily available online at BaseballReference.com

77   John Thorn, *Baseball in the Garden of Eden*, (New York: Simon and Schuster, 2011), 153-154.

78   "Dropped Dead While Making Arrest," New York Times, December 19, 1904, p 2; "'Johnny' Clapp Drops Dead," Syracuse Standard, December 19, 1904, p1; "'Honest John' Clapp Dead," Waverly Free Press.

79   Tim Wendel, *High Heat: The Secret History of the Fastball*, (Cambridge, MA: DaCapo Press, 2010), 14.

80   Thorn, 124.

81   Ibid.

82   David Fleitz, SABR Biography of Candy Cummings.

83   Peter Morris, *Catcher: The Evolution of an American Folk Hero*, (Chicago: Ivan R Dee, 2009), 124.

84   New York Tribune, March 30, 1883, 8; and January 13, 1894, 2. The Sporting Life of July 8, 1885, 3, reported the address to have been 2009 Third Avenue. The Sporting Life of September 16, 1885, 4, said it was "between one hundred and eighth and one hundred and ninth streets."

85   "Base-Ball Notes," The New York Times, March 30, 1883, 1.

86   "Base-Ball," Chicago Tribune, March 23, 1884, 3; and "Base Ball Briefs," Boston Globe, October 3, 1884, 5.

87   "An Aesthetic Headquarters," The St. Louis Post-Dispatch, February 14, 1884, 8.

88 Ibid.

89 "Important to Players," The Cincinnati Enquirer, August 12, 1880, 8.

90 Charles Alexander, *Turbulent Seasons: Baseball in 1890-1891*, (Dallas: SMU, 2011), 11.

91 Ross, 56

92 National Baseball Hall of Fame Almanac, 2014 edition, 460

93 Ross, 56

94 Ross, 53

95 While BaseballReference.com indicates Clapp played for minor league St. Paul in 1884, media stories at the time indicate his younger brother Aaron played for St. Paul (example: St Louis Post-Dispatch, February 14, 1884, 8.) Meanwhile, several stories place John Clapp in New York for 1884 (examples: Cincinnati Enquirer, May 25, 1884, 10; and "Base Ball," Boston Globe, November 9, 1884, 6.) The story that indicated Clapp & Lynch had to close due to "the sickness of John Clapp and Lynch's inability to attend to business" was found in: "Diamond Dust," St. Louis Post-Dispatch, July 8, 1885, 7.

96 "Toronto's Great Team," The Sporting News, July 5, 1886, 5.

97 Waverly Free Press, May 21, 1887, 3.

98 Waverly Academy first became a "free school" in or about 1872 under principal Stephen C. Hall (also a founder of the Hall and Lyons furniture factory), according to Hall's obituary in the Elmira Star Gazette, February 1, 1929, 23.

99 Leroy W. Kingman, *Our County and Its People*, (Elmira, NY: W.A. Fergusson and Company, 1900), 633.

100 Reiss, 118.

101 U.S. Department of Education. *120 Years of American Education: A Statistical Portrait*. Table 28, 82-83.

102   "The Diamond," Waverly Free Press, June 11, 1887, 1.

103   Sporting Life, July 12, 1890, 4.

104   "Fires," Athens Gleaner, July 13, 1871, 2.

105   "Drowned," Athens Gleaner, August 3, 1871.

106   "White Caps," Elmira Daily Gazette and Free Press, August 15, 1891.

107   "Speedy Pitcher Doran," Rome Daily Sentinel, October 20, 1890.

108   One local newspaper (The Bradford Era) contains a box score on July 24, 1886, p 1, that lists a "Doran," but that is the only one the author could locate prior to 1887. In addition to the other speculations, it's possible that since Doran was a left-hander, there were fewer positions available to him to easily play on the semi—professional circuit.

109   "The Diamond," Waverly Free Press, July 2, 1887.

110   Waverly Free Press, July 2, 1887.

111   Dubofsky, 22

112   Factory Inspectors of the State of New York, Second Annual Report, (Troy, NY: Troy Press, 1888), 7.

113   Waverly Advocate, November 5, 1885.

114   Waverly Advocate, December 25, 1884.

115   The analysis was done by matching up information from the Historical Gazetteer of Tioga County with New York State and U.S. Census Records.

116   Waverly Free Press, October 29, 1909, 2.

117   Waverly Free Press, December 10, 1892.

118   Charlie Bevis, SABR Biography of Harry Taylor.

119   Hammondsport Herald, November 13, 1889 and Naples Record, June 5, 1946.

120 "Great Baseball Player is Dead," Elmira Gazette and Free Press, December 19, 1904, 1.

121 "Aaron Clapp," Ithaca Journal, January 14, 1914, 6.

122 Ross, 12.

123 John J. McGraw, *My Thirty Years in Baseball*, (New York: Boni and Liveright, 1923; Reprint edition: Lincoln, Nebraska: Bison Books, 1995), 66.

124 Riess, 75

125 Frank V. Phelps, from Tiemann and Rucker, eds, *Nineteenth Century Stars*, 210.

126 Brian McKenna, SABR Biography of Dickey Pearce.

127 "Base-Ball," New York Tribune, June 15, 1870, 5.

128 Brian McKenna, SABR Biography of Dickey Pearce.

129 John C. Chapman, "Reminiscences of a Baseball Manager," Wilkes-Barre Times Leader, August 8, 1900, 5.

130 "The Colored League a Failure," Sporting Life, June 1, 1887, 9.

131 L. Robert Davids, from Tiemann and Rucker, eds., *Nineteenth Century Stars*, 98.

132 "The Binghamton Team," The Sporting News, April 16, 1887, 1.

133 *National Baseball Hall of Fame Almanac, 2014 Edition*, 460.

134 Michael Haupert, "MLB's annual salary leaders since 1874." SABR.

135 Jerry Malloy, from Tiemann and Rucker, eds., *Nineteenth Century Stars*, 110.

136 Bliss Perry, *The Plated City*, (New York: Charles Scribner's Sons, 1895), 8.

137 Eric Lott, *Love & Theft: Blackface Minstrelsy & the American Working Class, 20th Anniversary Edition*. (New York:

Oxford University Press, 2013), 23.

138   Lott, 4.

139   Lott, 15.

140   Lott, 17.

141   Sporting Life, June 1, 1887, 10.

142   Sporting Life, April 13, 1887

143   Sporting Life, April 20, 1887, 11.

144   Sporting Life, April 13, 1887.

145   "Bishop's Good Work," Pittsburgh Daily Post, April 12, 1887, 6.

146   Sporting Life, May 4, 1887, 11.

147   "Diamond Dust," Glens Falls Times, May 23, 1887.

148   Sporting Life, April 27, 1887.

149   National Police Gazette (New York), May 27, 1887.

150   Buffalo Daily Courier, May 8, 1887.

151   "The Binghamton Club." The Sporting News, April 23, 1987, 5.

152   "The Binghamton Club." The Sporting News, April 23, 1987, 5.

153   Buffalo Daily Courier, May 8, 1887.

154   Buffalo Daily Courier, May 10, 1887.

155   Robert Peterson, Only the Ball was White, (New York: Oxford University Press, 1970), 27.

156   Sporting Life, June 1, 1887, 10.

157   The Sporting News, June 4, 1887, 1.

158   "The Syracuse Plotters," The Sporting News, June 4, 1887, 1.

159   "Dug Crothers Suspended," The Sporting News, June 11, 1887, p 1, and "Fisticuffs in the Star Club," Syracuse Stan-

dard, June 6, 1887, 4.

160 The Sporting News, June 11, 1887, 4.

161 "Dug Crothers Suspended," The Sporting News, June 11, 1887, 1.

162 "Fisticuffs in the Star Club," Syracuse Standard, June 6, 1887, 4.

163 "Notes from the International League," New York Sun, June 19, 1887, 12.

164 Sporting Life, August 24, 1887, 5.

165 "Newark Notes," Sporting Life, July 20, 1887, 4.

166 "International League Meeting," Sporting Life, July 20, 1887, 1.

167 "International League Meeting," Sporting Life, July 20, 1887, 1.

168 "The Ohio League," Sporting Life, November 23, 1887, 3.

169 Brian McKenna, SABR Biography of Frank Grant.

170 Sporting Life, March 14, 1888, 1.

171 Sporting Life, April 18, 1888, 7.

172 "A Loss to the Game," Sporting Life, December 28, 1887, 5.

173 Riess, 113.

174 Brian McKenna, SABR Biography of Frank Grant.

175 "The Sporting Chapter," Buffalo Courier, September 29, 1888.

176 "The Sporting World," Buffalo Courier, April 14, 1889.

177 Brian McKenna, SABR Biography of Frank Grant.

178 "The Sporting World," Buffalo Courier, April 14, 1889.

179 U.S. House of Representatives, *Labor Troubles in the Anthracite Regions 1887-1888*, (Washington, DC: Government Printing Office, 1889), 536.

180   U.S. House of Representatives, 513.

181   U.S. House of Representatives, 554.

182   Sporting Life, February 8, 1888, 5.

183   Sporting Life, February 29, 1888, 4.

184   "For the Aid of the Oppressed Miners of the Lehigh Region," Elmira Telegram, January 22, 1888, 4.

185   Dubofsky, 6.

186   Matthew Algeo, *Pedestrianism: When Watching People Walk Was America's Favorite Spectator Sport*, (Chicago: Chicago Review Press, 2014), 26.

187   Algeo, 213.

188   Homer Republican, October 30, 1879.

189   Algeo, 248.

190   Waverly Advocate, September 10, 1880.

191   Corning Journal, September 10, 1880.

192   Oswego Times-Express, December 17, 1885.

193   Dubofsky, p 17.

194   "Death Recalls Athletic Work," Elmira Star-Gazette, May 13, 1914, 12.

195   The Sporting News, July 9, 1887, 2.

196   "Elmira Enthusiastic," Sporting Life, November 30, 1887, 5.

197   "Elmira's Great Ball Club," Elmira Telegram, April 8, 1888, 8.

198   "Elmira the Victor," Elmira Telegram, April 22, 1888.

199   "At Elmira," Elmira Telegram, May 20, 1888, 1.

200   "At Elmira," Elmira Telegram, May 20, 1888, 1.

201   "At Elmira," Elmira Telegram, July 1, 1888, 1.

202   "The Central League Not Solid," July 1, 1888, 1.

203   "At Elmira," Elmira Telegram, July 15, 1888, 1.

204 Charles C. Alexander, *John McGraw,* (New York: Viking Penguin, 1988), 11.

205 US Census records

206 Alexander, *John McGraw,* 11.

207 Blanche S. McGraw, *The Real McGraw.* (New York: David McKay, 1953), 24.

208 Alexander, *John McGraw,* 11.

209 Blanche McGraw, 32.

210 Blanche McGraw, 35.

211 Blanche McGraw, 36.

212 Blanche McGraw, 37.

213 Ibid.

214 "Man Who Gave McGraw Chance Dies Monday," Olean Times Herald, September 29, 1931, 11.

215 Mark Lamster, *Spalding's World Tour,* (New York: Public Affairs, 2006), 269.

216 Riess, 38

217 Thorn, 12.

218 Alexander, *Turbulent Seasons*, 12.

219 Gordon, 207.

220 "The Sporting World," Buffalo Courier, April 8, 1889.

221 Lamster. 241.

222 Lamster, xiv.

223 William B. Mead and Paul Dickson, *Baseball – The President's Game.* (Washington, DC: Farragut Publishing, 1993), 17.

224 Lamster, xvi.

225 Seymour, 224.

226 Ross, 136.

227   "In Hostile Array," Sporting Life, November 13, 1889.

228   Ross, 138.

229   "Louisville Lines," Sporting Life, June 14, 1890, 8.

230   The Sporting News, July 26, 1890, 4.

231   Sporting Life, August 2, 1890, 4.

232   "Louisville Less Lucky," Sporting Life, September 6, 1890, 9.

233   "The Coming Champions," Sporting Life, October 11, 1890, 8.

234   "Notes and Comment," Sporting Life, October 11, 1890, 2.

235   Thorn, 241.

236   Ross, 191.

237   Thorn, 241.

238   Ross, 194.

239   "Stray Sparks from the Diamond," New York Clipper, December 6, 1890.

240   "Base Ball's Nightmare," Sporting Life, September 27, 1890, 8.

241   Alexander, John McGraw, 15.

242   "Players All Signed," Olean Democrat, January 23, 1890, 16.

243   "The Second Game," Olean Democrat, May 8, 1890, 10.

244   "Defeated at Bradford," Olean Democrat, May 15, 1890, 16.

245   "The First at Home Game," Olean Democrat, May 15, 1890, 12.

246   Alexander, John McGraw, 16.

247   John McGraw, 35.

248   Sporting Life, August 23, 1890, 4.

249   Athens Daily News, June 6, 1890, 4.

250   Ibid.

251 Sporting Life, August 2, 1890, 4.

252 "Lightly Regarded," Sporting Life, June 14, 1890, 8.

253 Quoted from the Harrisburg Patriot as reported by the South Advocate, October 5, 1994, 7; Frank Grant player file, National Baseball Library, Cooperstown, NY.

254 Sporting Life, July 26, 1890, 8.

255 Ibid.

256 Sporting Life, August 2, 1890, 4.

257 "Harrisburg Hits," Sporting Life, August 9, 1890, 9.

258 Sporting Life, August 9, 1890, 9.

259 Sporting Life, August 23, 1890, 6.

260 Sporting Life, August 30, 1890, 12.

261 Sporting Life, August 2, 1890, 4.

262 Sporting Life, August 30, 1890, 12.

263 "Will Stay in New Haven," Elmira Telegram, July 20, 1890.

264 Sporting Life, June 7, 1890.

265 Sporting Life, August 16, 1890, 5.

266 "Rochester Ripples," The Sporting News, July 12, 1890, 1.

267 "Rewards in Ball," Sporting Life, September 20, 1890, 11.

268 "New Haven Notes," Sporting Life, June 14, 1890, 8.

269 Sporting Life, August 30, 1890, 12.

270 Jack Smiles, *"Ee-Yah": The Life and Times of Hughie Jennings, Baseball Hall of Famer,* (Jefferson, NC: McFarland, 2005), 12-13.

271 Sporting Life, September 13, 1890, 11.

272 Sporting Life, September 27, 1890, 11.

273 Sporting Life, October 4, 1890, 10.

274 Ibid.

275   "Harrisburg In Line," Sporting Life, October 4, 1890, 6.

276   "The Atlantic," Sporting Life, November 2, 1890.

277   "Capital City News," Sporting Life, July 12, 1890, 15.

278   Sporting Life, August 23, 1890, 4.

279   "Hard on Grant," Sporting Life, August 9, 1890, 4.

280   "Fowler's Great Scheme," The Sporting News, July 19, 1890, 2.

281   Michael E. Lomax, Black Baseball Entrepreneurs, 1860-1901, (Syracuse, NY: Syracuse University Press, 2003), 117.

282   Athens Daily News, October 3, 1890, 5.

283   "Ward's New Pitcher," Sporting Life, October 4, 1890.

284   Ibid.

285

286   Alexander, McGraw, 19.

287   John McGraw, 39.

288   Sporting Life, August 22, 1891.

289   Smiles, 24.

290   Ibid.

291   Sporting Life, June 13, 1891, 4.

292   "Hugh Jennings Eager to Help First Captain," Buffalo Courier, October 7, 1913.

293   Smiles, 27.

294   "Lebanon's Base Ball Club," Philadelphia Inquirer, March 22, 1891, 3.

295   "Won by the Cuban Giants," Washington Post, September 1, 1891.

296   Ibid.

297   Sporting Life, May 9, 1891, 2.

298   Sporting Life, June 6, 1891, 2.

299   Sporting Life, June 6, 1891, 7.

300   "Hits and Errors," Buffalo Courier, June 13, 1891.

301   "Stabbed by a Catcher," Sporting Life, April 11, 1891.

302   "Moses Walker Acquitted," Hammondsport Herald, June 10, 1891.

303   Sporting Life, July 4, 1891, 4

304   "General Local Mention," Sporting Life, July 18, 1891, 9.

305   Sporting Life, July 25, 1891, 2.

306   "Ball Player Ed. Dailey Dead," Philadelphia Inquirer, October 22, 1891, 3; Also FindAGrave website for Ed Daily, https://www.findagrave.com/memorial/45814196/ edward-m.-daily

307   Jerrold Casway, "Bacteria Beat the Phillies" *SABR Baseball Research Journal*, (Volume 1, Number 45, Spring 2016), 116-122.

308   Michael Haupert, "MLB's annual salary leaders since 1874," SABR.

309   John McGraw, 55.

310   "Diamond Dashes," Elmira Daily Gazette and Free Press, June 1, 1892.

311   Sporting Life, June 18, 1892.

312   "Same Old Story," Buffalo Courier, June 13, 1892.

313   New York Telegram, July 19, 1892.

314   Ritter, 53.

315   Sporting Life, July 9, 1892.

316   Sporting Life, July 16, 1892.

317   Ibid.

318   Sporting Life, July 30, 1892.

319   Sporting Life, August 13, 1892.

320   Ibid.

321   Sporting Life, August 27, 1892.

322   Sporting Life, September 12, 1892.

323   "Eastern League," Sporting Life, October 1, 1892.

324   Ibid.

325   "The Champions," Sporting Life, October 8, 1892.

326   Ibid.

327   "Athletics vs. Normals," Otsego Farmer, August 5 and August 12, 1892.

328   Philadelphia Inquirer, August 29, 1892.

329   Hammondsport Herald, June 22, 1892. "Harry Taylor was injured while playing ball at Cleveland last week. He collided with another player while running bases, and two ribs were broken, besides internal injuries."

330   Charlie Bevis, SABR Biography of Harry Taylor.

331   Robert L. Tiemann, Nineteenth Century Stars, 117.

332   Burt Solomon, Where They Ain't, (New York: Free Press, 1999), 59.

333   Solomon, 43.

334   John McGraw, 58.

335   Sporting Life, September 23, 1893.

336   Sporting Life, September 30, 1893.

337   Sporting Life, June 24, 1893, 2.

338   Cortland Evening Standard, August 28, 1893.

339   David Fleitz, SABR Biography of Cap Anson

340   Sporting Life, July 22, 1893, 4.

341   "Advice to Amateurs," Times-Picayune," August 20, 1893, 8.

342   William Ivy Hair, Carnival of Fury, (Baton Rouge: LSU

Press, 1976), 71.

343   "Lake Charles, La." New Orleans Times-Democrat, October 18, 1893, 2.

344   "Jack's La Belle Creole Company," New Orleans Times-Picayune, October 29, 1893, 14.

345   Sporting Life, April 8, 1893.

346   Ibid.

347   Sporting Life, April 22, 1893.

348   Sporting Life, April 29, 1893.

349   Sporting Life, May 13, 1893.

350   Smiles, 54.

351   Ritter, 52.

352   Ritter, 52.

353   Christy Mathewson, *Pitching in a Pinch: Baseball from the Inside*, (New York: G.P. Putnam's Sons, 1912), 165-166.

354   Solomon, 77.

355   John McGraw, 78.

356   Ibid.

357   Solomon, 71.

358   "Taylor's Club Named," Buffalo Courier, March 16, 1894.

359   Lawson and his brother George remained involved in baseball promotion, creating the United States League in 1910 with the intent of it becoming a racially integrated league. This effort failed. Alfred would eventually be inducted into the Wisconsin Aviation Hall of Fame for his pioneering manufacturing work in Milwaukee.

360   "Buffalo Bits," Sporting Life, March 3, 1894, 5.

361   Gordon, 264.

362   "Scranton Scraps," Sporting Life, March 3, 1894, 5.

363 Sporting Life, September 15, 1894, 5.

364 "Binghamton Bits," Sporting Life, May 26, 1894, 6.

365 "Doran in Buffalo," Elmira Daily Gazette and Free Press, July 10, 1894.

366 Sayre Evening Times, August 17, 1894, 2.

367 "Nubbing of Sport," Harrisburg Telegraph, March 26, 1895, 1.

368 "Base Ball," Otsego Farmer, August 3, 1894, 5.

369 "Athletics vs. Cuban Giants," Otsego Farmer, September 8, 1893.

370 Perry, 3.

371 Middletown State Homeopathic Hospital, 24th Annual Report, 1895, 33.

372 Middletown State Homeopathic Hospital, 24th Annual Report, 1895, 33-34.

373 Middletown State Homeopathic Hospital, 24th Annual Report, 1895, 34.

374 Wayne McElreavy, SABR Biography of Jack Chesbro

375 "Base Ball," Otsego Farmer, August 3, 1894, 5.

376 "Base Ball," Otsego Farmer, August 31, 1894, 5.

377 "Nubbins of Sport," Harrisburg Telegraph, March 26, 1895, 1.

378 "Harrisburg Happenings," Sporting Life, March 3, 1894, 5.

379 Williamsport Sun-Gazette, July 26, 1894, 5.

380 "Big Braves Heap Good," The Harrisburg Telegraph, April 8, 1895. "Pitchers Willis and Talada were very unsteady."

381 "Slaughtered by Yanigans," Harrisburg Telegraph, April 13, 1895, 1.

382 "Another Exploded Phenom," Harrisburg Telegraph, April 16, 1895, 1.

383 "Nubbins of Sport," Harrisburg Telegraph, March 26, 1895, 1.

384 David Nemec, *The Rank and File of 19ᵗʰ Century Major League Baseball*, (Jefferson, NC: McFarland and Company, 2012), 29.

385 "Stony was Umpire," Williamsport Sun-Gazette, August 19, 1912, 6.

386 "Towanda Won in the Tenth," Bradford Star, September 5, 1895.

387 "The Players," Sporting Life, May 25, 1895, 6.

388 Sporting Life, June 1, 1895, 23.

389 Thorn, 98.

390 "Among the Amateurs," Philadelphia Inquirer, August 16, 1896, 8.

391 "A Baseball Club," Waverly Advocate, May 8, 1896, 7.

392 "A Gypsy Band," Waverly Advocate, March 13, 1896, 1.

393 "Base Ball," Waverly Free Press, May 16, 1896, 6.

394 "Base Ball," Waverly Free Press, May 16, 1896, 6.

395 "Baseball Talk," Waverly Advocate, May 14, 1896, 1.

396 "Base Ball," Waverly Free Press, May 16, 1896, 6.

397 Ibid.

398 "The Black Diamond," Waverly Free Press, May 23, 1896, 2.

399 Ritter, 33.

400 "Fine Baseball Game," Waverly Advocate, June 5, 1896, 7.

401 "Base Ball," Waverly Free Press, June 13, 1896, 1.

402 "Sayre Defeats Us," Waverly Advocate, June 19, 1896, 7.

403 Ibid.

404 "Base Ball," Waverly Free Press, June 20, 1896, 1.

405 "How Matty Became a Pitcher," The Literary Digest, May

11, 1912, accessed via www.leaptoad.com/raindelay/matty/became.shtml

406   "Sporting Notes," Waverly Free Press, April 1, 1910.

407   "Base Ball," Waverly Free Press, June 27, 1896, 2.

408   For more about Setley, please see the excellent biography *The Legend of Wild Bill Setley* by Tony Kissel and Scott Fiesthumel.

409   "Baseball Notes," Waverly Advocate, June 19, 1896, 1.

410   "Base Ball Briefs," Waverly Free Press, July 4, 1896, 1.

411   Waverly Free Press, June 27, 1896, 2.

412   "Now for Chicago," Waverly Free Press, June 27, 1896, 2.

413   "Colossal Excursion to New York," Waverly Free Press, June 27, 1896, 2.

414   "Base Ball Briefs," Waverly Free Press, July 4, 1896, 1.

415   Ibid.

416   Ibid.

417   "Interview with Ricker," Scranton Tribune, June 29, 1896, 3. Drawing from the Wilkes-Barre Weekly Times, July 2, 1896, 2.

418   "Base Ball Briefs," Waverly Free Press, July 4, 1896, 1.

419   Ibid.

420   Ibid.

421   "Base Ball Briefs," Waverly Free Press, July 11, 1896, 1.

422   Ibid.

423   "Business Play Ball," Waverly Free Press, July 11, 1896, 1.

424   Ibid.

425   "Base Ball Briefs," Waverly Free Press, July 11, 1896, 1.

426   Ibid.

427   "Base Ball Briefs," Waverly Free Press, July 18, 1896, 1.

428   "Base Ball Briefs," Waverly Free Press, July 11, 1896, 1.

429   "Base Ball Briefs," Waverly Free Press, July 25, 1896.

430   "Base Ball Briefs," Waverly Free Press, August 8, 1896, 1.

431   Ibid.

432   "Base Ball Briefs," Waverly Free Press, August 15, 1896, 1.

433   Waverly Free Press, August 22, 1896, 3.

434   "Base Ball Briefs," Waverly Free Press, August 15, 1896, 1.

435   "Sayre Beaten Again," Waverly Advocate, August 21, 1896, 1.

436   "Base Ball Briefs," Waverly Free Press, August 22, 1896, 4.

437   Ibid.

438   Ibid.

439   "Playing Football," Elmira Gazette and Free Press, September 2, 1896, 8.

440   "Waverly Defeated," Elmira Daily Gazette and Free Press, September 2, 1896, 8.

441   Thorn, 87.

442   "Great Ball Playing," Waverly Free Press, September 12, 1896, 1.

443   Ibid.

444   Ibid.

445   "Yellow Ball and Red," Waverly Free Press, September 19, 1896, 4.

446   Ibid.

447   Ibid.

448   Ibid.

449   "Star Scintillations," Sporting Life, May 23, 1896.

450   "Yellow Ball and Red," Waverly Free Press, September 19,

1896, 4.

451 "Base Ball Briefs," Waverly Free Press, September 26, 1896, 1.

452 Box scores from the Buffalo Courier (May 19, 1896) and the Albany Evening Journal (May 23, 1896).

453 "The Cuban Giants," Waverly Advocate, September 25, 1896, 3.

454 "Base Ball Briefs," Waverly Free Press, September 26, 1896, 1.

455 Ibid.

456 "The Agony is Over," Waverly Advocate, October 8, 1896, 7.

457 "Big Indebtedness," Waverly Advocate, October 16, 1896, 1.

458 Ibid.

459 "Waverly Wins at Football," Waverly Free Press, October 10, 1896, 1.

460 Sporting Life, October 17, 1896, 3.

461 "Athens and Sayre," Elmira Daily Gazette and Free Press, June 5, 1897.

462 Ibid.

463 "Charles P. Kutzner, High Mining Official Dies in City Hospital," Shamokin Dispatch, November 24, 1924.

464 "The Darkies Won," North Adams Transcript, May 29, 1897, 4.

465 "Williamsport Redivivus," Sporting Life, August 7, 1897, 8.

466 "Hartford Happy," Sporting Life, June 12, 1897, 6.

467 Ritter, 27-28.

468 Ritter, 59.

469 Sporting Life, June 12, 1897, 12.

470 ibid.

471 Ibid.

472 Guy Waterman, SABR Biography of Lee Viau.

473 Sporting Life, June 19, 1897, 12.

474 Ibid.

475 ibid.

476 Sporting Life, August 14, 1897, 16.

477 Charlie Bevis, SABR Biography of Tim Murnane

478 *National Baseball Hall of Fame Almanac, 2014 Edition*, 272.

479 Sporting Life, August 8, 1897.

480 Sporting Life, July 25, 1897.

481 Letter from National Baseball Hall of Fame Player File for John "Sandy" McDougal.

482 "Sandy McDougal," Elmira Morning Telegram, August 10, 1907.

483 Solomon, 35-36.

484 Perry K. Blatz, *Democratic Miners*, (Albany, New York: SUNY Press, 1994), 4.

485 1900 U.S. Census record for Mike "Pikus"

486 Johnstown, Pennsylvania, City Directory, 1896.

487 William C. Kashatus, *Diamonds in the Coalfields.* (Jefferson, NC: McFarland, 2002), 11.

488 U.S. Census Records for 1850, 1880 and 1900.

489 "Ball Players Leave," Hazleton Plain Speaker, January 18, 1898, 4.

490 "Base Ball Dots," Freeland Tribune, August 12, 1897, 1.

491 "Base Ball Dots," Freeland Tribune, September 9, 1897, 1.

492 "The Cause of it All," Freeland Tribune, September 6, 1897, 1.

493 Michael Novak, *The Guns of Lattimer*, (New York: Basic Books, 1978), 93.

494   "The Strike Situation," Freeland Tribune, September 9 1897, 1.

495   Sporting Life, September 18, 1897.

496   "Riotous Strikers Killed by Sheriff's Deputies," The (Philadelphia) Times, September 11, 1897, 1.

497   "Blood Flows at Lattimer," Scranton Republican, September 11, 1897, 1.

498   "Striking Miners Massacred at Lattimer," Freeland Tribune, September 13, 1897, 1.

499   Blatz, 59.

500   "Operators will Win," Syracuse Evening Herald, September 19, 1900, 1.

501   DeLeon, Daniel, "Hazleton-New York," The People, September 26, 1897.

502   Candace Falk, ed., Emma Goldman: Made for America, 1890-1901. (Champaign, IL: University of Illinois Press, 2008), 285.

503   Novak, 243.

504   "Told of Murders, Lost His Place," New York World, March 15, 1898, 4.

505   "Giants Defeated the Tigers," Freeland Tribune, September 20, 1897, 1.

506   Deford, 18.

507   "A Good Team," Sporting Life, October 2, 1897, 1.

508   Riess, 28.

509   "Forget the Maine," The Economist, January 1, 1998, is among many relatively recent published accounts and analyses that contain provocative arguments for the source of the explosion, which remains controversial. The author's undergraduate textbook noncommittally referred to the

incident as "explosions ripped through the Maine…" and further said "With no evidence, but considerable emotion, Americans jumped to the conclusion that Spain had committed the dastardly deed." From Thomas G. Paterson, J. Garry Clifford, and Kenneth J. Hagan, *American Foreign Policy: A History/to 1914*. (Lexington, Massachusetts: D.C. Heath and Company, 1983), p. 199.

510   "Cleveland Chatter," Sporting Life, May 7, 1898.

511   Ibid.

512   "War Not Injurious," Sporting Life, May 7, 1898.

513   "Sporting World," Akron Beacon Journal, May 7, 1898, 5.

514   Sporting Life, June 4, 1898.

515   Ibid.

516   Sporting Life, June 11, 1898.

517   Ibid.

518   Mullin's name was variously spelled "Mullen" throughout his baseball career, and was even sometimes spelled both ways in the same box score. Two of the three obituaries the author located, and the ones from newspapers closest to his Philadelphia residence, spelled his name "Mullin," so to reduce confusion the author has changed the spelling to "Mullin" throughout the book, regardless of how news stories at the time spelled it. His SABR Baseballresearch.com profile is also spelled "Mullin."

519   "Cortland 4 Canandaigua 2," Rochester Democrat, June 8, 1898.

520   "City Band Concert," Waverly Advocate, June 10, 1898.

521   Calculations based on information from Silas Wright Burt, *New York and the War with Spain: History of the Empire State Regiments*, (Albany, NY: Argus Company, 1903).

522   Found in "U.S. Army Registry of Enlistments, 1798-1914"

database under spelling "Jacob Covalaskie."

523 Ritter, 117.

524 "Abe Lincoln and Baseball," Baseball History Daily, July 26, 2012. https://baseballhistorydaily.com/2012/07/26/lincoln/

525 "Battle-Scarred Veteran," Sporting Life, September 10, 1898.

526 "Cortland Broke Even," Cortland Evening Standard, July 5, 1898, 7.

527 Ibid.

528 Cortland Evening Standard, July 5, 1898, 1.

529 "Glorious Victories," Cortland Evening Standard, July 5, 1898, 1.

530 Sporting Life, July 16, 1898.

531 Ibid.

532 "Palmyra Passes," Sporting Life, July 30, 1898, 19.

533 "Chipper Canandaigua," Sporting Life, July 30, 1898, 19.

534 "Baseball and the War Tax," Sporting Life, September 17, 1898, 1.

535 Ibid.

536 Sporting Life, November 5, 1898.

537 Sporting Life, September 17, 1898.

538 Ibid.

539 Tony Kissel, "Bound for the Klondike," The National Pastime, Issue 15 (Fall 1982), (Cleveland, OH: Society for American Baseball Research),132.

540 "Some Things the Magnates Must Do for the National Game," Sporting Life, December 3, 1898, 9.

Sources

Archive, Library, and Government Collections

Bradford County (PA) Historical Society (Towanda, PA)

Chemung County (NY) Historical Society (Elmira, NY)

National Archives and Records Administration (Washington, DC)

National Baseball Hall of Fame and Library (Cooperstown, NY)

New York State Library (Albany, NY)

Sayre (PA) Historical Society

Sayre (PA) Public Library

Spalding Memorial Library (Athens, PA)

Susquehanna River Archaeological Center (Waverly, NY)

Tioga County (NY) Historical Society (Owego, NY)

Waverly (NY) Free Library

Waverly (NY) Historical Society

Newspapers and Periodicals

Addison Advertiser, The (Addison, NY) 1879-1902

Akron Beacon Journal (Akron, OH) 1898

Albany Evening Journal (Albany, NY) 1896-1901

Albany Express, The (Albany, NY) 1888

Albany Times-Union, The (Albany, NY) 1892-1900

Allentown Leader, The (Allentown, PA) 1897

Altoona Tribune, The (Altoona, PA) 1910-11

Amsterdam Evening Recorder, The (Amsterdam, NY) 1950

Angelica Advocate, The (Angelica, NY) 1913

Athens Daily News, The (Athens, PA) 1890

Athens Gazette, The (Athens, PA) 1910

Athens Gleaner, The (Athens, PA) 1871

Auburn Bulletin, The (Auburn, NY) 1890-1902

Auburn Citizen-Advertiser, The (Auburn, NY) 1945 and 1975

Auburn Democrat, The (Auburn, NY) 1901

Auburn Democrat-Argus, The (Auburn, NY) 1901

Baseball Research Journal, SABR, Spring 2016

Binghamton Press, The (Binghamton, NY) 1903-1954

Bloomfield Independent Press, The (Bloomfield, NJ) 1933

Bradford Era, The (Bradford, PA) 1886

Bradford Star, The (Towanda, PA) 1895-1899

Broome Republican, The (Binghamton, NY) 1901-1902

Buffalo Courier, The (Buffalo, NY) 1887-1936

Buffalo Evening News, The (Buffalo, NY) 1881-1901

Buffalo Express, The (Buffalo, NY) 1890-94

Canaseraga Times, The (Canaseraga, NY) 1882

Canisteo Times, The (Canisteo, NY) 1900

Central News, The (Perkasie, PA) 1916

Chicago Tribune, The (Chicago, IL) 1898-1901

Cincinnati Enquirer, The (Cincinnati, OH) 1921

Citizen, The (Phelps, NY) 1904

Clifton Springs Press, The (Clifton Springs, NY) 1902

Columbia Herald, The (Columbia, PA) 1897

Cornell Daily Sun, The (Ithaca, NY) 1888-1952

Corning Journal, The (Corning, NY) 1878-1901

Corning Evening Leader, The (Corning, NY) 1942

Cortland Democrat, The (Cortland, NY) 1880-1913

Cortland Evening Standard, The (Cortland, NY) 1900-1902

Cortland News, The (Cortland, NY) 1885

Cortland Standard, The (Cortland, NY) 1900-1933

Daily Argus, The (Mount Vernon, NY) 1900

Daily Eagle, The (Brooklyn, NY) 1895-1901

Daily Eagle, The (Poughkeepsie, NY) 1902

Daily Journal, The (Lockport, NY) 1890

Daily News, The (Ithaca, NY) 1896-1902

Daily Sentinel, The (Rome, NY) 1890-1902
Daily Times, The (Oswego, NY) 1900-1903
Day, The (New London, CT) 1907
Democrat, The (Penn Yan, NY) 1901-1909
Democrat, The (Rochester, NY) 1895-1900
Democrat-Chronicle, The (Rochester, NY) 1897-1930
Detroit Free Press, The (Detroit, MI) 1907
Economist, The, 1998
Elmira Daily Gazette and Free Press (Elmira, NY) 1891-1902
Elmira Star-Gazette (Elmira, NY) 1910-1955
Elmira Telegram, The (Elmira, NY) 1888-1916
Emporia Weekly News, The (Emporia, KS) 1862
Evening Herald, The (Syracuse, NY) 1900-1901
Evening News, The (Jamestown, NY) 1887
Evening Telegram, The (Herkimer, NY) 1900
Evening Telegram, The (New York, NY) 1886
Evening Times, The (Little Falls, NY) 1897
Evening Times, The (Sayre, PA) 1891-1984
Free Press, The (Montour Falls, NY) 1895
Freeland Tribune, The (Freeland, PA) 1897
Geneva Daily Times, The (Geneva, NY) 1901
Geneva Gazette, The (Geneva, NY) 1887
Glens Falls Times, The (Glens Falls, NY) 1887
Gloversville Daily Leader, The (Gloversville, NY) 1901-1903
Greenpoint Daily Star, The (Long Island City, NY) 1886
Harrisburg Independent, The (Harrisburg, PA) 1897
Harrisburg Telegraph, The (Harrisburg, PA) 1895
Hartford Courant, The (Hartford, CT) 1901
Herald, The (Hammondsport, NY) 1886-1905
Herald, The (Honesdale, PA) 1898
Homer Republican, The (Homer, NY) 1879
Independent, The (New York, NY) 1902
Ithaca Daily News, The (Ithaca, NY) 1896
Ithaca Journal, The (Ithaca, NY) 1914-1919
Johnson City – Endicott Record, The (Johnson City, NY) 1916

Journal, The (Auburn, NY) 1907
Lebanon Daily News, The (Lebanon, PA) 1897-1916
Leavenworth Times, The (Leavenworth, KS) 1870
Lewiston Daily Sun, The (Lewiston, NY?) 1900
Lockport Journal, The (Lockport, NY) 1901
Los Angeles Herald, The (Los Angeles, CA) 1901
Mansfield Advertiser, The (Mansfield, PA) 1944
Mercury, The (Pottstown, PA) 1941-54
Miltonian, The (Milton, PA) 1910
Miners Journal, The (Pottsville, PA) 1897
Moravia Republican, The (Moravia, NY) 1900
Naples Record, The (Naples, NY) 1946
National Police Gazette, The (New York, NY) 1887
New York Age, The (New York, NY) 1937
New York Clipper, The (New York, NY) 1870-1885
New York Herald, The (New York, NY) 1887-1916
New York Morning Telegraph, The (New York, NY) 1901
New York Evening Post, The (New York, NY) 1901
New York Press, The (New York, NY) 1889-1902
New York Sun, The (New York, NY) 1887-90
New York Telegram, The (New York, NY) 1886-1892
New York Times, The (New York, NY) 1896-1901
New York Tribune, The (New York, NY) 1921
New York World, The (New York, NY) 1890-1898
Niagara Falls Gazette, The (Niagara Falls, NY) 1954-1968
North Adams Transcript, The (North Adams, MA) 1896
Otsego Farmer, The (Cooperstown, NY) 1892-1896
Oswego Daily Palladium, The (Oswego, NY) 1900
Oswego Times-Express, The (Oswego, NY) 1885
Ovid Gazette, The (Ovid, NY) 1901
Owego Daily Blade, The (Owego, NY) 1884-87
Owego Daily Record, The (Owego, NY) 1887-88
Palladium Times, The (Oswego, NY) 1941
People, The (New York, NY) 1897
Philadelphia Inquirer (Philadelphia, PA) 1892-1944

Pittsburgh Courier, The (Pittsburgh, PA) 1927-31

Pittsburgh Daily Post, The (Pittsburgh, PA) 1887-1911

Pittston Gazette, The (Pittston, PA) 1888-1901

Port Jervis Gazette, The (Port Jervis, NY) 1886

Post-Standard, The (Syracuse, NY) 1900

Potsdam-St. Lawrence Herald, The (Potsdam, NY) 1900

Pottstown Mercury, The (Pottstown, PA) 1935

Pottsville Republican, The (Pottsville, PA) 1897

Poughkeepsie Eagle News, The (Poughkeepsie, NY) 1889

Public Opinion, Volume 23, 1897

Reading Times, The (Reading, PA) 1891-1901

Record, The (Johnson City & Endicott, NY) 1916-1919

Record-Argus, The (Greenville, PA) 1900

Rome Citizen, The (Rome, NY) 1901-1902

San Francisco Call, The (San Francisco, CA) 1905

Scranton Republican, The (Scranton, PA) 1896-1922

Scranton Tribune, The (Scranton, PA) 1897

Sentinel, The (Carlisle, PA) 1890

Shamokin Dispatch, The (Shamokin, PA) 1924

Sporting Life (Philadelphia, PA) 1885-1908

Sporting News (St. Louis, MO) 1886-1902

Sports Illustrated, 2001-2012

Star, The (Long Island, NY) 1886-1898

Syracuse Evening Telegram, The (Syracuse, NY) 1900-1901

Syracuse Herald, The (Syracuse, NY) 1900-1902

Syracuse Journal, The (Syracuse, NY) 1897-1905

Syracuse Post-Standard, The (Syracuse, NY) 1901-1904

Syracuse Standard, The (Syracuse, NY) 1886-1887

Times, The (Philadelphia, PA) 1896-00

Times-Herald, The (Olean, NY) 1921-31

Times-Picayune, The (New Orleans, LA) 1895-96

Tioga County Record, The (Owego, NY) 1887-1905

Tribune, The (Bismarck, ND) 1890-1914

Troy Daily Times, The (Troy, NY) 1900-1901

Tyrone Herald, The (Tyrone, PA) 1897

Utica Daily Press, The (Utica, NY) 1902
Utica Herald, The (Utica, NY) 1896
Utica Journal, The (Utica, NY) 1901
Valley Sports Report (Sayre, PA) 2017
Washington Evening Star, The (Washington, DC) 1888
Washington Post, The (Washington, DC) 1891
Watkins Express, The (Watkins Glen, NY) 1880
Waverly Advocate, The (Waverly, NY) 1879-1901
Waverly Free Press, The (Waverly, NY) 1886-1914
Wayne County Herald, The (Wayne County, NY) 1898-1904
Weekly Bulletin, The (Auburn, NY) 1901
Weekly Tribune, The (Hornellsville, NY) 1893-1896
Wellsboro Gazette, The (Wellsboro, PA) 1897
Wilkes-Barre Record, The (Wilkes-Barre, PA) 1896-97
Wilkes-Barre Times Leader, The (Wilkes-Barre, PA)
     1890-1910
Williamsport Sun-Gazette (Williamsport, PA) 1901-12

Books and Journal Articles

Albertson, Capt. Charles L. *History of Waverly, NY, and Vicinity.* Waverly, NY: Waverly Sun, 1943.

Alexander, Charles C. *John McGraw.* New York: Viking Penguin, 1988.—. *Turbulent Seasons: Baseball in 1890-1891.* Dallas: Southern Methodist University Press, 2011.

Algeo, Matthew. *Pedestrianism: When Watching People Walk Was America's Favorite Spectator Sport.* Chicago: Chicago Review Press, 2014.

Appel, Marty, "Retroactive Rewards," *Memories and Dreams, the Official Magazine of the Hall of Fame* 38, no. 5 (Fall 2016). Also available via: http://www.appelpr.com/?page_id=3320

Aswad, Ed and Meredith, Suzanne M., *Images of America: Endicott-Johnson.* Charleston, SC: Arcadia, 2003.

Bernstein, Peter L. *Wedding of the Waters: The Erie Canal and the Making of a Great Nation.* New York: Norton, 2005.

Bevis, Charlie. *Jimmy Collins: A Baseball Biography.* Jefferson,

NC: McFarland, 2012.

Blatz, Perry K. *Democratic Miners.* Albany, New York: SUNY Press, 1994.

Brands, H.W. *The Reckless Decade: America in the 1890s.* Chicago: University of Chicago Press, 1995.

Brock, Darryl. *Two in the Field.* New York: Plume, 2002.

Browne, Paul. *The Coal Barons Played Cuban Giants.* Jefferson, NC: McFarland, 2013.

Browning, Reed. *Cy Young: A Baseball Life.* Amherst, MA: University of Massachusetts Press, 2000.

Burt, Silas W. *New York and the War with Spain: History of the Empire State Regiments.* New York: Argus Company, 1903.

Casway, Jerrold, "Bacteria Beat the Phillies," *SABR Baseball Research Journal*, Volume 1, Number 45 (Spring 2016): 116-122.

Cook, William A. *August "Garry" Herrmann: A Baseball Biography.* Jefferson, NC: McFarland, 2008.

Creamer, Robert W. *Babe: The Legend Comes to Life.* New York: Simon and Schuster, 1974.

Deford, Frank. *The Old Ball Game.* New York: Atlantic Monthly Press, 2005.

DeMotte, Charles. *Bat, Ball & Bible: Baseball and Sunday Observance in New York.* Washington, DC: Potomac, 2013.

Deutch, Jordan A., Richard M, Cohen, Roland T. Johnson and David S. Neft. *The Scrapbook History of Baseball.* New York: Bobbs-Merrill, 1975.

Dubofsky, Melvyn. *Industrialism and the American Worker 1865-1920.* Arlington Heights, IL: Harlan Davidson, 1975.

Factory Inspectors of the State of New York. *Second Annual Report.* Troy, NY: Troy Press, 1888.

Falk, Candace, editor. *Emma Goldman: Made for America, 1890-1901.* Champaign, IL: University of Illinois Press, 2008.

Friedlander, Brett and Robert Reising. *Chasing Moonlight: The True Story of Field of Dreams' Doc Graham.* Winston-Salem, NC: John F. Blair, 2009.

Frick, Ford C. *Games, Asterisks and People.* New York: Crown, 1973.

Gay, W.B. *Historical Gazetteer of Tioga County, New York, 1785-1888.* Interlaken, NY: Heart of the Lakes Publishing, 1985.

Goldman, Steven. *Forging Genius: The Making of Casey Stengel.* Washington, DC: Potomac, 2005.

Golenbock, Peter. *Dynasty: The New York Yankees 1949-1964.* Englewood Cliffs, NJ: Prentice-Hall, 1975.

Goodrich, Thomas. *Bloody Dawn: The Story of the Lawrence Massacre.* Kent, OH: Kent State University Press, 1991.

Goodwin, Doris Kearns. *The Bully Pulpit.* New York: Simon & Schuster, 2013.

Gordon, John Steele. *An Empire of Wealth.* New York: Harper Collins, 2004.

Green, Guy W. *The Nebraska Indians and Fun and Frolic with an Indian Ball Team. Edited by Jeff P. Beck.* Jefferson, NC: McFarland, 2010.

Hair, William Ivy. *Carnival of Fury: Robert Charles and the New Orleans Race Riot of 1900.* Baton Rouge: LSU Press, 1976.

Hardy, James D. *The New York Giants Base Ball Club.* Jefferson, NC: McFarland, 2006.

Helyar, John. *Lords of the Realm.* New York: Ballantine Books, 1994.

Hogan, Lawrence D. *Shades of Glory.* Washington, DC: National Geographic Society, 2006.

Honig, Donald. *The American League: An Illustrated History.* New York: Crown, 1983.

Horigan, Michael. Elmira – *Death Camp of the North.* Mechanicsburg, Pennsylvania: Stackpole Books, 2002.

Howells, William Dean. *A Hazard of New Fortunes.* New York: Harper and Brothers, 1890.

Jobs, Sebastian. *Welcome Home Boys: Military Victory Parades in New York City, 1899-1945.* New York: Campus Verlag, 2013.

Jones, Mary Harris. *Autobiography of Mother Jones.* Chicago, Illinois: Charles H. Kerr and Company, 1925.

Kashatus, William C. *Diamonds in the Coalfields.* Jefferson, NC: McFarland, 2002.

Kazin, Michael. *A Godly Hero: The Life of William Jennings Bryan.* New York: Alfred A. Knopf, 2006.

Kingman, Leroy W. *Our County and Its People.* Elmira, NY: W.A. Fergusson and Company, 1900.

Kirsch, George B. *Baseball in Blue & Gray: The National Pastime during the Civil War.* Princeton, NJ: Princeton University Press, 2003.

Kissel, Tony, "Bound for the Klondike," *The National Pastime,* Issue 15 (Fall 1982), Cleveland, OH: Society for American Baseball Research: 131-132.

Kissel, Tony and Scott Fiesthumel. *The Legend of Wild Bill Setley.* Kearney, NE: Morris Publishing, 2002.

Krist, Gary. *Empire of Sin.* New York: Crown, 2014.

Kurkjian, Tim. *America's Game.* New York: Crown, 2000.

Lamster, Mark. *Spalding's World Tour.* New York: Public Affairs, 2006.

Layden, Tim, "Tinker to Evers to Chance . . . to Me," *Sports Illustrated,* December 3, 2012.

Lang, Louis J., ed. *The Autobiography of Thomas Collier Platt.* New York: B.W. Dodge, 1910.

Lardner, Ring. *Selected Stories.* New York: Penguin, 1997.

Linker, Andrew. *One Patch of Grass.* Harrisburg, PA: Andrew Linker, 2012.—. *Clippings.* Harrisburg, PA: Andrew Linker, 2012.

Lomax, Michael E. *Black Baseball Entrepreneurs, 1860-1901.* Syracuse, NY: Syracuse University Press, 2003.

Lott, Eric. *Love & Theft: Blackface Minstrelsy & the American Working Class, 20th Anniversary Edition.* New York: Oxford University Press, 2013.

Lowenfish, Lee. *The Imperfect Diamond.* Lincoln, Nebraska: University of Nebraska Press, 1980.

Lowman, Seymour. *The Lowmans in Chemung County.* Elmira, NY: The Commercial Press, 1938.

Martin, Billy and Golenbock, Peter. *Number 1.* New York: Dell, 1980.

Mathewson, Christy. *Pitching in a Pinch: Baseball from the Inside.* New York: G.P. Putnam's Sons, 1912.

Mayer, Ronald A. *Christy Mathewson: A Game-by-Game Profile of a Legendary Pitcher.* Jefferson, NC: McFarland, 2008.

McDonald, Brian. *Indian Summer.* New York: Rodale, 2003.

McGraw, Blanche S. *The Real McGraw.* New York: David McKay, 1953.

McGraw, John J. *My Thirty Years in Baseball.* New York: Boni and Liveright, 1923. Reprint edition: Lincoln, NE: Bison Books, 1995.

McKelvey, G. Richard. *For It's One, Two, Three, Four Strikes You're Out at the Owners' Ball Game.* Jefferson, NC: McFarland, 2001.

McNamara, Robert F. *The Diocese of Rochester in America, 1868-1993.* Rochester, NY: Diocese of Rochester, NY, 1998.

McPherson, James M. *Drawn With the Sword – Reflections on the American Civil War.* New York: Oxford University Press, 1996.

Mead, William B. and Paul Dickson. *Baseball – The President's Game.* Washington, DC: Farragut Publishing, 1993.

Melone, Harry R. *150 Years of Progress.* Auburn, NY: Finger Lakes Press, 1929.

Middletown State Homeopathic Hospital, *24th Annual Report*, Albany, NY: James B. Lyon, State Printer,1895.

Miller, Scott. *The President and the Assassin.* New York: Random House, 2011.

Morgan, Lewis Henry. *League of Ho-de-no-sau-nee, or Iroquois.* (Two Volumes in One.) New York: Dodd, Mead and Company, 1922

Morris, Edmund. *Theodore Rex.* New York: Random House, 2001.

Morris, Peter. *Catcher: The Evolution of an American Folk Hero.* Chicago: Ivan R Dee, 2009.

Murphy, Cait. *Crazy '08.* New York: Harper Collins, 2007.

Murray, Elsie. *Teaoga – Annals of a Valley.* Athens, Pennsylvania: Tioga Point Museum, 1939.

Nack, William, with special reporting by Mike Donovan, "Collision at Home" *Sports Illustrated*, June 4, 2001.

Nash, Bruce and Zullo, Allan. *The Baseball Hall of Shame: The Best of Blooperstown*. Guilford, CT: Lyons, 2012.

National Baseball Hall of Fame Almanac 2014 Edition. Durham, NC: Baseball America, Source Interlink Magazines, Inc., 2014.

Nemec, David. *The Rank and File of 19th Century Major League Baseball*. Jefferson, NC: McFarland, 2012.

Nemec, David and Saul Wisnia. *Baseball: More than 150 Years*. Lincolnwood, IL: Publications International, 1996.

Novak, Michael. *The Guns of Lattimer*. New York: Basic Books, 1978.

Overmyer, James. *Frank Grant*. Baseball History 4.

Palmer, Richard. *The Coming of the Railroad to Sayre*. Sayre, PA: Sayre Historical Society, 2017.

Paterson, Thomas G., Clifford, J. Garry and Hagan, Kenneth J. *American Foreign Policy: A History/to 1914*. Lexington, Massachusetts: D.C. Heath and Company, 1983.

Pellechia, Thomas. *Over a Barrel – The Rise and Fall of New York's Taylor Wine Company*. Albany, NY: State University of New York Press, 2015.

Pennington, Bill. *Billy Martin: Baseball's Flawed Genius*. New York: Houghton Mifflin Harcourt, 2015.

Perry, Bliss. *The Plated City*. New York: Charles Scribner's Sons, 1895.

Peterson, Robert. *Only the Ball Was White*. New York: Oxford University Press, 1970.

Publishing Society of New York. *Republicans of New York*. 1902

Quest, Richard. *Tioga County, New York*. Charleston, SC: Arcadia, 1999

Rice, Edward Le Roy. *Monarchs of Minstrelsy, from "Daddy" Rice to Date*. New York: Kenny Publishing Company, 1911.

Riess, Steven A. *Sport in Industrial America 1850-1920*. Arlington Heights, IL: Harlan Davidson, 1995.

Ritter, Lawrence S. *The Glory of Their Times*. New York: Macmillan and Company, 1966.

Roberts, Randy & Carson Cunningham, eds. *Before the Curse: The Chicago Cubs' Glory Years, 1870-1945.* Champaign, IL: University of Illinois Press, 2012.

Rosenberg, Howard W. *Cap Anson 3: Mugsy McGraw and the Tricksters: Baseballs' Fun Age of Rule-Bending.* Arlington, Virginia: Tile Books, 2005.

Ross, Robert B. *The Great Baseball Revolt.* Lincoln, NE: University of Nebraska Press, 2016

Schiff, Andrew J. *The Father of Baseball: A Biography of Henry Chadwick.* Jefferson, NC: McFarland, 2008.

Schultz, Duane. *Quantrill's War: The Life and Times of William Clarke Quantrill.* New York: St. Martins Press, 1996.

Seymour, Harold. *Baseball: The Early Years.* New York: Oxford University Press, 1960.

Shipton, Alyn. *A New History of Jazz.* New York: Continuum, 2001.

Smiles, Jack. *"Ee-Yah": The Life and Times of Hughie Jennings, Baseball Hall of Famer.* Jefferson, NC: McFarland, 2005.

Solomon, Burt. *Where They Ain't.* New York: Free Press, 1999.

Somers, Dale A. *The Rise of Sports in New Orleans.* New Orleans: Pelican Publishing, 1972

Stacy, Bonnie. *Athens, Sayre and Waverly.* Dover, NH: Arcadia, 1996.

Standiford, Les. *Meet You in Hell.* New York: Three Rivers Press, 2005.

Stump, Al. *Cobb – A Biography.* Chapel Hill, NC: Algonquin, 1996.

Terry, James L. *Long Before the Dodgers: Baseball in Brooklyn, 1855-1884.* Jefferson, NC: McFarland, 2002.

Thompson, E.P. *The Making of the English Working Class.* New York: Vintage Books, 1966.

Thorn, John, ed. *The National Pastime.* New York: Warner Books, 1987.—. *Baseball in the Garden of Eden.* New York: Simon & Schuster, 2011.

Tiemann, Robert L. and Rucker, Mark, eds. *Nineteenth Century*

Stars, 2012 Edition. Phoenix, Arizona: Society for American Baseball Research, 2012.

Tye, Larry. *Satchel: The Life and Times of an American Legend*. New York: Random House, 2009.

United States House of Representatives, Select Committee on Existing Labor Troubles in Pennsylvania. *Labor Troubles in the Anthracite Regions of Pennsylvania 1887-1888*. Washington, DC: Government Printing Office, 1889.

Wagenheim, Kal. *Babe Ruth: His Life and Legend*. Washington, DC: Waterfront Press, 1990.

Ward, Geoffrey, et al. *Mark Twain: An Illustrated Biography*. New York: Alfred A. Knopf, 2001.

Welch, Lewis Sheldon and Camp, Walter. *Yale, Her Campus, and Athletics*. Boston: L.C. Page and Company, 1899.

Wendel, Tim. *High Heat: The Secret History of the Fastball*. Cambridge, MA: DaCapo Press, 2010.

Wilbert, Warren N. *A Cunning Kind of Play: the Cubs-Giants Rivalry, 1876-1932*. Jefferson, NC: McFarland, 2002.—*The Arrival of the American League*. Jefferson NC: McFarland, 2007.

Wood, Allan. *Babe Ruth and the 1918 Red Sox*. New York: Writer's Club Press, 2000.

Zoss, Joel and John Bowman. *Diamonds in the Rough: The Untold History of Baseball*. New York: Macmillan, 1989.

Index

A

African-American 61, 70, 73, 74, 75, 76, 80, 90, 91, 98, 125, 134, 143, 176, 193, 205, 216, 224

Akron (OH) 74

Albany (NY) 148, 149, 150, 154, 178, 190, 191

Aldrich, Vernie 58

Alexander, Charles 105, 106, 108

Algeo, Matthew 98

Allegany College 122, 158

Allen, George 251, 256

Allentown (PA) 28, 101, 102, 104, 115, 129, 132, 251

Allison, James 101

Altoona (PA) 120

American Association 45, 48, 67, 74, 109, 110, 113, 114, 115, 117, 119, 128, 137, 139, 141, 145, 146, 156, 163, 189

Ames, Ed 181

Amsterdam (NY) 191

Anson, Adrian "Cap" 40, 60, 76, 89, 160, 170, 224

Ansonia (CT) 142

Anthracite 11, 12, 13, 95, 234, 235, 236

Appalachia 158

Athens (PA) 9, 37, 51, 124, 125, 128, 134, 166, 175, 176, 180, 182, 191, 198, 200, 206, 210, 211, 214, 220, 221, 223, 270

Atlantic Association 109, 120, 121, 124, 126, 127, 128, 132, 133, 139, 141, 176, 182

Atlantic Shades 67

Auburn (NY) 108, 136, 194, 251, 253, 262

Australia 110

125, 126, 127, 133, 141, 142, 163, 215, 216, 218, 224, 252
Colored All Americans 133
Columbus (OH) 82, 83, 118, 160, 190, 245, 256
Comiskey, Charles 128, 163
Confederate (States of America) 20, 21, 22, 73, 75, 89
Congdon, Lynn 58
Connor, Roger 45, 46
Cooper, James Fenimore 176
Cooperstown (NY) 2, 4, 68, 154, 175, 176, 178, 181, 272
Cornell University 32, 49, 60, 102, 141, 155, 156, 172, 220, 261
Corning (NY) 191, 195, 196, 197, 206, 211, 214, 217, 269, 270
Cortland (NY) 99, 104, 105, 106, 107, 191, 251, 252, 253, 256,
    257, 258
Coveleski, Jacob 254
Coveleski, Stan 12, 18, 30, 254
Cox, John 129
Cranberry (PA) 240
Crawford, Sam 148, 168, 169, 228
Creighton, Jim 43, 65, 66
Cricket 42
Cristall, Bill 251
Cronin, Jerry 99
Crothers, Douglas "Doug" or "Dug" 75, 85, 86, 87
Cuban Giants 91, 92, 93, 125, 126, 134, 141, 142, 144, 176, 178,
    215, 216, 217, 218, 224, 252, 271
Cuban X Giants 224, 246
Cudworth, Jim 129
Cumberland (MD) 168
Cumberland Valley (PA) 190
Cummings, Candy 43
Cuppy, George 247

D

Dahlen, Bill 247
Daily, Vince 34

McGill, Willy 182
McGraw, John 2, 63, 104, 105, 106, 107, 109, 121, 122, 123,
    137, 138, 139, 146, 147, 148, 157, 158, 159, 161, 167, 168,
    169, 170, 171, 228
McGreevy, Pat 178
McGuire, Jim 251
McKee, Joe 203, 205, 207, 210, 266
McKee, John 129
McKibbon, Henry 58
McKinley, William 222, 248
McQuaid, James 251, 253, 256, 258
Meadville (PA) 121
Meaney, Patrick 241
Meki, Joseph 246
Memphis (TN) 75, 83, 85, 90
Messitt, John 34
Metropolitans "Mets" 2, 44, 45, 48
Michigan State League 97
Middletown (NY) 176, 177
Middletown (OH) 40
Middletown State Homeopathic Hospital 177
Milnesville (PA) 95, 238
Milton (PA) 190, 223, 252
Milwaukee (WI) 66, 190
Minneapolis (MN) 190
Minstrel 73, 78, 193
Mitchell (umpire) 178
Mix, Ervin 193, 195, 196, 205, 210, 266
Mobile (AL) 165, 166, 180
Molesworth, Carlton 251, 256
Molly McGuires 235
Montgomery (AL) 165
Montpelier (VT) 88
Montreal (QC) 91, 174
Moore, Tom 29, 49, 266

W